Side
by
Side
A Handbook

Side by Side

by

A Handbook

Steve & Lois Rabey,
General Editors

First Printing, 2000
Printed in the United States of America

1 2 3 4 5 6 7 8 9 10 Printing / Year 04 03 02 01 00

Editor: Greg Clouse
Cover Design: Smith/Lane Associates
Cover Photo Illustration: Jeff Lane
Cover Photography: © 2000 Stone Images
Interior Design: Pat Miller

Library of Congress Cataloging-in-Publication Data

Rabey, Steve.
    Side by side: a handbook/Steve and Lois Rabey.
        p. cm.
    Includes bibliographical references.
    ISBN 0-78143-468-8
    1. Christian life. I. Rabey, Lois Mowday.

BV4501.2 .R24 2000
248.4--dc21

CONTENTS

Section Three

Section Four

Section Five

FOREWORD

I wonder how you would sum up the Christian situation in the world today. For me, it's a strange, rather tragic, and disturbing paradox. On the one hand, in many parts of the world the church is growing by leaps and bounds. But on the other hand, throughout the church, superficiality is everywhere. That's the paradox. Growth without depth.

No doubt God is not pleased with superficial discipleship. The apostolic writers of the New Testament declare with one voice that God wants His people to grow up and to grow into maturity in Christ. Remember, for example, Paul told the Corinthians, "I could not address you as spiritual, but carnal, as mere infants in Christ." The writer to the Hebrews said, "Though by this time you ought to be teachers, you need somebody to teach you all over again the elementary truths of the Word of God." Or Peter's words, "Like newborn babies, thirst after the pure spiritual milk that "by it you may grow up in or into salvation." Or Colossians 1:28: "We proclaim Christ. Warning everybody, teaching everybody in all wisdom." Why? "In order that we may present everybody mature in Christ."

What is Christian maturity? What does it mean to grow up into mature discipleship? The fact is, maturity is a very elusive quality. Most of us, if we're honest with ourselves and one another, are suffering from lingering immaturities. Even inside the grown adult, the little child still hides somewhere. Besides, there are different types of maturity. There is physical maturity. There's intellectual maturity. You remember Paul saying in 1 Corinthians 14, "In the sphere of evil, be as innocent as a little child, but in your thinking, for heaven's sake, grow up!" There's moral maturity, referring to people who have trained themselves to distinguish good from evil (Hebrews 5:14). And there's emotional maturity—having a balanced personality so that we are able to establish good relationships with one another and bear responsibility.

But above all, there is spiritual maturity, that is, having a mature relationship to Jesus Christ. To be in Christ is to enjoy a vibrant, vital, organic relationship with Him, so that His life flows into us and we share His very life. And this is a relationship characterized by faith, love, worship, and obedience. We cannot possibly claim to be mature disciples if we are living in disbelief or disobedience. Mature disciples are so closely related to Jesus Christ that they trust His promises, obey His commands, and fall down and worship Him, acknowledging Him as Lord.

In the introduction of J.I. Packer's great classic of the 20th century, *Knowing God,* he writes, "We are pygmy Christians, because we have a pygmy God." I venture to alter that slightly to say, "We are pygmy Christians, because we have a pygmy Christ." The truth is that there are many Jesuses on offer in the world's religious supermarkets. And most of them are false Christs, distorted Christs, caricatures of the authentic Jesus of the New Testament witness.

This great Jesus is not one we carry around in our pockets like a hypodermic syringe. No, away with these petty and pygmy Jesuses— Jesus the clown; Jesus the pop star; Jesus the political messiah; Jesus the revolutionary; Jesus the reactionary—if this is how we think of Christ, and if this is how we proclaim Christ, no wonder we continue in our immaturities.

Where then shall we find the authentic Jesus so that we may grow in our understanding of Him and in our relationship with Him? The answer, of course, is in the Scriptures. Scripture is God's portrait of His Son, painted by the Holy Spirit. The Scripture, Christ said, "bears witness to Me." Jerome, the great church father, said, "Ignorance of Scripture is ignorance of Christ." If only the veil could be taken away from our eyes, if only we could see Jesus in the fullness of His divine human person and His saving work, then we would see that He's worthy of our complete allegiance, our love, and our worship. Nothing is more important.

So the discipleship principle is clear. The poorer our vision of Christ, the poorer our discipleship will be. The brighter and richer our vision of Christ, the richer our discipleship will be.

Note the Apostle Paul's ministry objective. The popular image of Paul is that he was a pioneer missionary, whose goal was to win people for Christ, start a church, and then move on. But that is only part of the picture. Paul did not see himself only as an evangelist. He was also a pastor and teacher, and his longing was to go beyond evangelism to discipleship, to present everybody mature in Christ. That was his goal, and to that goal he "bent his energies" (Colossians 1:29). With all the energy that Christ inspired within him, Paul toiled and struggled in prayer, in study, in preaching, in teaching.

Oh for that divine energy with which we also could toil and strive, that we ourselves may grow into mature disciples and bend our energies to present everybody for whom we are responsible mature in Christ.

THE REV. DR. JOHN STOTT
Rector Emeritus of All Souls Church, Langham Place
London, England

From the opening address at the First International Consultation on Discipleship

INTRODUCTION:
Putting Discipleship on the Map

M illions of Christians around the world are either personally involved in evangelism, or actively supporting missionary work, or aggressively engaged in defending Christian policies in the public square.

But look for believers actively involved in discipleship, and it will be harder to find a crowd. That's because for many people, discipleship is a nonissue that isn't even in their minds or on their maps. As a result, Christianity has a billion or more adherents but far fewer true disciples.

It was with this challenge in mind that 450 Christian leaders from 50 nations met in Eastbourne, England, in September 1999 for the First International Consultation on Discipleship sponsored by Cook Communications Ministries. Born out of the vision of Dr. Appianda Arthur, president of Global Leaders Initiative, and David Mehlis, president of Cook, the delegates spent several days discussing the pressing need for disciple-making in the 21st century.

As the American magazine *Christianity Today* said in an editorial following the consultation, "Too often disciple-making has been understood as preaching the gospel, helping a penitent pray the sinner's prayer, or offering a compelling case for Christian belief. Disciple-making surely includes all these things, but it has as its goal Christian maturity." [1]

It was because of the consultation that the book you are holding in your hands came to be. In England, many participants bemoaned the lack of a comprehensive overview volume featuring some of the best of 20 centuries' worth of discipleship theory and practice. Within weeks of the conference, publishers in England and America had begun setting the wheels in motion to bring this book to the public.

Like the organizers of the consultation, we hope our efforts will help people think more biblically and act more Christianly about the urgent and important task of discipleship.

Twenty Centuries of Ministry

Jesus didn't invent the concept of discipleship. After all, teachers like Socrates and Plato had disciples centuries earlier. But just as He did with virtually everything else He touched, Jesus radically transformed the whole notion of teacher and disciples.

For one thing, students who wanted to learn from philosophers like Socrates sought them out, but Jesus turned the tables by seeking out disciples who would follow Him. In addition, Jesus upped the ante, transforming discipleship from an educational program into a matter of wholehearted, life-changing devotion.

At the beginning of His ministry, Jesus called 12 disciples to follow Him and devote their lives to Him. Over the next few years, other people would follow Jesus either occasionally or at a distance. Throughout the Gospels, *disciple* was the only term regularly applied to followers of Jesus. The New Testament uses the word more than 250 times.

A Reader's Guide to This Book

The pages that follow don't presume to present an exhaustive or definitive manual on discipleship. Rather, they seek to explore some of the nuggets of wisdom from men and women who lived all over the world over the past 20 centuries, following Jesus with a passion and trying to help others do likewise.

If there is any one single God-ordained discipleship method (and we are among the many people who don't believe there is), it isn't found here. Rather, we have attempted to compile some of the words and insights of those who have walked this path before us. Instead of providing one surefire method, we present some of the many themes that disciples of Jesus have emphasized century after century. If C.S. Lewis had been organizing this book, it might have been called *Mere Discipleship*.

The material is organized into five major sections:

Section 1. Come, Follow Me: Being a Disciple of Jesus.

The purpose of this section is to examine what Jesus meant when He called people to follow Him, and what following Him has meant in the centuries since. Among the many marks of a disciple discussed in this section, one that saints throughout the ages have praised is humility.

Section 2. Go and Make Disciples: Helping Others Follow Jesus.

Using Jesus as our model, we look at how He called, worked with, and trained His own disciples. Clearly, Jesus was a master teacher but frequently it was His incarnational lifestyle and commitment to backing up His pronouncements with His actions that helped His often hardheaded disciples get the picture.

Section 3. I Am With You: We All Do the Work of Discipleship.

This is the "who" section. Here, we dismiss the myth that discipleship is something that *they* do, whether the they is ordained clergy, or professional evangelists, or others. The truth of the matter is that discipleship is something we *all* do, and we all do it in our own unique way by utilizing the gifts and calling God has given us.

Section 4. Teaching Them to Obey: Disciple-making Methods and Models.

This is the "how" section, and it's the book's longest. Here we review some of the many approaches, programs, and methods believers have devised through the ages to disciple others. Along the way, we show that discipleship—like much of the human life—is destined to always be something that exists beyond human methods and programs.

Section 5. Issues: Applying God's Wisdom in Changing Times.

God is timeless and unchanging, but we don't enjoy that luxury. Hence, this section examines the ways in which things like postmodernism, individualism, and political activism have helped or hindered the work of discipleship.

Finally, there is a brief section on recommended resources at the end of the book.

Working on this project has been both eye-opening and invigorating. We only hope that the material collected here will help us learn from the trials and tribulations of the past 20 centuries and do a better job in the next.

Blessings,
STEVE AND LOIS RABEY, General Editors

COME, FOLLOW ME:
Being a Disciple of Jesus

During the few brief years that Jesus walked this earth and proclaimed the message of the kingdom of God, He called many men and women to follow Him and be His disciples.

Often, His call was brief and direct, as we see in this terse example from the Gospel of John:

"The next day Jesus decided to leave for Galilee. Finding Philip, he said to him, 'Follow me'" (John 1:43).

Christ beats his drum, but he does not press men;
Christ is served with volunteers.

*≈*JOHN DONNE

In some of His other entreaties, Jesus beckoned His hearers with lengthier explanations and more appealing solicitations:

"Come to me, all you who are weary and burdened, and I will give you rest. Take my yoke upon you and learn from me, for I am gentle and humble in heart, and you will find rest for your souls. For my yoke is easy and my burden is light" (Matthew 11:28-30).

Many of those who heard Jesus' call failed to understand it or didn't know what to do about it, but some heard and followed in His footsteps, traveling with Him down the Middle East's dusty roads, hearing His words, and marveling at His example as He compellingly demonstrated the radical message He proclaimed.

The Call Still Goes Out

Today, Jesus no longer presents Himself as a man, looking us straight in the eyes and inviting us to join Him in His unique mission. But still, the call continues to go out, and amazingly, people continue to hear it and respond, as Elisabeth Elliot writes:

▶ God calls me. In a deeper sense than any other species of earthbound creature, I am called. And in a deeper sense I am free, for I can ignore the call. I can turn a deaf ear. I can say that no call came. I can deny that God called or even that God exists. What a gift of amazing grace—that the One who made me allows me to deny His existence! God created me with the power to disobey, for the freedom to obey would be nothing at all without the corresponding freedom to disobey.

I can answer no, or I can answer yes. My fulfillment as a human being depends on my answer, for it is a loving Lord who calls me through the world's fog to His island of peace. If I trust Him, I will obey Him gladly." 1 ◄

Who is it that wants to live, and desires to see good days? What can be more agreeable, my dear brothers, than the voice of the Lord inviting us! See! In his lovingkindness he shows us the way of life.

~Benedict

In the centuries since His death and resurrection, Jesus has continued to call each one of us to follow Him in a particular style that is custom-tailored to our life experience and personality. Over the ages, some have heard a call to be victors for Christ, while others have heard a call to serve the unlovely and lowly. Some have come to receive much-needed inner healing and forgiveness, while others have responded to Jesus' offer of godly direction, companionship, and comfort.

If God has called you, do not spend time looking over your shoulder to see who is following you.

~Corrie ten Boom

Joyce Rupp, a member of the Servants of Mary Catholic community, heard the call of Jesus as an invitation to a divine dance:

► Thus says the Lord God to these bones: "I will cause breath to enter you, and you shall live." Ezekiel 37:5 (NSRV)
 there I am in Ezekiel's valley, one heap among many, just another stack of old, dry bones.
 some Mondays feel this way, and Tuesdays, too, to say nothing of Wednesday, Thursday, Friday.
 lost dreams and forgotten pleasures, sold like a soul to a gluttonous world feeding on my frenzy and anxious activity.
 but just when the old heap of bones seems most dry and deserted, a strong Breath of Life stirs among my dead.

Someone named God comes to my fragments and asks, with
twinkling eye: "May I have this dance?"
the Voice stretches into me, a stirring leaps in my heart, lifting up
the bones of death.
then I offer my waiting self to the One who's never stopped
believing in me, and the dance begins. 2 ◄

The Greatest Commandment

Jesus doesn't call people primarily to a social or political movement, or even first and foremost to a life or religiosity or ethical
living. More than anything, He calls us to love God—a call that was
first stated in the laws of Moses: "Hear O Israel: The Lord our God,
the Lord is one. Love the Lord your God with all your heart and with
all your soul and with all your strength" (Deuteronomy 6:4-5).

Repeatedly throughout His earthly ministry, Jesus called this the
greatest commandment. "God is love," the Apostle John reiterated in
his first epistle. "Whoever lives in love lives in God, and God in him"
(1 John 4:16b).

Centuries later, Protestant theologians restated this simple call to
love God. "What is the chief end of man?" asked the 1646 *Westminster
Confession of Faith.* "Man's chief end is to glorify God, and to enjoy
Him for ever."

---

*God does not love us because we are valuable. We are
valuable because God loves us.*

≈FULTON JOHN SHEEN

Throughout the first 20 centuries of Christian history, many disciples of Jesus have described the immense love of God. Perhaps
none has done so as eloquently as St. Bernard of Clairvaux
(1091–1153), a Cistercian monk who was both an intellectual and a
mystic, and whose French monastery had a worldwide influence.
Bernard's most famous work is *On Loving God,* which contains the
following passage:

► You want me to tell you why God is to be loved and how

**The Praise
of Love**
Who can describe
the [blessed]
bond of the love
of God? What
man is able to tell
the excellence of
its beauty, as it
ought to be told?
The height to
which love exalts
is unspeakable.
Love unites us to
God. Love covers
a multitude of
sins. Love beareth
all things, is long-
suffering in all
things. There is
nothing base,
nothing arrogant
in love. Love
admits of no
schisms: love
gives rise to no
seditions: love
does all things in
harmony. By love
have all the elect
of God been
made perfect;
without love
nothing is well-
pleasing to God.
In love has the
Lord taken us to
Himself. 3

—*St. Clement*

*St. Clement (30–100)
was one of the earli-
est bishops of Rome.
His* Epistle to the
Corinthians, *quoted here, was
written around the
year 97 and is the
oldest surviving post-
apostolic writing.*

19

much. I answer, the reason for loving God is God Himself; and the measure of love due to Him is immeasurable love. Is this plain?

We are to love God for Himself, because of a twofold reason; nothing is more reasonable, nothing more profitable. When one asks, Why should I love God? he may mean, What is lovely in God? or What shall I gain by loving God? In either case, the same sufficient cause of love exists, namely, God Himself.

And first, of His title to our love. Could any title be greater than this, that He gave Himself for us unworthy wretches? And being God, what better gift could He offer than Himself? Hence, if one seeks for God's claim upon our love here is the chiefest: Because He first loved us (1 John 4:19).

Ought He not to be loved in return, when we think who loved, whom He loved, and how much He loved? For who is He that loved? The same of whom every spirit testifies: "Thou art my God: my goods are nothing unto Thee" (Psalm 16:2, Vulgate). And is not His love that wonderful charity which "seeketh not her own"? (1 Corinthians 13:5). But for whom was such unutterable love made manifest? The apostle tells us: "When we were enemies, we were reconciled to God by the death of His Son" (Romans 5:10).

So it was God who loved us, loved us freely, and loved us while yet we were enemies. And how great was this love of His? St. John answers: "God so loved the world that He gave His only-begotten Son, that whosoever believeth in Him should not perish, but have everlasting life" (John 3:16). St. Paul adds: "He spared not His own Son, but delivered Him up for us all" (Romans 8:32); and the Son says of Himself, "Greater love hath no man than this, that a man lay down his life for his friends" (John 15:13).

This is the claim which God the holy, the supreme, the omnipotent, has upon men, defiled and base and weak.

The Rewards of Love. Having written as best I can, though unworthily, of God's right to be loved, I have still to treat of the recompense which that love brings. For although God would be loved without respect of reward, yet He wills not to leave love unrewarded. True charity cannot be left destitute, even though she is unselfish and seeketh not her own (1 Corinthians 13:5).

Love is an affection of the soul, not a contract: it cannot rise from a mere agreement, nor is it so to be gained. It is spontaneous in its origin and impulse; and true love is its own satisfaction. It has its reward; but that reward is the object beloved. For whatever you seem to love, if it is on account of something else, what you do really love is that something else, not the apparent object of desire. St. Paul did not preach the Gospel that he might earn his bread; he ate that he might be strengthened for his ministry. What he loved was not bread, but the Gospel. True love does not demand a reward, but it deserves one. Surely no one offers to pay for love; yet some recompense is due to one who loves, and if his love endures he will doubtless receive it.

Neither fear nor self-interest can convert the soul. They may change the appearance, perhaps even the conduct, but never the object of supreme desire. Sometimes a slave may do God's work; but because he does not toil voluntarily, he remains in bondage. So a mercenary may serve God, but because he puts a price on his service, he is enchained by his own greediness. For where there is self-interest there is isolation; and such isolation is like the dark corner of a room where dust and rust befoul.

Fear is the motive which constrains the slave; greed binds the selfish man, by which he is tempted when he is drawn away by his own lust and enticed (James 1:14). But neither fear nor self-interest is undefiled, nor can they convert the soul. Only charity can convert the soul, freeing it from unworthy motives. 4 ◄

Loving Our Beloved

If, as St. Bernard believed, love is not a contract but "an affection of the soul," how does one come to experience such love? Answering this question has been a top priority for disciples of Jesus throughout the ages.

Don't try to reach God with your understanding; that is impossible. Reach him in love; that is possible.

Carlo Caretto

Thomas à Kempis (1380–1471) was a German-born contemplative who entered a monastery at about the age of 20 and died there

Tranquillity All the Time

The time of labor does not with me differ from the time of prayer; and, in the noise and confusion of the kitchen where I am at work, while several persons are at the same time calling for different things, I possess God in a great tranquillity as if I were upon my knees at the Blessed Sacrament. 5

—*Brother Lawrence*

Brother Lawrence, who was born Nicholas Herman, was a 17th-century French monk.

when he was 90. During his decades of quiet submission to God, Thomas worked on a devotional book called *The Imitation of Christ,* which continues to be hailed as a classic of the faith.

The book's many evocative passages demonstrate that its author was caught up in a deep love for God:

▶ Ah, Lord God, my holy Lover, when You come into my heart, all that is within me will rejoice. You are my glory and the exultation of my heart. You are my hope and refuge in the day of my tribulation. But because my love is as yet weak and my virtue imperfect, I must be strengthened and comforted by You.

Visit me often, therefore, and teach me Your holy discipline. Free me from evil passions and cleanse my heart of all disorderly affection so that, healed and purified within, I may be fit to love, strong to suffer, and firm to persevere.

Love is an excellent thing, a very great blessing, indeed. It makes every difficulty easy, and bears all wrongs with equanimity. For it bears a burden without being weighted and renders sweet all that is bitter. The noble love of Jesus spurs to great deeds and excites longing for that which is more perfect. Love tends upward; it will not be held down by anything low. Love wishes to be free and estranged from all worldly affections, lest its inward sight be obstructed, lest it be entangled in any temporal interest and overcome by adversity. Nothing is sweeter than love, nothing stronger or higher or wider; nothing is more pleasant, nothing fuller, and nothing better in heaven or on earth, for love is born of God and cannot rest except in God, who is above all created things.

If a man loves, he will know the sound of this voice. For this warm affection of soul is a loud voice crying in the ears of God, and it says:

"My God, my love, You are all mine and I am all Yours. Give me an increase of love, that I may learn to taste with the inward lips of my heart how sweet it is to love, how sweet to be dissolved in love and bathe in it. Let me be rapt in love. Let me rise above self in great fervor and wonder. Let me sing the hymn of love, and let me follow You, my Love, to the heights. Let my soul exhaust itself in praising You, rejoicing out of love. Let me love You more than myself, and let me not love myself except for Your sake. In You let me love all those who truly love You, as the law of love, which shines forth from You, commands." 6 ◄

Gaining a New Perspective

For some people, loving God is difficult. Though they intellectually assent to the truths of Scripture and are volitionally committed to serving Him, their hearts remain relatively untouched, and their relationship with God yields little warmth.

What is Christian perfection? Loving God with all our heart, mind, soul and strength.

JOHN WESLEY

In some cases, this absence of love can be caused by a religious upbringing that stresses obedience over devotion, legalism over love. Ken Gire, the author of popular Christian books like *Intimate Moments with the Savior,* captured this dilemma in an article entitled "He Looks at Me with Delight," which explores the powerful impact our own mental images of Jesus can have in our spiritual lives.

▶ In the pictures I saw of Jesus when I was a child, He appeared mostly stoic and devoid of extremes. I saw in Him neither joy nor sorrow, laughter nor tears, elation nor depression. His facial expressions were all somewhere safely in the middle. Similar to the way He was portrayed physically—not quite a Jew yet not quite a gentile either. Somewhere in between.

The picture of Him I remember most hung on a wall in our home. His skin was smooth and tan. His hair, silken and brown. His posture, stately. His features, airbrushed to perfection. His head was turned slightly to one side, His eyes looking away, almost as if He had been posed by a photographer who told Him not to look at the camera.

As a kid who got into my share of mischief, snitching cookies from the cupboard or sneaking loose change from my mother's purse, I was glad His eyes looked away.

I remember one picture, though, in which His eyes didn't look away. While on vacation in California, our family visited a chapel where

Fuel of God

From prayer that
    asks that I may
    be
Sheltered from
    winds that beat
    on Thee,
From fearing
    when I should
    aspire,
From faltering
    when I should
    climb higher,
From silken self, O
    Captain, free
Thy soldier who
    would follow
    Thee.
From subtle love
    of softening
    things,
From easy choices,
    weakenings,
Not thus are spirits
    fortified,
Not this way went
    the Crucified,
From all that dims
    Thy Calvary,
O Lamb of God,
    deliver me.
Give me the love
    that leads the
    way,
The faith that
    nothing can dis-
    may,
The hope no dis-
    appointments
    tire,
The passion that
    will burn like
    fire.
Let me not sink to
    be a clod:
Make me Thy
    fuel, O Flame of
    God. 7

—*Amy
Carmichael*

*Amy Carmichael
(1867–1951), a native
of Northern Ireland,
was the founder of the
Dohnavur Fellowship,
a mission society
devoted to caring for
children in South
India.*

a picture of Jesus was the main attraction. We filed reverently into the wooden pews of the small room, and, as the lights dimmed, we watched the arched doors in front of us slowly open, revealing a huge portrait of Christ.

The eyes were remarkable.

Wherever you sat, they looked at you. Not only at you but through you. Or so it seemed to me as a young boy with plenty inside I didn't want Him seeing. And if that wasn't spooky enough, if you stood up to walk around the room, the eyes followed you. I never knew how they did it. I still don't. But I vividly remember those eyes locked on me with their unblinking scrutiny.

A Gaze of Pleasure. I saw different things in the eyes of all those portraits. I saw detachment. I saw disappointment. What I never saw was delight.

I see it now, though, as I peer into the pages of the Scriptures.

As I read, I try not only to hear what the people heard, but to see what they saw. I imagine, for example, looking at Jesus through the eyes of the hemorrhaging woman (Mark 5:25-34). After His eyes had picked her out of the crowd as the one who touched Him, she fell at His feet, trembling.

When He said, "Daughter, your faith has healed you. Go in peace and be freed from your suffering," I'm sure she looked up at Him. And I try to imagine what she saw in His eyes.

Was it a far-off look? An intrusive gaze into the dark closets of her soul?

I don't think so. I think she saw delight. I think she saw His pleasure in her faith, however brief the touch of her hand, however feeble the grasp on His garment.

Beholding the Beloved. On a literal level, the Bible's *Song of Solomon* portrays the romantic love between a bridegroom and his bride. On an allegorical level, it portrays the relationship between Christ and His bride, the church.

As you listen to Solomon's words, look into his eyes. Can you see the delight in them as he looks into the eyes of his beloved?

"O my dove . . . let me see your form, let me hear your voice; for your voice is sweet, and your form is lovely" (Song 2:14, NASB).

"You have made my heart beat faster, my sister, my bride; you

24

have made my heart beat faster with a single glance of your eyes" (Song 4:9, NASB).

"How beautiful and how delightful you are, my love" (Song 7:6, NASB).

It seems impossible, something our thoughts can hardly contain, but, if the allegory holds true, that is the way Jesus looks at us.

In that tonal portrait of Christ, we see the truest expression of how He feels about us. We see it in His eyes. And it's not detachment. It's not disapproval. It's delight.

Anthony de Mellow once said, "Behold God beholding you . . . and smiling." Looking at my bride, who has brought so many smiles to my face over the years, has helped me see what I never could in my youth. That this is a true picture of how God looks at us.

Maybe even the truest. [8] ◄

From Fear to Friendship

Have you ever had a friend who stood by you, stuck up for you, and comforted you when times were tough? Jesus desires to be such a friend to us all. Thomas à Kempis paints us a picture of what such friendship with Jesus looks like:

► When Jesus is near, all is well and nothing seems difficult. When He is absent, all is hard. When Jesus does not speak within, all other comfort is empty, but if He says only a word, it brings great consolation.

You cannot live well without a friend, and if Jesus be not your friend above all else, you will be very sad and desolate. Thus, you are acting foolishly if you trust or rejoice in any other. Choose the opposition of the whole world rather than offend Jesus. Of all those who are dear to you, let Him be your special love. Let all things be loved for the sake of Jesus, but Jesus for His own sake. Jesus Christ must be loved alone with a special love for He alone, of all friends, is good and faithful. [9] ◄

Enter nearly any bookstore and you can find many titles that promise to give you the secrets of making friends. But how does one learn to become closer friends with God? Writer Cynthia Heald found the answer she was looking for in the Psalms:

▶ Three years ago I prayed, "Lord, I want to go deeper with You." His answer was to lead me into a comprehensive study of the Psalms. In essence He said, "If you want to know Me, study the longing, the honesty, the depth of feeling the psalmists expressed to Me. This is how I want you to fellowship with Me, and to grow in intimacy with Me."

From studying the hearts of the psalmists, I have begun to deepen my understanding of what friendship with God is like and of how it is developed.

David's longing for God was insatiable, and the Apostle Paul counted "everything as loss compared to the possession of the price-less privilege—the overwhelming preciousness, the surpassing worth and supreme advantage—of knowing Christ Jesus my Lord" (Philippians 3:8, AMP).

True intimacy with God leaves us with a desire for deeper intimacy. And a desire to know only the Lord and His character must be our motive for intimacy. If all I seek are His gifts or what He can do for me, I have a self-centered relationship based on God's "perform-ance" in meeting my perceived needs. Instead, my desire to seek Him must be based on a longing just to know Him, to fellowship with Him, to enjoy His company.

God's love sets us truly free. Our love finds its fulfill-ment in being transformed into God's love, and only then will our works be truly fruitful.

~SIMON TUGWELL

In order to seek God in this way, I must be willing to admit that I am not the center of the universe, and that I am not self-sufficient. I cannot depend on anyone else but the Living God to fully and con-sistently care about what is best for me. To earnestly seek God, I must be willing to enter into relationship with Him on His terms—by acknowledging my need and dependence upon Him. David wrote, "Find rest, O my soul, in God alone; my hope comes from him. He alone is my rock and my salvation" (Psalm 62:5-6).

In my life the greatest hindrance to developing intimacy with the Father is my bent to live my life in my own strength, to rely on my own insight, to think that I know what God wants me to do. I can easily distance myself from the Lord by trusting my feelings and my inclinations.

Abiding and Obeying. If I truly desire to be intimate with someone, then I plan to be with that person as much as I can. David wrote: "The one thing I want from God, the thing I seek most of all, is the privilege of meditating in his Temple, living in his presence every day of my life, delighting in his incomparable perfections and glory" (Psalm 27:4, TLB).

Realistically, though, how can we live in His presence every day of our lives? Psalm 91:1 tells us: "He who dwells in the shelter of the Most High will rest in the shadow of the Almighty." To dwell means to remain, abide, sit. It conveys a constancy, a continuity, a daily communion with the Lord.

The relationship spoken of here is not an erratic visitation as need dictates. Jesus, in John 15:5, taught, "I am the vine, you are the branches; he who abides in Me, and I in him, he bears much fruit; for apart from Me you can do nothing" (NASB). To bear the fruit of His character, which can only come from the intimacy of living with Him, we must choose to dwell in His shelter.

Desiring Him and acknowledging God's rightful place in our lives are important aspects of intimacy. Yet, even with God's great love and desire for us, we cannot presume upon His character. Our God is a holy God. David wrote, "Friendship with God is reserved for those who reverence him. With them alone he shares the secrets of his promises" (Psalm 25:14, TLB).

Reverence, respect, and fear of God are essential to abiding in Him. To reverence the Lord is to stand in awe of His majesty, His holiness, His power, His glory. To fear the Lord is to be concerned about ever displeasing Him. John White wrote, "While we must never on the one hand lose the freedom to enter boldly and joyfully by faith into God's presence during our lives on earth, we must also learn how to revere God in our relationship with Him. . . . Intimacy cannot occur without respect."

In Psalm 15:1-2, David described the heart of those who dwell with God. "Lord, who may dwell in your sanctuary? Who may live on your holy hill? He whose walk is blameless and who does what is righteous, who speaks the truth from his heart."

Wholly Devoted to God

I withdrew to my usual place of retirement, in great tranquillity. I knew only to breathe out my desire for a perfect conformity to Him in all things. God was so precious that the world with all its enjoyments seemed infinitely vile. I had no more desire for the favor of men than for pebbles. At noon I had the most ardent longings after God which I ever felt in my life. In my secret retirement, I could do nothing but tell my dear Lord in a sweet calmness that He knew I desired nothing but Him, nothing but holiness, that He had given me these desires and He only could give the thing desired. I never seemed to be so unhinged from myself, and to be so wholly devoted to God. My heart was swallowed up in God most of the day. [10]

—David Brainerd

David Brainerd (1718–1747) was a heroic missionary to the Indians of northeastern America who kept a diary, which was published as Brainerd's Journal. He died of tuberculosis before he could marry the daughter of the Great Awakening's Jonathan Edwards.

One of the most succinct verses on intimacy with God is John 14:21: "Whoever has my commands and obeys them, he is the one who loves me. He who loves me will be loved by my Father, and I too will love him and show myself to him." If we love God and want to grow in our knowledge of Him, we will obey His commands. It is in our obedience that God discloses Himself to us. Jesus said, "You are my friends if you do what I command" (John 15:14).

If I desire to share in "the secrets of His promises," then I will choose to pursue a lifestyle of purity.

A Settled Assurance. If intimacy with God is our ardent desire, then we will diligently seek Him for the friendship that only He can provide. We will trust Him with our lives and we will choose to honor Him by desiring to live righteously before Him.

If we are willing to know the Lord in this way, what will our lives be like? Will we continually experience spiritual ecstasy? Will we always feel "unhinged" as Brainerd did that special day in his life? Do we need to withdraw from the demands of daily life and just sit at the feet of Jesus?

Intimacy, for me, is essentially a settled assurance that God is with me and for me even though my feelings and circumstances may seem to deny His commitment to our relationship. It is trusting Him and His promise to never leave me or forsake me. It is knowing that He is with me in the reality of my life. It is not expecting some continual emotional assurance that He is my friend.

God does not have a secret society of intimate friends. We are as intimate with God as we choose to be. It is our desire, our abiding, our purity that will determine the depth of our intimacy with Him. Intimacy is understanding that I may feel "hinged" or "unhinged." It is knowing that I must sit at the feet of Jesus, so that I can walk with integrity as His friend. It is experiencing the closeness of the Lord and at other times wondering if He is near. Essentially, intimacy is abandonment of ourselves to the Lord—abandonment born out of trust and an intense longing to know the living God. [11] ◂

Being and Doing

Some of Jesus' disciples were commissioned by Him to go out and preach, teach, and heal. But before conducting their missions of mercy, these disciples learned much from their master. In their case, being preceded doing. Loving God came before serving God. And that's the way it should be for us too.

"Come, follow me," Jesus said to the brothers Peter and Andrew, "and I will make you fishers of men" (Matthew 4:19). Following Jesus preceded casting their nets for more followers. Discipleship preceded evangelism.

I do not know whether God can bestow upon a man anything greater than this grace, that by his work wayward men might be changed into better, and sons of the devil be changed into sons of God.

—RICHARD OF ST. VICTOR

"Preach always," said St. Francis of Assisi. "If necessary, use words." Centuries earlier, St. Ignatius (35?–107?), the Bishop of Antioch, expressed similar thoughts:

▶ It is better for a man to be silent and be [a Christian], than to talk and not to be one. It is good to teach, if he who speaks also acts. There is then one Teacher, who spake and it was done; while even those things which He did in silence are worthy of the Father. He who possesses the word of Jesus is truly able to hear even His very silence, that he may be perfect, and may both act as he speaks, and be recognized by his silence. There is nothing which is hid from God, but our very secrets are near to Him. Let us therefore do all things as those who have Him dwelling in us, that we may be His temples, and He may be in us as our God, which indeed He is, and will manifest Himself before our faces. Wherefore we justly love Him. [12] ◀

Throughout church history, many movements have sought to quickly turn converts into missionaries, and in some cases, such efforts have yielded much good. On the other hand, each person is

Disciples Bear Much Fruit

How is it possible for us sinful, finite creatures to glorify God? How can we—with all our limitations—add anything at all to the majesty and the blessedness of the everlasting Creator? It seems so impossible. Almost incredible. Jesus assures us, however, that we can do so by "bearing much fruit." It is through such spiritual productivity, He says, that we become His disciples. Maybe, then, we should make a distinction. Maybe there are Christians who never pass from mere belief into the category of discipleship. For only in proportion as, and to the degree that, we bear fruit are we entitled to call ourselves the disciples of Jesus.

What is the supreme purpose of human life? A Christ-like discipleship that glorifies God. And how do we become Christlike disciples? By bearing fruit. No, by bearing much fruit, becoming maximally productive for the praise of our heavenly Father. [13]

—*Vernon Grounds*

29

unique, and many new disciples seem to require a significant period of learning and training before they are truly prepared to minister in God's name.

As Richard Baxter (1615–1691), a Puritan pastor in England, often said, "Let us consider what it is to take heed to ourselves." As Baxter wrote:

▶ See that the work of saving grace be thoroughly wrought in your own souls. Take heed to yourselves, lest you be void of that saving grace of God which you offer to others, and be strangers to the effectual working of that gospel which you preach; and lest, while you proclaim to the world the necessity of a Savior, your own hearts should neglect him, and you should miss of an interest in him and his saving benefits.

Take heed to yourselves, lest you perish, while you call upon others to take heed of perishing; and lest you famish yourselves while you prepare food for them. Though there is a promise of shining as the stars, to those "who turn many to righteousness," that is but on supposition that they are first turned to it themselves. Their own sincerity in the faith is the condition of their glory, simply considered, though their great ministerial labors may be a condition of the promise of their greater glory. [14] ◀

There are some people who at first are hardhearted
and persist in sin; somehow the good God in his
mercy sends them the chastisement of affliction, so
that they grow weary of their ways and come to their
senses, and are converted. They draw near to God
and come to knowledge and repent wholeheartedly,
and attain to the true way of life.

~ANTONY OF EGYPT

Secret Sins

In the 1980s, two prominent American televangelists gained worldwide media attention after they were confronted with charges of lying, financial mismanagement, and sexual misconduct. Such charges would have been libelous if they hadn't been true. Although this wasn't the first time in 20 centuries that Christian leaders had been exposed as hypocrites, it was certainly one of the most widely publicized scandals in church history.

But hidden sins are no new problem for believers. Catholic Cardinal John Henry Newman of England (1801–1890) had concern for the many believers who harbored what he called "secret faults." As he wrote:

▶ Strange as it may seem, multitudes called Christians go through life with no effort to obtain a correct knowledge of themselves. They are contented with general and vague impressions concerning their real state; and, if they have more than this, it is merely such accidental information about themselves as the events of life force upon them. But exact systematic knowledge they have none, and do not aim at it.

[Yet] unless we have some just idea of our hearts and of sin, we can have no right idea of a Moral Governor, a Savior, or a Sanctifier that is, in professing to believe in Them, we shall be using words without attaching distinct meaning to them. Thus self-knowledge is at the root of all real religious knowledge; and it is in vain—worse than vain, it is a deceit and a mischief—to think to understand the Christian doctrines as a matter of course, merely by being taught by books, or by attending sermons, or by any outward means, however excellent, taken by themselves. For it is as we search our hearts and understand our own nature that we understand what is meant by an Infinite Governor and Judge; in proportion as we comprehend the nature of disobedience and our actual sinfulness, that we feel what is the blessing of the removal of sin, redemption, pardon, sanctification, which otherwise are mere words.

Most men [however] are contented with a slight acquaintance with their hearts. Men are satisfied to have numberless secret faults. They do not think about them, either as sins or as obstacles to strength of faith, and live on as if they had nothing to learn.

You cannot cure the soul of others or "help people"
without having changed yourself.
                       —ALEXANDER ELCHANINOV

Self-knowledge Takes Work. Call to mind the impediments that are in the way of your knowing yourselves or feeling your ignorance, and then judge. First of all, self-knowledge does not come as a matter of course; it implies an effort and a work. Now the very effort of steadily reflecting is itself painful to many men; not to speak of the difficulty of reflecting correctly. To ask ourselves why we do this or that, to take account of the principles which govern us, and see whether we act for conscience's sake or from some lower inducement, is painful.

And then comes in our self-love. We hope the best; this saves us the trouble of examining.

Next we must consider the force of habit. Conscience at first warns us against sin; but if we disregard it, it soon ceases to upbraid us; and thus sins, once known, in time become secret sins.

To the force of habit must be added that of custom. Every age has its own wrong ways; and these have such influence, that even good men, from living in the world, are unconsciously misled by them. The most religious men, unless they are especially watchful, will feel the sway of the fashion of their age.

Now what is our chief guide amid the seducing customs of the world? Obviously, the Bible. Our conscience gets corrupted, true; but the words of truth, though effaced from our minds, remain in Scripture, bright in their eternal youth and purity.

Ask yourselves what do you know of the Bible? Do you know very much more of your Savior's works and words than you have heard read in church? Have you compared His precepts, or St. Paul's, or any other Apostle's, with your own daily conduct, and prayed and endeavored to act upon them? If you have, so far is well; go on to do so. If you have not, it is plain you do not possess, for you have not sought to possess, an adequate notion of that perfect Christian character nor an adequate notion of your actual sinful state. [15] ◄

Jesus Himself dealt with the issue of secret sins: "This is the verdict," He said. "Light has come into the world, but men loved darkness instead of light because their deeds were evil. Everyone who does evil hates the light, and will not come into the light for fear that his deeds will be exposed. But whoever lives by the truth comes into the light, so that it may be seen plainly that what he has done has been done through God" (John 3:19-21).

Jesus calls those who would follow Him to walk in the light, not keep portions of life hidden away in the dark.

Discipleship Defined

Jesus didn't interrogate those He called to be His disciples, nor did He require them to take a spiritual aptitude test before permitting them to follow Him. And He never gave a lengthy, definitive sermon on the essence of discipleship.

"If you hold to my teaching, you are really my disciples," He once told some of the Jews who had believed Him. "Then you will know the truth, and the truth will set you free" (John 8:31-32).

The commandment of absolute truthfulness is really only another name for the fullness of discipleship.

—DIETRICH BONHOEFFER

But over the centuries, many saints and scholars have attempted to provide a more detailed definition of what discipleship entails.

David Watson, a canon in the Anglican Church, wrote this description in 1980:

▶ "When Christ calls a man, he bids him come and die," declared Dietrich Bonhoeffer. In this startling statement we see the radical nature of Christian discipleship. There are different ways in which we may die; not every Christian is called to literal martyrdom, as was Bonhoeffer. But every Christian is called to clear, dedicated discipleship, whatever the personal cost may be.

The concept of discipleship was by no means new when Jesus called men and women to follow him, so it is not surprising that, although the verb "disciple" occurs only 25 times in the New Testament (6 in the Gospels), the noun "disciple" appears no less than 264 times, exclusively in the Gospels and Acts. In secular Greek the word meant an apprentice in some trade, a student of some subject, or a

---

Discipleship Includes Everything

A disciple of Jesus is not necessarily one devoted to doing specifically religious things as that is usually understood. To repeat, I am learning from Jesus how to lead my life, my whole life, my real life.

So as his disciple I am not necessarily learning how to do religious things, either as a part of "full-time service" or as a "part-time service." My discipleship to Jesus is, within clearly definable limits, not a matter of what I do, but of how I do it. And it covers everything, "religious" or not. [16]

—*Dallas Willard*

Jesus Is Near
Discipleship means living one day at a time as though Jesus were near, near in time, near in place, the witness of our motives, our speech, our behavior. As indeed He is.

Religiosity per se is not discipleship; in fact, it may be a safe refuge from the revolutionary lifestyle proposed by Jesus.

What is the relationship between discipleship and religious practices? The latter sustain the Christian life. It is impossible to keep Christian values in focus if we do not read Scripture and pray and lean on others for support and direction.

Insofar as prayer, reading, sacraments and spiritual direction support genuine Christian living, that is, Christian attitudes, relationships, choices and actions, they are useful. When they become an escape from the more difficult demands of Christian living, they are the corruption of discipleship." [18]

—*Brennan Manning*

pupil of some teacher. In the New Testament times we find the same primary meaning in the terms "disciples of Moses"' (students of the Mosaic law) and "disciples of the Pharisees" (those preoccupied with a detailed knowledge of Jewish tradition as given in the Torah). These disciples would submit themselves entirely to their rabbi, and were not permitted to study the Scriptures without the guidance of their teacher, although they expected to become teachers themselves after extensive training.

Nearer to the specifically Christian concept of discipleship were the followers of John the Baptist who attached themselves to this New Testament prophet. Following their teacher, they fasted and prayed, confronted the Jewish leaders, and remained loyal to John during his imprisonment and at his death. Unlike the disciples of Moses or of the Pharisees, they were fully committed to their master as well as to his message.

Thus we see that the basic idea of discipleship was widely accepted when Jesus began his ministry. At the same time, when Jesus took the initiative in calling people to follow him, when he called them primarily to himself and not just to his teaching, when he expected from them total obedience, when he taught them to serve and warned them that they would suffer, and when he gathered around him a diverse group of very ordinary people, he was obviously creating a radical and unique pattern of discipleship. [17] ◄

Another summary of discipleship was provided by William MacDonald, who identified seven of what he calls "terms of discipleship as laid down by the Savior of the world":

► 1. *A supreme love for Jesus Christ.* Our love to Christ should be so great that all other loves are hatred by comparison. Not until we are willing to lay down our very lives for Him are we in the place where He wants us.

2. *A denial of self.* Denial of self is not the same as self-denial. The latter means foregoing certain foods, pleasures, or possessions. But denial of self means such complete submission to the lordship of Christ that self has no rights or authority at all. It means that self abdicates the throne.

3. *A deliberate choosing of the cross.* The cross is not some physical infirmity or mental anguish; these things are common to all men. The cross is a pathway that is deliberately chosen. The cross symbolizes the shame, persecution and abuse which the world heaped upon the Son of God, and which the world will heap on all who choose to stand against the tide.

4. *A life spent in following Christ.* What characterized the life of the Lord Jesus? It was a life of obedience to the will of God. It was a life lived in the power of the Holy Spirit. It was a life of unselfish service for others. It was a life of patience and long-suffering in the face of the gravest wrongs.

5. *A fervent love for all who belong to Christ.* This is the love that esteems others better than oneself. It is the love that covers a multitude of sins. It is the love that suffers long and is kind. It vaunts not itself and is not puffed up (1 Corinthians 13). Without this love, discipleship would be a cold, legalistic asceticism.

6. *An unswerving continuance in His Word.* For real discipleship there must be continuance. It is easy enough to start well, to burst forth in a blaze of glory. But the test of reality is endurance to the end. Spasmodic obedience to the Scriptures will not do. Christ wants those who will follow Him in constant, unquestioning obedience.

7. *A forsaking of all to follow Him.* This is perhaps the most unpopular of all Christ's terms of discipleship, and Luke 14:33 may well prove to be the most unpopular verse in the Bible. What is meant by forsaking all? It means abandonment of all one's material possessions that are not absolutely essential and that could be used in the spread of the Gospel. [19] ◄

While some authors have focused on defining discipleship, others have tried instead to describe the "marks" or characteristics of those who are true disciples of Jesus.

Heavenly Things

O my soul, lift up thyself above thyself; fly away in the contemplation of heaven and heavenly things; make not thy further abode in this inferior region, where is nothing but travail and trials, and sorrow, and woe, and wretchedness, and sin, and trouble, and fear, and all deceiving and destroying vanities. Bend all thine affections upward unto the superior places where thy Redeemer liveth and reigneth, and where thy joys are laid up in the treasury of his merits which shall be made thy merits, his perfection thy perfection, and his death thy life eternal, and his resurrection thy salvation. Esteem not the trifling pleasures of this life to be the way to this wealth, nor thy ignominious estate here to be any bar to prevent thee from the full use and joyful fruition of the glory there prepared for thee. [20]

—*John Bradford*

John Bradford (1510?–1555) was a Protestant preacher and martyr who was executed during the reign of England's "bloody" Queen Mary.

35

The Marks of a Disciple

Following Christ's Example: Eight Steps toward Discipleship

1. First of all, *the purity and holiness* of the life of Christ is proposed as a glorious pattern for the saints' imitation.

2. *The obedience* of Christ to his Father's will is a pattern for the imitation of Christians.

3. The *self-denial* of Christ is the pattern of believers, and their conformity to it is their indispensable duty.

4. The *activity and diligence* of Christ in finishing the work of God committed to him was a pattern for all believers to imitate.

5. *Delight in God and his service* was eminently conspicuous in the life of Christ, and is a pattern for the believer's imitation.

6. The *inoffensiveness* of the life of Christ upon earth is an excellent pattern for all his people; he injured none, but was holy and harmless.

continued on the next page

It seems that when Jesus' disciples weren't following Him from town to town, or listening to His powerful words, or performing miracles in His name, they were competing and squabbling amongst themselves.

"Who is the greatest in the kingdom of heaven?" they asked Him once. Jesus answered them with a powerful illustration of what the kingdom was like:

"He called a little child and had him stand among them. And he said: 'I tell you the truth, unless you change and become like little children, you will never enter the kingdom of heaven. Therefore, whoever humbles himself like this child is the greatest in the kingdom of heaven. And whoever welcomes a little child like this in my name welcomes me'" (Matthew 18:2-5).

Nearly a century after Jesus spoke these words, a man who had personally observed the peculiar habits of the early Christians described their activities in a letter to a friend:

▶ For the Christians are distinguished from other men neither by country, nor language, nor the customs which they observe. For they neither inhabit cities of their own, nor employ a peculiar form of speech, nor lead a life which is marked out by any singularity. The course of conduct which they follow has not been devised by any speculation or deliberation of inquisitive men; nor do they, like some, proclaim themselves the advocates of any merely human doctrines. But, inhabiting Greek as well as barbarian cities, according as the lot of each of them has determined, and following the customs of the natives in respect to clothing, food, and the rest of their ordinary conduct, they display to us their wonderful and confessedly striking method of life. They dwell in their own countries, but simply as sojourners. As citizens, they share in all things with others, and yet endure all things as if foreigners. Every foreign land is to them as their native country, and every land of their birth as a land of strangers. They marry, as do all [others]; they beget children; but they do not destroy their offspring. They have a common table, but not a common bed. They are in the flesh, but they do not live after the flesh. They pass their days on earth, but they are citizens of heaven. They obey the prescribed laws, and at the same time surpass the laws by their lives. They love all men, and are persecuted by all. They are unknown and condemned; they are put to death, and restored to life. They are poor, yet make many rich; they are in lack of all things, and yet abound in all; they are dishonored, and yet in their very dishonor are glorified. They are evil spoken of, and yet are justified; they are reviled, and bless; they are insulted, and repay the insult with honor; they do good, yet are punished as evil-doers. When punished, they rejoice as if quickened into life; they are assailed by the Jews as for-eigners, and are persecuted by the Greeks; yet those who hate them are unable to assign any reason for their hatred. [21] ◀

This letter seems to indicate that some of those who became Jesus' disciples in the years after His death and resurrection possibly understood the message of the kingdom better than His own disci-ples initially did.

In later centuries, Christian thinkers continued to offer their views of what factors constituted the marks of a true disciple. Jeremiah Bur-roughs considered contentment an important—but scarce—aspect of the Christian life. His work, *The Rare Jewel of Christian Contentment,* discussed the following four ways Christians could experience greater happiness.

▶ *All the rules and helps in the world will do us little good unless we get a good temper within our hearts.* You can never make a ship go steady by propping it outside; you know there must be ballast within the ship, to make it go steady. And so, there is nothing out-side us that can keep our hearts in a steady, constant way, but what is within us: grace is within the soul, and it will do this.

If you would get a contented life, do not grasp too much of the world, do not take in more of the business of the world than God calls you to. Do not be greedy of taking in a great deal of the world, for if a man goes among thorns, when he may take a simpler way, he has no reason to complain that he is pricked with them. You go among thorns—is it your way? Must you of necessity go among them? Then it is another matter. But if you voluntarily choose that

---

7. The humility and lowliness of Christ is pro-pounded by him-self as a pattern for his people's imitation.

8. The content-ment of Christ in a low condition in the world is an excellent pattern for his people's imitation. [22]

—*John Flavel*

John Flavel (1630–1691) was a Presbyterian pastor in England and the author of many works about practi-cal religion.

True Repentance

If Jesus Christ is Lord, men must be confronted with his authority over the totality of life. Evangelism is not, and cannot be, a mere offer of benefits avail-able through Jesus Christ. Christ's work is inseparable from his person; the Jesus who died for our sins is the Lord of the whole universe, and the announcement of forgiveness in his name is insepara-ble from the call to repentance, the call to turn from "the rulers of this world" to the Lord of glory. [23]

—*Rene Padilla*

**Follow God:
Do Good
Works**

What shall we do,
then, brethren?
Shall we become
slothful in well-
doing, and cease
from the practice
of love? God for-
bid that any such
course should be
followed by us!
But rather let us
hasten with all
energy and readi-
ness of mind to
perform every
good work. For
the Creator and
Lord of all Him-
self rejoices in His
works. For by His
infinitely great
power He estab-
lished the heav-
ens, and by His
incomprehensi-
ble wisdom He
adorned them.
He also divided
the earth from
the water which
surrounds it, and
fixed it upon the
immovable foun-
dation of His own
will. The animals
also which are
upon it He com-
manded by His
own word into
existence. So like-
wise, when He
had formed the
sea, and the liv-
ing creatures
which are in it, He
enclosed them
[within their
proper bounds]
by His own
power.
Above all, with His
holy and unde-
filed hands He
formed man, the
most excellent [of
His creatures], and
truly great
through the
understanding

*continued on the
next page*

way, when you may go another, then you have no cause to complain. If men and women will thrust themselves on things of the
world which they do not need, then no wonder that they are pricked
and meet with what disturbs them.

Labor to be spiritually minded. That is, be often in meditation of
the things that are above. "If we be risen with Christ," say the Scriptures, "let us seek the things that are above, where Christ is, that sits
at the right hand of God." Be much in spiritual thoughts, in conversing with things above. Many Christians who have an interest in the
things of heaven converse but very little with them; their meditations
are not much upon heavenly things.

*Be not inordinately taken up with the comforts of this world when
you have them.* When you have them, do not take too much satisfaction in them. It is a certain rule: however inordinate any man or
woman is in sorrow when a comfort is taken from them, so were they
immoderate in their rejoicing in the comfort when they had it. 24 ◄

In a similar vein, Thomas à Kempis declared that believers who
were committed to God and focused on doing God's work were
most peaceful and contented:

► The more recollected a man is, and the more simple of heart
he becomes, the easier he understands sublime things, for he
receives the light of knowledge from above. The pure, simple, and
steadfast spirit is not distracted by many labors, for he does them all
for the honor of God. And since he enjoys interior peace he seeks
no selfish end in anything. What, indeed, gives more trouble and
affliction than uncontrolled desires of the heart?

A good and devout man arranges in his mind the things he has
to do, not according to the whims of evil inclination but according to
the dictates of right reason. Who is forced to struggle more than he
who tries to master himself? This ought to be our purpose, then: to
conquer self, to become stronger each day, to advance in virtue. 25 ◄

The Beauty of Humility

T hrough the ages, people have marveled at Jesus' compassion, His miracles, and His wisdom, as well as His amazing ability to explain mysterious concepts of the kingdom of God in simple, clear language. People have also debated about which of the many characteristics of Jesus are most central to His ministry and the life of His disciples.

One characteristic of Jesus that many believers consider extremely important is His humility, an attitude Vernon Grounds described as "the Gethsemane mindset":

▶ It is the attitude of trustful self-surrender demonstrated by Jesus as He prayed, "Not my will, Father, but your will be done." It is the renunciation of our own very human feelings, desires, hopes, dreams, and ambitions in order that the purposes of God may be accomplished. [26] ◀

As we saw in a passage from Matthew cited earlier, Jesus silenced His disciples, who were battling over positions of prominence in His entourage, with these startling words: "Whoever humbles himself like this child is the greatest in the kingdom of heaven."

Jesus demonstrated humility in the way He served the people who followed Him, in the way He washed His disciples' feet, and more importantly, in the way He came to earth to serve us.

From the earliest times, Christians have written about Christ's humility. St. Clement of Rome explored the subject in his *Epistle to the Corinthians:*

▶ For Christ is of those who are humble-minded, and not of those who exalt themselves over His flock. Our Lord Jesus Christ, the Scepter of the majesty of God, did not come in the pomp of pride or arrogance, although He might have done so, but in a lowly condition. If the Lord thus humbled Himself, what shall we do who have through Him come under the yoke of His grace. [27] ◀

Centuries later Teresa of Avila (1582–1582), a devout nun who is now honored as the patron saint of Spain, filled journals and books

given him—the express likeness of His own image. For thus says God: "Let us make man in Our image, and after Our likeness. So God made man; male and female He created them." Having thus finished all these things, He approved them, and blessed them, and said, "Increase and multiply." We see, then, how all righteous men have been adorned with good works, and how the Lord Himself, adorning Himself with His works, rejoiced. Having therefore such an example, let us accede to His will, and let us work the work of righteousness with our whole strength. [28]
—*St. Clement*

Vanity or Humility?
How many there are who perish because of vain worldly knowledge and too little care for serving God. They became vain in their own conceits because they chose to be great rather than humble. He is truly great who has great charity. He is truly great who is little in his own eyes and makes nothing of the highest honor. He is truly wise who looks upon all earthly things as folly that he may gain Christ. [29]
—*Thomas à Kempis*

with reflections on the kind of selfless love that was exhibited by Jesus and is demanded of His followers:

▶ When we hope to gain affection from others, we always seek it because of some interest, benefit, or pleasure we hope to receive from them.

However "pure" our affection for another may seem in our own eyes, it is natural that we should want them to feel affection for us. Too often, though, we begin to analyze the affection they show us. Do they feel the same toward us as we feel toward them? Would they do as much for us? Soon we determine that, compared with the way we feel for them, compared with what we would do for them, their love for us has little substance. "It is like a piece of chaff in the wind, insignificant and easily blown away."

I want you to consider this, though: No matter how dearly we have been loved by any human being—what is there in human love that is not "chaff"? And what is it that remains?

The one who truly loves in spirit cares nothing whether he receives the affection of another or not. When I say this, you may think it odd and unnatural. You may think that such a person will be cold and compassionless toward people while they are occupied with loving God.

Nothing is further from the truth. A man or woman who learns to love in a detached manner, for the sake of God's love, will love others a great deal. They will love with greater compassion and greater intensity. Their only concern will be to see the person they love grow in the Lord, no matter what it takes.

To love others for their spiritual profit and not for our own comfort or benefit—that is what love really is. People who love in this way are always more happy to give than to receive, even in their relationship with the Creator Himself!

So many other things have been described as affection, when they are really only base and self-seeking. What I have described to you is true holy affection. It is the only thing that deserves to be called by its high and holy name: Love. [30] ◀

One of the most powerful biblical passages about humility can be found in Philippians 2:5-8, in which Paul challenges believers that "your attitude should be the same as that of Christ Jesus."

Andrew Murray (1828–1917), a minister in South Africa's Dutch Reformed church and an author of many devotional books, incorporated portions of this passage into one of his many readings on humility:

▶ "Let this mind be in you, which was also in Christ Jesus, who being in the form of God made himself of no reputation . . . and as a man humbled himself." We must be like Christ in His self-emptying and self-humiliation. In this first great act He emptied himself of His divine glory and power and laid it aside; this was followed up by the no less wondrous humbling of himself as man to the death of the cross. In this amazing twofold humiliation, the astonishment of the universe and the delight of the Father, Holy Scripture with the utmost simplicity tells us how we must be like Christ.

And does God really expect this of us? Why not? or rather, how can He expect anything else? He fully knows the power of human pride. But He also knows that Christ has redeemed us from the power of sin, and that He gives us His resurrection life and power to enable us to live as He did on earth. It is as our example that we not only live through Him but like Him. And further, as our head, He lives in us, and continues in us the life He once led on earth. With such a Christ, and such a plan of redemption, can it be otherwise? The follower of Christ must have the same mind as was in Christ; he must be like Him especially in His humility. [32] ◀

Downward Mobility

Ours is a world in which many people seek first and foremost to better themselves, even if this means doing so at the expense of others. In such a world of self-centered upward mobility, writers like Roy Hession have advocated that Christians pursue lifestyles of downward mobility in the service of God and humanity.

All for God and nothing for self.
❈MARY MAGDALENE DEI PAZZI

In this moving passage from his classic work, *The Calvary Road,* Hession argues that humility should be a defining mark of Jesus' disciples:

▶ Nothing is clearer from the New Testament than that the Lord Jesus expects us to take the low position of servants. This is not just an extra obligation, which we may or may not assume as we please. It is the very heart of that new relationship which the disciple is to take if he is to know fellowship with Christ and any degree of holiness in his life.

When we come to the New Testament, the word in the Greek for the servant of the Lord Jesus Christ is not "hired servant"—one who receives wages and has certain rights—but "bond-servant," meaning that our position is one where we have no rights and no appeal, where we are the absolute property of our Master, to be treated and disposed of just as he wishes.

Further, we shall see more clearly still what our position is to be when we understand that we are to be the bond-servants of One who was himself willing to be a bond-servant. He took "the very nature of a servant" (Philippians 2:7)—without rights, willing to be treated as the will of the Father and the malice of men might decree, if only he might thereby serve men and bring them back to God.

You and I are to be the bond-servants of him who was and always is a bond-servant whose disposition is ever that of humility and whose activity is ever that of humbling himself to serve his creatures.

How utterly low, then, is our true position! How this shows us what it means to be ruled by the Lord Jesus!

That leads us to something further. Our servanthood to the Lord Jesus is to express itself in our servanthood to our fellows. The low position we take toward the Lord Jesus is judged by him by the low position we take in our relationship with our fellows. An unwillingness to serve others in costly, humbling ways he takes to be an unwillingness to serve him.

The Five Marks of a Bond-servant. In Luke 17, Jesus compares the person who would be his disciple to a bond-servant. The five marks of the bond-servant are as follows.

First of all, he must be willing to have one thing on top of another put upon him, without any consideration being given him. On top of a hard day in the field, the servant in the parable had immediately to prepare his master's meal, and on top of that he had to wait on him at table—and all that before he had any food himself. He just went and did it, expecting nothing else. How unwilling we are for this! How quickly there are murmurings and bitterness in our hearts when that sort of thing is expected of us. But the moment we start murmuring, we are acting as if we had rights, and a bond-servant hasn't any!

Secondly, in doing this he must be willing not to be thanked for it. How often we serve others, but what self-pity we have in our hearts and how bitterly we complain that they take it as a matter of course and do not thank us for it. But a bond-servant must be willing for that. Hired servants may expect something, but not bond-servants.

Thirdly, having done all this, he must not charge the other with selfishness. As I read the passage, I could not but feel that the master was rather selfish and inconsiderate. But there is no such charge from the bond-servant. He exists to serve the interests of his master, and the selfishness or otherwise of his master does not enter into it with him.

But we? We can perhaps allow ourselves to be "put upon" by others, and are willing perhaps not to be thanked for what we do, but how in our minds we charge the other with selfishness!

Yet that is not the place of a bond-servant. He is to find in the selfishness of others a further opportunity to identify himself with his Lord as the servant of all.

Fourth, having done all that, there is no ground for pride or self-congratulation, but we must confess that we are unworthy servants—we are of no real use to God or man in ourselves. We must confess again and again that in our flesh, there dwelleth no good thing; that if we have acted as willing servants, it is no thanks to us, whose hearts are naturally proud and stubborn, but only to the Lord Jesus, who dwells in us and who has made us willing.

The fifth and last step is the admission that doing and bearing what we have in the way of meekness and humility, we have not done one stitch more than it was our duty to do. God made man in the first place simply that he might be God's bond-servant. Man's sin has simply consisted in his refusal to be God's bond-servant. His restoration can only be, then, a restoration to the position of a bond-servant. A man has not done anything specially meritorious when he has consented to take that position, for he was created and redeemed for that very thing.

This, then, is the Way of the Cross. It is the way that God's lowly Bond Servant first trod for us, and should not we, the bond-servants of that Bond Servant, tread it still? 33 ◄

Pressured, But Not Crushed

We are hard pressed on every side, but not crushed; perplexed, but not in despair; persecuted, but not abandoned; struck down, but not destroyed. We always carry around in our body the death of Jesus, so that the life of Jesus may also be revealed in our body. For we who are alive are always being given over to death for Jesus' sake, so that his life may be revealed in our mortal body. So then, death is at work in us, but life is at work in you (2 Corinthians 4:8-12).

Taking Up the Cross

A Visit to Vanity Fair

Then I saw in my dream, that when they were got out of the wilderness, they presently saw a town before them, and the name of that town is Vanity; and at the town there is a fair kept, called Vanity Fair. It beareth the name of Vanity Fair because the town where it is kept is lighter than vanity, and also because all that is there sold, or that cometh thither, is vanity.

This fair is no new erected business, but a thing of ancient standing. At this fair are all such merchandise sold, as houses, lands, trades, places, honors, preferments, titles, countries, kingdoms, lusts, pleasures; and delights of all sorts, as whores, bawds, wives, husbands, children, masters, servants, lives, blood, bodies, souls, silver, gold, pearls, precious stones, and what not. And, moreover, at this fair there is at all times to be seen juggling cheats, games, plays, fools, apes, knaves, and rogues, and that of every kind. Here are to be seen, too, and that for nothing, thefts, murders, adulteries, false swearers, and that of a bloodred color.

continued on the next page

During the 20th century, one of the most popular evangelistic appeals went something like this: "God loves you and has a wonderful plan for your life."

Though true, this selective summary told only a small part of the story about the Christian life, and its sunny, optimistic presentation of the Christian life stood in sharp contrast to the picture Jesus repeatedly painted to His own disciples:

"If anyone would come after me, he must deny himself and take up his cross and follow me," He told His disciples and those in a crowd following Him. "For whoever wants to save his life will lose it, but whoever loses his life for me and for the gospel will save it" (see Mark 8:34-35).

"If the world hates you, keep in mind that it hated me first," He says in the Gospel of John. "If you belonged to the world, it would love you as its own. As it is, you do not belong to the world, but I have chosen you out of the world. That is why the world hates you. Remember the words I spoke to you: 'No servant is greater than his master.' If they persecuted me, they will persecute you also" (see John 15:18–16:4).

"All men will hate you because of me," Jesus tells His disciples in Matthew, "but he who stands firm to the end will be saved" (see Matthew 10:17-23).

Later in this passage from Matthew, Jesus tells His disciples that taking up one's cross is a requirement, not an option: "Anyone who loves his father or mother more than me is not worthy of me; anyone who loves his son or daughter more than me is not worthy of me; and anyone who does not take his cross and follow me is not worthy of me. Whoever finds his life will lose it, and whoever loses his life for my sake will find it" (Matthew 10:37-39).

The stoning of Stephen (Acts 7) gave the early Christians a preview of the persecution that would follow. And as Paul told Timothy, persecution was not an anomaly in the Christian life. "In fact," he wrote, "everyone who wants to live a godly life in Christ Jesus will be persecuted" (2 Timothy 3:12-13).

Peter, whose faith would lead to him being crucified as Christ was, wrote about the cost of following Jesus:

"Dear friends, do not be surprised at the painful trial you are suffering, as though something strange were happening to you. But rejoice that you participate in the sufferings of Christ, so that you may be overjoyed when his glory is revealed. If you are insulted because of the name of Christ, you are blessed, for the Spirit of glory and of God rests on you. If you suffer, it should not be as a murderer or thief or any other kind of criminal, or even as a meddler. However, if you suffer as a Christian, do not be ashamed, but praise God that you bear that name" (1 Peter 4:12-16).

The Cost of Commitment

The church of Jesus was born amidst severe persecution of believers, and Christians are still harassed, intimidated, injured, or killed in many parts of the world today. Persecution purifies the church and challenges believers to live out their commitment during times of tremendous evil and destructiveness.

Perhaps no modern believer better understood these things than Dietrich Bonhoeffer, who was the director of a German seminary that resisted Adolf Hitler's totalitarian Third Reich. Lecturing in the United States in 1939, Bonhoeffer could have remained in America, safe from the growing conflagration at home. But he chose to return to Germany and share in the suffering of his people.

Our peace is not a well-being; it is a participation in Christ, in God in the flesh against all other things in the flesh.

CHRISTOPH FRIEDRICH BLUMHARDT

His continuing opposition to the Third Reich's evil policies and efforts to control the church led to his imprisonment in 1943 and his execution on April 9, 1945, which was less than one month before Germany surrendered to the Allied forces.

A series of lectures he had delivered were published in 1937 under the title *The Cost of Discipleship*. In that book, Bonhoeffer contrasts "cheap grace" with the true cost of following Christ:

Now, as I said, the way to the Celestial City lies just through this town where this lusty fair is kept; and he that will go to the city, and yet not go through this town, "must needs go out of the world." The Prince of princes himself, when here, went through this town to his own country, and that upon a fair day too; yea, and as I think, it was Beelzebub, the chief Lord of this fair, that invited him to buy of his vanities; yea, would have made him Lord of the fair, would he but have done him reverence as he went through the town. Yea, because he was such a person of honor, Beelzebub had him from street to street, and showed him all the kingdoms of the world in a little time, that he might, if possible, allure the Blessed One to cheapen and buy some of his vanities; but he had no mind to the merchandise, and therefore left the town, without laying out so much as one farthing upon these vanities. [34]

—*John Bunyan*

**The Suffer-
ings of Our
Lord**

It is with the holi-
est fear that we
should approach
the terrible fact
of the sufferings
of our Lord.

Let no one think
that they were
less because He
was more. The
more delicate the
nature, the more
alive to all that is
lovely and true,
lawful and right,
the more does it
feel the antago-
nism of pain, the
inroad of death
upon life. The
more sensitive
the nature, the
more dreadful is
that breach of the
harmony of
things whose
sound is untrue.

Jesus felt more
than [a mere]
man could feel,
because He had a
larger feeling. He
was therefore
worn out even
sooner than
another man
would have been.
These sufferings
were awful
indeed when
they began to
invade the region
about the will.
Then did Jesus
bear the weight
of our sin, when
the struggle to
keep consciously
trusting in God
began to sink in
darkness, when
the will of the
man put forth in
its last deter-
mined effort in
that cry after the
vanishing vision
of the Father, "My

*continued on the
next page*

▶ Cheap grace is the deadly enemy of our Church. We are fight-ing today for costly grace.

Cheap grace means grace sold on the market like cheapjacks' wares. The sacraments, the forgiveness of sin, and the consolations of religion are thrown away at cut prices. Grace is presented as the Church's inexhaustible treasury, from which she showers blessings with generous hands, without asking questions or fixing limits. Grace without price; grace without cost! The essence of grace, we suppose, is that the account has been paid in advance; and, because it has been paid, everything can be had for nothing. Since the cost was infi-nite, the possibilities of using and spending it are infinite. What would grace be if it were not cheap?

Cheap grace means grace as a doctrine, a principle, a system. It means forgiveness of sins proclaimed as a general truth, the love of God taught as the Christian "conception" of God. An intellectual assent to that idea is held to be of itself sufficient to secure remission of sins. The Church which holds the correct doctrine of grace has, it is supposed, ipso facto a part in that grace. In such a Church the world finds a cheap covering for its sins; no contrition is required, still less any real desire to be delivered from sin. Cheap grace therefore amounts to a denial of the living Word of God, in fact, a denial of the Incarnation of the Word of God.

_____

*Our immersion in the world's suffering is like tickling
our toes in the ocean of sorrow and need, in
comparison with the Calvary-life which plunges
into the whole flood.*

◈ THOMAS KELLY

_____

Grace Without Discipleship. Cheap grace is the preaching of forgiveness without requiring repentance, baptism without Church discipline, Communion without confession, absolution without per-sonal confession. Cheap grace is grace without discipleship, grace without the cross, grace without Jesus Christ, living and incarnate.

Costly grace is the treasure hidden in the field; for the sake of it a man will gladly go and sell all that he has. It is the pearl of great price to buy which the merchant will sell all his goods. It is the kingly rule of Christ, for whose sake a man will pluck out the eye which causes him to stumble; it is the call of Jesus Christ at which the disciple leaves his nets and follows him.

Costly grace is the gospel which must be sought again and again, the gift which must be asked for, the door at which a man must knock.

Such grace is costly because it calls us to follow, and it is grace because it calls us to follow Jesus Christ. It is costly because it costs a man his life, and it is grace because it gives a man the only true life. It is costly because it condemns sin, and grace because it justifies the sinner. Above all, it is costly because it cost God the life of his Son: "ye were bought at a price," and what has cost God much cannot be cheap for us. Above all, it is grace because God did not reckon his Son too dear a price to pay for our life, but delivered him up for us. Costly grace is the Incarnation of God.

Costly grace is the sanctuary of God; it has to be protected from the world, and not thrown to the dogs. It is therefore the living word, the Word of God, which he speaks as it pleases him. Costly grace confronts us as a gracious call to follow Jesus, it comes as a word of forgiveness to the broken spirit and the contrite heart. Grace is costly because it compels a man to submit to the yoke of Christ and follow him; it is grace because Jesus says: "My yoke is easy and my burden is light." [35] ◄

Choosing the Way of the Cross

In many parts of the developed world, the second half of 20th century brought millions of people untold wealth and comfort. But do prosperity and affluence make it more difficult for people to pick up the cross of Jesus and follow Him? Perhaps. Still, disciples of Jesus have long struggled with this challenge.

"Jesus has always many who love His heavenly kingdom, but few who bear His cross," wrote Thomas à Kempis more than five centuries ago:

▶ He has many who desire consolation, but few who care for trial. He finds many to share His table, but few to take part in His fasting. All desire to be happy with Him; few wish to suffer anything for Him. Many follow Him to the breaking of bread, but few to the

God, my God, why hast thou forsaken me?" Never before had He been unable to see God beside Him. Yet never was God nearer Him than now. For never was Jesus more divine. He could not see, could not feel God near; yet it was "My God" that He cried. Still it was to His Father He turned in His very agony. Thus the will of Jesus, in the very moment when His faith seemed about to yield, was finally triumphant. It had no feeling then to support it, no blissful vision to absorb it. It stood naked in His soul and tortured, as He stood naked and scourged before Pilate. Pure and simple and surrounded by fire, His will declared for God. [36]

—*George MacDonald*

George MacDonald (1824–1905) was a Scottish pastor, author, poet, hymnist, and novelist whose work contributed significantly to C.S. Lewis' Christian conversion. This excerpt is taken from one of his nonfiction works, Unspoken Sermons *(1866).*

May God Give You Strength

I do not pray that you may be delivered from your pains; but I pray God earnestly that He would give you strength and patience to bear them as long as He pleases. Comfort yourself with Him who holds you fastened to the cross: He will loose you when He thinks fit. Happy those who suffer with Him: accustom yourself to suffer in that manner, and seek from Him the strength to endure as much, and as long, as He shall judge to be necessary for you. The men of the world do not comprehend these truths, nor is it to be wondered at, since they suffer like what they are, and not like Christians: they consider sickness as a pain to nature, and not as a favor from God; and seeing it only in that light, they find nothing in it but grief and distress. But those who consider sickness as coming from the hand of God, as the effects of His mercy, and the means which He employs for their salvation, commonly find in it great sweetness and sensible consolation.

continued on the next page

drinking of the chalice of His passion. Many revere His miracles; few approach the shame of the Cross. Many love Him as long as they encounter no hardship; many praise and bless Him as long as they receive some comfort from Him. But if Jesus hides Himself and leaves them for a while, they fall either into complaints or into deep dejection. Those, on the contrary, who love Him for His own sake and not for any comfort of their own, bless Him in all trial and anguish of heart as well as in the bliss of consolation. Even if He should never give them consolation, yet they would continue to praise Him and wish always to give Him thanks.

There is no Easter without a Good Friday.

~MATTHEW FOX

What power there is in pure love for Jesus—love that is free from all self-interest and self-love! Do not those who always seek consolation deserve to be called mercenaries? Do not those who always think of their own profit and gain prove that they love themselves rather than Christ? Where can a man be found who desires to serve God for nothing? Rarely indeed is a man so spiritual as to strip himself of all things. And who shall find a man so truly poor in spirit as to be free from every creature? No one, however, is more wealthy than such a man; no one is more powerful, no one freer than he who knows how to leave all things and think of himself as the least of all. 37 ◄

Hadewijch of Brabant was a Belgian author, poet, and spiritual counselor who was a member of the Beguine religious order. She lived in the 13th century, and even then, there was widespread evidence of the malaise of spiritual selfishness. The following passage, taken from one of her many letters, encourages disciples of Jesus to take up His cross:

► Whatever troubles may come to you, do not commit the folly of believing that you are set for any other goal than the great God Himself, in the fullness of His being and of His love. Do not let folly or doubt deflect you from any good practice which can lead you to this goal. If you will confide yourself to His love, you will soon grow to your full stature, but if you persist in doubting, you will become sluggish and grudging, and everything which you ought to do will be a burden to you.

Let nothing trouble you. Do not believe that anything which you must do for Him whom you seek will be beyond your strength, that you cannot surmount it, that it will be beyond you. This is the fervor, this is the zeal which you must have, and all the time your strength must grow.

You must choose and love God's will alone in all things—His will for you, for your friends, for Himself, even though your own wish might be for Him to give you consolation, so that you might live your life here in peace and rest.

But today, instead of loving God's will, everyone loves himself. It is everyone's will to have peace and rest, to live with God in riches and might, and to be one with Him in His joy and glory. We all want to be God along with God; but God knows that there are few of us who want to be man with Him in His humanity, to carry His cross with Him, to hang upon it with Him, to pay with Him the debt of humankind.

What people don't realize is how much religion costs.
They think faith is a big electric blanket,
when of course it is the cross.
FLANNERY O'CONNOR

If we look at ourselves we can see that this is true. We will not suffer anything; we will not endure. Just let our hearts be stabbed by the slightest grief, just let someone say a scornful or slanderous word about us, let anyone act against our reputation or our peace or our will, and at once we are mortally injured.

We know exactly what we want and what we do not want; there are so many different things which give us pleasure or pain; now we want this and now we want that. Our joy today is our sorrow tomorrow. We would like to be here, we would like to be there; we do not want something and then we want it; and in everything all we are thinking of is our own satisfaction and how we can best seek it. [38] ◄

Be satisfied with the condition in which God places you: however happy you may think me, I envy you. Pains and suffering would be a paradise to me, while I should suffer with my God, and the greatest pleasure would be hell to me, if I could relish them without Him; all my consolation would be to suffer something for His sake. [39]

—Brother Lawrence

Quenching the Spirit

The man, however, who would presume on God's forgiveness, and despise God's holiness and His claim upon His people, by doing deliberately the thing that he knows to be contrary to God's will, that man will find spiritual dearth and spiritual death inevitably follow. His communion with God is brought to an end, and it is hard to say how far Satan may not be permitted to carry such a backslider in heart and life. It is awfully possible not merely to "grieve" and to "resist," but even to "quench" the Spirit of God. [40]

—J. Hudson Taylor

The Discipline of a Disciple

"I Will Not Be Mastered by Anything"

"Everything is permissible for me"—but not everything is beneficial. "Everything is permissible for me"—but I will not be mastered by anything. "Food for the stomach and the stomach for food"—but God will destroy them both. The body is not meant for sexual immorality, but for the Lord, and the Lord for the body. By his power God raised the Lord from the dead, and he will raise us also. Do you not know that your bodies are members of Christ himself? Shall I then take the members of Christ and unite them with a prostitute? Never! Do you not know that he who unites himself with a prostitute is one with her in body? For it is said, "The two will become one flesh." But he who unites himself with the Lord is one with him in spirit (1 Corinthians 6:12-17).

On the Practice of Virtue

Stand fast, therefore, in these things, and follow the example of the Lord, being firm and unchangeable in the faith, loving

continued on the next page

In the time of Jesus, those who taught rhetoric and philosophy had disciples—or students—who learned from them. These students were required to memorize portions of their teachers' lectures and utilize the principles they had learned in lectures of their own.

Jesus was a teacher, too, and His disciples memorized many of His addresses. But Jesus was more than a teacher; He was the Son of God. As a result, He demanded more than intellectual growth from His disciples; He demanded complete love and total obedience.

"If you love me, you will obey what I command," Jesus told His disciples. "Whoever has my commands and obeys them, he is the one who loves me. He who loves me will be loved by my Father, and I too will love him and show myself to him" (see John 14:15-21).

Twice in his first epistle, John explained the importance of obeying Jesus:

"We know that we have come to know him if we obey his commands. The man who says, 'I know him,' but does not do what he commands is a liar, and the truth is not in him. But if anyone obeys his word, God's love is truly made complete in him. This is how we know we are in him: Whoever claims to live in him must walk as Jesus did" (1 John 2:3-6).

"This is love for God: to obey his commands. And his commands are not burdensome, for everyone born of God overcomes the world. This is the victory that has overcome the world, even our faith. Who is it that overcomes the world? Only he who believes that Jesus is the Son of God" (1 John 5:3-5).

Today, Jesus still calls those who would follow Him to a life of holy obedience, as Jerry Bridges writes in his classic work, *The Pursuit of Holiness:*

▶ God has called every Christian to a holy life. There are no exceptions to this call. It is not a call only to pastors, missionaries, and a few dedicated Sunday School teachers. Every Christian of every nation, whether rich or poor, learned or unlearned, influential or totally unknown, is called to be holy. The Christian plumber and the

Christian banker, the unsung housewife and the powerful head of state are all alike called to be holy.

This call to a holy life is based on the fact that God Himself is holy. Because God is holy, He requires that we be holy. Many Christians have what we might call a "cultural holiness." They adapt to the character and behavior pattern of Christians around them. As the Christian culture around them is more or less holy, so these Christians are more or less holy. But God has not called us to be like those around us. He has called us to be like Himself. Holiness is nothing less than conformity to the character of God.

The concept of holiness may seem a bit archaic to our current generation. To some minds the very word *holiness* brings images of bunned hair, long skirts, and black stockings. To others the idea is associated with a repugnant "holier than thou" attitude. Yet holiness is very much a scriptural idea. The word *holy* in various forms occurs more than 600 times in the Bible. One entire book, Leviticus, is devoted to the subject, and the idea of holiness is woven elsewhere throughout the fabric of Scripture. More important, God specifically commands us to be holy (see Leviticus 11:44).

We must face the fact that we have a personal responsibility for our walk of holiness. [41] ◄

Hearing the Call to Holiness

William Law (1686–1761), an Anglican thinker and mystic whose works were praised by John Wesley and others, wrote many works about the need for holy obedience. In *A Serious Call to a Devout and Holy Life,* which was his most popular work, Law challenges all believers:

► He, therefore, is the devout man, who lives no longer to his own will, or the way and spirit of the world, but to the sole will of God, who considers God in everything, who serves God in everything, who makes all the parts of his common life parts of piety, by doing everything in the Name of God, and under such rules as are conformable to His glory.

You see two persons: one is regular in public and private prayer, the other is not. Now the reason of this difference is not this, that one

---

the brotherhood, and being attached to one another, joined together in the truth, exhibiting the meekness of the Lord in your intercourse with one another, and despising no one. When you can do good, defer it not, because "alms delivers from death." Be all of you subject one to another, having your conduct "blameless among the Gentiles," that ye may both receive praise for your good works, and the Lord may not be blasphemed through you. But woe to him by whom the name of the Lord is blasphemed! Teach, therefore, sobriety to all, and manifest it in your own conduct. [42]

—*Polycarp*

Holiness: A Joint Venture
The pursuit of holiness is a joint venture between God and the Christian. No one can attain any degree of holiness without God working in his life, but just as surely no one will attain it without effort on his own part. God has made it possible for us to walk in holiness. But He has given to us the responsibility of doing the walking; He does not do that for us. [43]

—*Jerry Bridges*

has strength and power to observe prayer, and the other has not; but the reason is this, that one intends to please God in the duties of devotion, and the other has no intention about it.

Now the case is the same in the right or wrong use of our time and money. You see one person throwing away his time in sleep and idleness, in visiting and diversions, and his money in the most vain and unreasonable expenses. You see another careful of every day, dividing his hours by rules of reason and religion, and spending all his money in works of charity: now the difference is not owing to this, that one has strength and power to do thus, and the other has not; but it is owing to this, that one intends to please God in the right use of all his time, and all his money, and the other has no intention about it. Here, therefore, let us judge ourselves sincerely; let us not vainly content ourselves with the common disorders of our lives, the vanity of our expenses, the folly of our diversions, the pride of our habits, the idleness of our lives, and the wasting of our time, fancying that these are such imperfections as we fall into through the unavoidable weakness and frailty of our natures; but let us be assured, that these disorders of our common life are owing to this, that we have not so much Christianity as to intend to please God in all the actions of our life, as the best and happiest thing in the world. So that we must not look upon ourselves in a state of common and pardonable imperfection, but in such a state as wants the first and most fundamental principle of Christianity, viz., an intention to please God in all our actions. [44] ◄

In a later work, Law issued a specific challenge to those who ministered in Jesus' name. This brief passage is from that work, *An Humble, Earnest, and Affectionate Address to the Clergy:*

► Many are the marks, which the learned have given us of the true church; but be that as it will, no man, whether learned or unlearned, can have any mark or proof of his own true church-membership, but his being dead unto all sin, and alive unto all righteousness. This cannot be more plainly told us, than in these words of our Lord, "He that committeth sin, is the servant of sin"; but surely that servant of sin, cannot at the same time be a living member of Christ's body, or that new creature, who dwells in Christ, and Christ in him. To suppose a man born again from above, yet under a necessity of continuing to sin, is as absurd as to suppose that the true Christian is only to have so much of the nature of Christ born in him as is consistent with as real a power of Satan still dwelling in him. "If the Son," says Christ, "shall make you free, then ye shall be free indeed."

What is this, but saying, if Christ be come to life in you, then a true freedom from all necessity of sinning is given to you. Now if this is hindered, and cannot come to pass in the faithful follower of Christ, it must be, because both the willing and working of Christ in man is too weak to overcome that, which the devil wills and works in him. [46] ◄

From Holy Discipline to the Spiritual Disciplines

Jesus demanded that His disciples obey Him, but at the same time, He realized that there was more to discipleship than mere outward behavior. Once He was talking with a group of Pharisees and teachers of the Law. These men were convinced that legalism brought them as close to godliness as humans could ever be. Jesus reminded them that there was more to following God than moral behavior:

"What comes out of a man is what makes him 'unclean.' For from within, out of men's hearts, come evil thoughts, sexual immorality, theft, murder, adultery, greed, malice, deceit, lewdness, envy, slander, arrogance and folly. All these evils come from inside and make a man 'unclean'" (Mark 7:20-23).

We get no deeper into Christ than we allow him to get into us.

≈JOHN HENRY JOWETT

Over the ages, many followers of Jesus have turned their attention to the inner dimensions of the faith. And in many cases, they base their practices on Jesus, who balanced an extremely active ministry with periods of deep silence and solitude.

The Problem Is Sin

The dilemma of the human race, this dilemma that twentieth-century man is wrestling with so much, is moral. The basic problem of the human race is sin and guilt—a real moral guilt, not just guilt feelings, and a real moral sin, because we have sinned against a God who is there and a God who is holy. In opposition to neo-orthodoxy and all the other modern theologies, we must understand that sin and guilt are really moral. They are not simply due to certain metaphysical or psychological limitations. Man is really guilty before a holy God who exists and against whom we have sinned. Except on these bases, the hope given by Scripture concerning freedom from the bonds of sin is only a cruel illusion. [47]

—*Francis A. Schaeffer*

The Vine and Its Branches

Remain in me, and I will remain in you. No branch can bear fruit by itself; it must remain in the vine. Neither can you bear fruit unless you remain in me. I am the vine; you are the branches. If a man remains in me and I in him, he will bear much fruit; apart from me you can do nothing. If anyone does not remain in me, he is like a branch that is thrown away and withers; such branches are picked up, thrown into the fire and burned. If you remain in me and my words remain in you, ask whatever you wish, and it will be given you. This is to my Father's glory, that you bear much fruit, showing yourselves to be my disciples (John 15:4-8).

For example, Matthew tells us of an instance when Jesus left the chaos and commotion of the crowd to pray in solitude:

"Immediately Jesus made the disciples get into the boat and go on ahead of him to the other side, while he dismissed the crowd. After he had dismissed them, he went up on a mountainside by himself to pray" (Matthew 14:22-23a).

Writer Richard Foster has done more than anyone to reacquaint Western Christians with spiritual disciplines that have been practiced by believers for centuries but are largely unfamiliar to many Protestants and evangelicals. These spiritual practices, which Foster calls "doors to liberation," include inward disciplines (meditation, prayer, fasting, study); outward disciplines (simplicity, solitude, submission, service); and corporate disciplines (confession, worship, guidance, celebration).

———

No man need stay the way he is.

—Harry Emerson Fosdick

———

"The classical Disciplines of the spiritual life (The Disciplines are classical because they are central to experiential Christianity) call us to move beyond surface living into the depths," writes Foster in his acclaimed work, *Celebration of Discipline* [Harper & Row Publishers, 1978]. "They invite us to explore the inner caverns of the spiritual realm. They urge us to be the answer to a hollow world."

———

I have had a deep conviction for many years that practical holiness, and entire self-consecration to God are not sufficiently attended to by modern Christians in this country. Politics, or controversy, or party-spirit, or worldliness, have eaten out the heart of piety in many of us.

—John Charles Ryle

———

The Disciplines Are for All Disciples

Like holy obedience, there are many people who say the spiritual disciplines are designed only for, and can be achieved only by, an elite group of Christian superstars. Foster disagrees:

"We must not be led to believe that the Disciplines are for spiritual giants and hence beyond our reach, or for contemplatives who devote all their time to prayer and meditation. Far from it. God intends the Disciplines of the spiritual life to be for ordinary human beings: people who have jobs, who care for children, who must wash dishes and mow lawns."

To believe in God is one thing, to know God another.
Both in heaven and on earth the Lord is made known
only by the Holy Spirit,
and not through ordinary learning.

        ◆STARETZ SILOUAN

But practicing the disciplines doesn't make us spiritual any more than behaving morally makes us righteous. "Inner righteousness is a gift from God to be graciously received," writes Foster. "The needed change within us is God's work, not ours. The demand is for an inside job, and only God can work from the inside. We cannot attain or earn this righteousness of the kingdom of God; it is a grace that is given." But far from advocating that we do nothing and leave everything up to God, Foster argues that the disciplines "allow us to place ourselves before God so that He can transform us."

An Introduction to the Disciplines

Here is a brief summary of eleven of the disciplines from Foster's influential book:

▶ 1. *Meditation.* Meditation has always stood as a classical and central part of Christian devotion, a crucial preparation for and adjunct to the work of prayer. No doubt part of the surge of interest in Eastern meditation is because the churches have abrogated the field.

Meditation was certainly not foreign to the authors of Scripture. "And Isaac went out to meditate in the field in the evening" (Genesis 24:63). "I think of thee upon my bed, and meditate on thee in the watches of the night" (Psalm 63:6). These were people who were

Silence and Solitude

Anyone, then, who aims to live the inner and spiritual life must go apart, with Jesus, from the crowd. No man appears in safety before the public eye unless he first relishes obscurity. No man is safe in speaking unless he loves to be silent. No man rules safely unless he is willing to be ruled. No man commands safely unless he has learned well how to obey. No man rejoices safely unless he has within him the testimony of a good conscience. [48]

—*Thomas à Kempis*

Willing to Learn

The One who knew said, "Blessed are the poor in spirit, for theirs is the kingdom of Heaven." Happy, that is, are those people who know that their spiritual power is small, that their creeds are imperfect, that their instruction concerning God and man is incomplete. Happy are those who know that they do not know all of truth. For only those who admit their spiritual poverty are willing to learn. [49]

—*Agnes Sanford*

Dealing with Distractions

Temptations, as well as distractions, are a major problem you will encounter at the outset of your adventure into God. Be very careful in your attitude toward them. If you attempt to struggle directly with these temptations, you will only strengthen them; and in the process of this struggle, your soul will be drawn away from its intimate relationship with the Lord.

You see, a close, intimate relationship to Christ should always be your soul's only purpose. Therefore, when you are tempted toward sin or toward outward distractions—no matter the time, no matter the place, nor the provocation—simply turn away from that sin. And as you turn, draw nearer to your Lord. It is that simple. 50

—*Jeanne Guyon*

close to the heart of God. God spoke to them not because they had special abilities, but because they were willing to listen.

2. *Prayer.* Prayer catapults us onto the frontier of the spiritual life. It is original research in unexplored territory. Meditation introduces us to the inner life, fasting is an accompanying means, but it is the Discipline of prayer itself that brings us into the deepest and highest work of the human spirit. Real prayer is life creating and life changing.

The purpose of all prayer is to find God's will
and to make that will our prayer.
—CATHERINE MARSHALL

To pray is to change. Prayer is the central avenue God uses to transform us. If we are unwilling to change, we will abandon prayer as a noticeable characteristic of our lives. The closer we come to the heartbeat of God the more we see our need and the more we desire to be conformed to Christ.

Prayer does not change God,
but it changes him who prays.
—SØREN KIERKEGAARD

3. *Fasting.* Throughout Scripture fasting refers to abstaining from food for spiritual purposes. It stands in distinction to the hunger strike, the purpose of which is to gain political power or attract attention for a good cause. It is also distinct from health dieting, which stresses abstinence from food, but for physical not spiritual purposes.

When the stomach is full it is easy to talk of fasting.
—JEROME

4. *Study.* The purpose of the Spiritual Disciplines is the total transformation of the person. It aims at replacing old destructive habits of thought with new life-giving habits. Nowhere is this purpose more clearly seen than in the Discipline of study. The Apostle Paul tells us that the way we are transformed is through the renewal of the mind

(Romans 12:2). The mind is renewed by applying it to those things that will transform it. "Finally, brethren, whatever is true, whatever is honorable, whatever is just, whatever is pure, whatever is lovely, whatever is gracious, if there is anything worthy of praise, think about these things" (Philippians 4:8). The Discipline of study is the primary vehicle to bring us to "think about these things."

We take excellent care of our bodies, which we have
for only a lifetime; yet we let our souls shrivel,
which we will have for eternity.

BILLY GRAHAM

---

5. *Simplicity.* The Christian Discipline of simplicity is an inward reality that results in an outward life-style. Both the inward and outward aspects of simplicity are essential. To attempt to arrange an outward life-style of simplicity without the inward reality leads to deadly legalism.

Experiencing the inward reality liberates us outwardly. Speech becomes truthful and honest. The lust for status and position is gone, because we no longer need status and position. We cease from showy extravagance, not on the grounds of being unable to afford it, but on the grounds of principle.

6. *Solitude.* There is a solitude of the heart that can be maintained at all times. Crowds or the lack of them have little to do with this inward attentiveness. It is quite possible to be a desert hermit and never experience solitude. But if we possess inward solitude we will not fear being alone, for we know that we are not alone. Neither do we fear being with others, for they do not control us. In the midst of noise and confusion we are settled into a deep inner silence.

Outward silence is indispensable for the cultivation
and improvement of inner silence.

JEANNE GUYON

Inward solitude will have outward manifestations. There will be the freedom to be alone, not in order to be away from people but in order to hear better. Jesus lived in inward "heart solitude." He also frequently experienced outward solitude. He inaugurated His ministry by spending forty days alone in the desert (Matthew 4:1-11). Before He chose the twelve He spent the entire night alone in the desert hills (Luke 6:12). When He received the news of the death of John the Baptist, "He withdrew from there in a boat to a lonely place apart" (Matthew 14:13). After the miraculous feeding of the five thousand Jesus made His disciples leave; then He dismissed the crowd and "went up into the hills by himself" (Matthew 14:23). Following a long night of work "in the morning, a great while before day, he rose and went out to a lonely place" (Mark 1:35). When the twelve had returned from a preaching and healing mission, Jesus instructed them, "Come away by yourselves to a lonely place" (Mark 6:31). Following the healing of a leper Jesus "withdrew to the wilderness and prayed" (Luke 5:16). With three disciples He sought out the silence of a lonely mountain as the stage for the transfiguration (Matthew 17:1-9). As He prepared for His highest and most holy work, Jesus sought the solitude of the garden of Gethsemane (Matthew 26:36-46). One could go on, but perhaps this is sufficient to show that the seeking out of a solitary place was a regular practice with Jesus. So it should be for us.

7. *Submission.* The biblical teaching on submission focuses primarily on the spirit with which we view other people. Scripture is not attempting to set forth a series of hierarchical relationships but to communicate to us an inner attitude of mutual subordination.

8. *Service.* As the cross is the sign of submission, so the towel is the sign of service. When Jesus gathered His disciples for the Last Supper they were having trouble over who was the greatest. This was no new issue for them. "And an argument arose among them as to which of them was the greatest" (Luke 9:46). Whenever there is trouble over who is the greatest there is trouble over who is the least. That is the crux of the matter for us, isn't it? Most of us know we will never be the greatest; just don't let us be the least.

Having lived out servanthood before them He called them to the way of service: "If I then, your Lord and Teacher, have washed your feet, you also ought to wash one another's feet. For I have given you an example, that you also should do as I have done to you" (John 13:14,15).

In the Discipline of service there is also great liberty. Service enables us to say "no!" to the world's games of promotion and authority. It abolishes our need (and desire) for a "pecking order."

9. *Confession.* Confession is so difficult a Discipline for us partly because we view the believing community as a fellowship of saints before we see it as a fellowship of sinners. We come to feel that everyone else has advanced so far into holiness that we are isolated and alone in our sin. We could not bear to reveal our failures and shortcomings to others. We imagine that we are the only ones who have not stepped onto the high road to heaven. Therefore we hide ourselves from one another and live in veiled lies and hypocrisy.

But if we know that the people of God are first a fellowship of sinners we are freed to hear the unconditional call of God's love and to confess our need openly before our brothers and sisters. We know we are not alone in our sin. The fear and pride which cling to us like barnacles cling to others also. We are sinners together. In acts of mutual confession we release the power that heals. Our humanity is no longer denied but transformed.

10. *Worship.*Worship is our responding to the overtures of love from the heart of the Father. Its central reality is found "in spirit and truth." It is kindled within us only when the Spirit of God touches our human spirit. Forms and rituals do not produce worship, nor does the formal disuse of forms and rituals. We can use all the right techniques and methods, we can have the best possible liturgy, but we have not worshiped the Lord until Spirit touches spirit. Singing, praying, praising all may lead to worship, but worship is more than any of them. Our spirit must be ignited by divine fire.

11. *Celebration.* Celebration is central to all the Spiritual Disciplines. Without a joyful spirit of festivity the Disciplines become dull, death-breathing tools in the hands of modern Pharisees. Every Discipline should be characterized by carefree gaiety and a sense of thanksgiving.

Joy is one of the fruits of the Spirit (Galatians 5:22). Often I am inclined to think that joy is the motor, the thing that keeps everything else going. Without joyous celebration to infuse the other Disciplines we will sooner or later abandon them. Joy produces energy. Joy makes us strong. 51 ◀

Waiting, Watching, and Praying

When Jesus taught His disciples, they spent much of their time waiting, watching, and praying. Today, those who want to follow Jesus and be His disciples must do the same.

The time of waiting, that is the ordeal. I will warrant that the suffering endured in having a few nails driven through one's hands, in being crucified, is something purely mechanical that lifts the soul into an ecstasy comparable with nothing else. But the waiting in the garden—that hour drips with blood.

≈KIM MALTHE-BRUUN

Waiting sounds simple, but for many people, it is one of the most difficult things to do. But according to Andrew Murray, it is a necessary prerequisite to growing closer to God:

► If salvation indeed comes from God, and is entirely His work, just as our creation was, it follows that our first and highest duty is to wait on Him to do the work that pleases Him. Waiting then becomes the only way to experience full salvation, the only way to truly know God as the God of our salvation. All the difficulties that are brought forward, keeping us back from full salvation, have their cause in this one thing: our lack of knowledge and practice of waiting on God.

Let us strive to see what the elements are that make up this most blessed and needful waiting on God. It may help us to look into the reasons why this grace is so neglected and to feel how infinitely desirable it is that the church, that is we believers, should learn this blessed secret at any price. [52] ◄

A Life of Discipleship

Through reading the Bible and studying church history, we know what happened to early saints like Paul and Peter. But whatever became of the many other people who followed Jesus—either closely or at a distance? Were they in it for the long haul, or did they merely become disciples for a short time?

Jerry Bridges writes that "the Christian life is not a sprint—it's a marathon." And in the following article, he challenges believers of all ages with these words: "It's not enough just to begin well. To be faithful in the Christian life requires finishing well—usually after a long, sometimes grueling race of some twenty, forty, or even sixty years."

▶ One of my favorite Bible characters is a little-known man named Enoch. Enoch rates only seven verses in the entire Bible, yet he merits a spot in "Faith's Hall of Fame" in Hebrews 11. You might say Enoch lived an unusual life: He and Elijah are the only ones in the history of humanity to escape the experience of death.

Inclusion among the heroes of faith and a direct transport to the presence of God—surely this is evidence that Enoch was a man who finished well. He must have stayed faithful to God through the years. We could say that he's an example of a marathon runner in the Christian faith.

What can we learn from Scripture's brief description of Enoch's life? What was the secret of this unusual man's perseverance? How did he hang in there for the long haul? Three characteristics of Enoch's life stand out.

He Walked with God. Enoch walked with God (Genesis 5:21-24). This is without doubt the most basic and fundamental characteristic necessary to remain faithful through the years.

To walk with God means that we live consistently in the awareness of God's presence and that we fellowship with Him through His Word and through prayer. David is an example of someone who lived in a constant awareness of God's presence. He said to God, "You know when I sit and when I rise; you perceive my thoughts from afar" (Psalm 139:2). David was mindful that his every action—yes, even his every thought—was known by God.

But it's not enough just to be aware that we live in the presence of God. We must cultivate a consistent fellowship with Him through meditation on His Word, through prayer, and through a daily quiet time.

Fellowship with God must not be limited, however, to the quiet time. To walk with God means fellowship with Him all day long.

Keep at It

Perseverance does not mean "perfect." It means that we keep going. We do not quit when we find that we are not yet mature and that there is a long journey still before us.

For perseverance is not resignation, putting up with things the way they are, staying in the same old rut year after year after year, or being a doormat for people to wipe their feet on. Endurance is not a desperate hanging on but a traveling from strength to strength. There is nothing fatigued or humdrum in Isaiah, nothing flat-footed in Jesus, nothing jejune in Paul. Perseverance is triumphant and alive. [53]

—*Eugene H. Peterson*

Jesus calls us; o'er the tumult
Of our life's tempestuous sea
Day by day his sweet voice soundeth,
Saying, "Christian, follow me."
~Cecil Frances Alexander

When you let your thoughts wander, what do you think about? If you will cultivate the habit of thinking about God and His Word and prayerfully expressing your thoughts to Him, you will find that the most ordinary activities of your life are permeated by the presence of God. You will discover how His Word is relevant to your actions, your decisions, your problems.

He Pleased God. Enoch pleased God (Hebrews 11:5). How do we please God?

First, resist bitterness. Bitterness is resentment toward God or another person. It starts with a perceived or real injustice. If allowed to, it festers until it develops into a deep rancor and hostility.

Bitterness has probably sidetracked more people than any other cause. Sometimes we become bitter at God because of a tragic event: the death of a child, the unfaithfulness of a spouse, the failure of a business or career. Sometimes we become bitter at a person who has wronged us in some way.

All of us suffer tragic events of some degree, and all of us are treated unfairly at different times in our lives. Each time something like this occurs, bitterness is a pitfall we must avoid.

We can learn how to deal with the temptation of bitterness from Joseph. His own brothers sold him into slavery. Talk about injustice! But Joseph avoided the malignancy of bitterness through his trust in God. He did not deny the heinousness of his brothers' sin but saw beyond it to the sovereignty of God. He believed, in the words of Paul, that even though he was the victim of someone else's sin, God was at work in it for his good (Genesis 45:8; Romans 8:28).

Second, avoid disobedience. Defiance of God means engaging in direct, willful disobedience. King Solomon is a vivid example of one who fell into this snare. Although his life began well and was exceptionally blessed by God, Solomon's life ended tragically. He deliberately and willfully disobeyed God. This is a sobering lesson for us all. Exceptional gifting, or the unusual blessing of God upon our lives or ministries, does not guarantee that we will remain faithful to the end.

I have seen some of the most capable Christians turn aside—who, in some cases, had experienced an unusual blessing from God upon their ministries. But at some point they knowingly and deliberately acted in direct disobedience to God. For some, it was indulging in extramarital dalliances. They knew these actions were wrong but felt they could get away with them, until eventually they were sucked into an immoral relationship.

Whether it is the temptation to immorality, or the many snares in the love of money, or some other area of disobedience, none of us is immune to the temptation to direct disobedience. This is where walking with God can help us. We are less likely to defy God if we consciously live in His presence; if we strive to bring every plan and action under the scrutiny of His Word; if we pray over all aspects of our lives.

Third, banish pride. Pride, in essence, is believing that we don't need God. This was the problem of King Uzziah: another tragic example of someone who began well and was unusually blessed of God, but who did not end well. But "his pride led to his downfall" (2 Chronicles 26:16), and Uzziah died a leper, isolated from his family and estranged from God.

Pride often accompanies success, whether in business, athletics, scholarship, or Christian ministry. I have seen gifted young men sidetracked even in their twenties because of pride. More often, though, it seems to come a little later in life, with achievement of some measure of personal or professional success. Like Uzziah, we can become resistant to reproof or counsel. We think we know it all. Eventually we turn aside altogether, or perhaps God's hand of blessing is removed. We do not finish well, even though we may think we are staying faithful to God. We cease to be fruitful in His kingdom.

Serving God for the Long Haul. Enoch served God. Enoch did not walk with God in a cloistered environment; he was a spokesman for God in the ungodly marketplace of his day (Jude 14-15). The Bible doesn't tell us how long Enoch did this, but from the Genesis and Hebrews passages, we can safely infer that Enoch served God

---

Pilgrims Who Did Not Complete Their Journey

Yes, they turned several out of the way. There was Slow-pace that they persuaded to do as they. They also prevailed with one Short-wind, with one No-heart, with one Linger-after-lust, and with one Sleepy-head, and with a young woman, her name was Dull, to turn out of the way and become as they. Besides, they brought up an ill-report of your Lord, persuading others that he was a hard taskmaster. They also brought up an evil report of the good land, saying it was not half so good as some pretended it was. They also began to vilify his servants, and to count the best of them meddle-some, trouble-some busybodies. Further, they would call the bread of God husks; the comforts of his children fancies; the travel and labor of pilgrims, things to no purpose. [54]

—*John Bunyan*

right up to the day God took him [home to heaven].

It seems to me that as Christians approach the so-called senior years, many of them stagnate because they retire not only from their secular work, but from the Lord's work as well. I hear statements such as, "I've paid my dues," or "I've done my share: now it's time for the younger folks to take over." True, as we grow older we do lose some of the physical stamina of our earlier years. Even God made provision for the priests serving at the tabernacle to retire at age fifty from the more physically demanding work connected with the sacrificial system. But they were not to retire from their walk with God, and they could continue to assist the younger priests.

> *Here in this world He bids us come, there in the next*
> *He shall bid us welcome.*
>
> *▬JOHN DONNE*

"[The righteous] will still bear fruit in old age," declares the psalmist, "they will stay fresh and green" (Psalm 92:14). I think of an older friend of mine, now in her eighties, who is still bearing fruit. She is limited in her physical mobility, but in her prayer life she ranges all over the globe, praying for Christian works and workers worldwide. She is not turning aside from God's work, nor is she stagnating in her inner spiritual life. She will stay fruitful to the end because she will continue to serve God to the end.

None of us will ever finish "doing our share." We can never repay the debt of love we owe to Christ. If we are running for the long haul we must determine never to quit His service. If we want to run with endurance we must keep asking as long as we live, "Lord, what do you want me to do?" Only in that way can we expect to stay faithful to the end and be greeted at the finish by our Lord's voice saying, "Well done, good and faithful servant!" 55 ◀

Those people who hear Jesus' call, heed it with their lives, and endure until the end cannot only be Jesus' disciples, but as we will see in the following section, they can also disciple others.

Section *Two*

GO AND MAKE DISCIPLES:
Helping Others Follow Jesus

At the beginning of His earthly ministry, Jesus' call to those who would be His disciples was simple and direct: "Come, follow Me." Then, during the waning moments of His time on earth—in the days between His resurrection and ascension—Jesus left His disciples with a final command that was just as simple and direct: "Go and make disciples."

The full text of this command, a passage many people call "the Great Commission," is found at the end of Matthew's Gospel:

"Then Jesus came to them and said, "All authority in heaven and on earth has been given to me. Therefore go and make disciples of all nations, baptizing them in the name of the Father and of the Son and of the Holy Spirit, and teaching them to obey everything I have commanded you. And surely I am with you always, to the very end of the age" (Matthew 28:18-20).

With this command, it was becoming increasingly clear that those who had been Jesus' disciples would now go out on their own and disciple others.

In the pages that follow, we will closely look at a number of biblical passages and classic Christian writings that help us understand what Jesus meant by this command, what His first disciples did about it, and how we can find relevant and creative ways to apply it in our own day.

If God sends us on stony paths,
he provides strong shoes.
—CORRIE TEN BOOM

Christ's Ambassadors

The Great Commission wasn't the first time Jesus told His disciples to go out and minister in His name. On a number of occasions throughout His earthly ministry, He commissioned some of His 12 disciples and other followers to go out and do the work of the kingdom of God. Luke describes one such commissioning:

"After this the Lord appointed seventy-two others and sent them two by two ahead of him to every town and place where he was about to go. He told them, 'The harvest is plentiful, but the workers are few. Ask the Lord of the harvest, therefore, to send out workers into his harvest field. Go! I am sending you out like lambs among wolves'" (Luke 10:1-4).

Later in Luke, we get a indication of how truly plentiful the harvest would be. The Gospel writer tells how Jesus traveled to the house of a prominent Pharisee, teaching about the kingdom through many stories, including the parable of the great banquet. Most biblical scholars interpret this parable as one of many explanations Jesus would give about how His message of redemption would go beyond the confines of Jewish religion and encompass the whole world.

The parable describes a man who prepared a banquet and invited many guests. But one after another, the invited guests responded that they were caught up in the affairs of daily life, and couldn't attend the banquet. Unfazed, the host instructed his servant to enlarge the circle of those who were invited: "Go out quickly into the streets and alleys of the town and bring in the poor, the crippled, the blind and the lame" (Luke 14:21b). The message of this seemingly simple parable was radical: through Jesus, God was inviting everyone to join Him in His heavenly banquet.

After commissioning one group of disciples, Jesus prayed about them to His Heavenly Father: "As you sent me into the world, I have sent them into the world" (John 17:18).

Some want to live within the sound
Of Church or Chapel bell;
I want to run a rescue shop
Within a yard of hell.
—C.T. STUDD

And the Apostle Paul, who received his call to follow Jesus from an ascended Christ, explained the call to make disciples to the believers in Corinth: "We are therefore Christ's ambassadors," he wrote, "as though God were making his appeal through us" (2 Corinthians 5:20a).

Over the past 20 centuries, there have been many occasions when it seemed that God should have come up with a better plan than entrusting to frail human beings the mission of proclaiming the gospel and inviting men and women to become Jesus' disciples. But for reasons that are destined to remain mysterious, that is precisely the approach Jesus chose to take.

Into the World

The call to go out into the world as Christ's ambassadors is a supremely significant assignment. Thomas Coke (1747–1814), who was born in Wales and ordained in England before going to America to serve as superintendent of the Methodist Episcopal Church, wrote about the seriousness of this in his work, *The Duties of the Minister of the Gospel:*

▶ The work of the ministry must be acknowledged, by all who believe the truths of revelation, and hope for happiness beyond the grave, to be the most important in which a human being can possibly engage. It extends, in its effects and consequences, beyond the boundaries of time, and involves the future happiness or misery of millions, by leading them to felicities or woes which baffle all our calculations.

The ministerial office is the most important to the human race of any which is exercised on earth for, according to the order of the dispensation of grace, the preaching of the gospel is indispensably necessary to raise mankind out of the ruins of their fall, to deliver them from all the miseries which spring from an everlasting banishment from God, and to bring them to the eternal enjoyment of him, the Sovereign God, at whose right hand are pleasures for evermore.

The good which one single minister, true to the cause in which he has engaged, can do in the course of his life by a faithful ministry of the Word, is not easily to be described. How many of the ignorant he may instruct, how many sleepy consciences arouse, how many daring sinners confound; how many mourners he may bring into the liberty of the children of God, how many believers confirm in grace, yea, lead into the enjoyment of perfect love!

If we will be disciples, much more ministers of Christ, we must daily take up his cross. Without this, he refuses to acknowledge us as his disciples, or to make us partakers of that glory into which he

Wayward Apostles

We profess to be strangers and pilgrims, seeking after a country of our own, yet we settle down in the most un-stranger-like fashion, exactly as if we were quite at home and meant to stay as long as we could. I don't wonder apostolic miracles have died. Apostolic living certainly has.

—Amy Carmichael

entered not himself but by the way of the cross.

Those who are acquainted with the religious history of Christendom, well know, that in proportion as the ministers of a church are holy, holiness will reign among the people. The purity of Christianity, wherever it has flourished, never has begun to decay but with the fall of the ministry; and disorder has generally begun at the house of God. Thus it is in a considerable measure we who decide, if I may so speak, on the salvation or damnation of the people: upon us, in some sense, depends the increase or diminution of the reign of Jesus Christ upon earth, the consummation or destruction of his work, the utility or inutility of his blood and mission, the glory or reproach of his religion, and all the designs of God concerning the salvation of man.

Attention to, and fidelity in the exercise of, the duty of prayer, is not one of those obligations which are peculiar to the ministry of the gospel. It is one of the most essential duties of Christianity. Every real Christian is a man of prayer: his views, his desires, his hopes, his affections, yea, even his conversation, are all in heaven. Every Christian is a citizen of the world to come, and a stranger here below: all exterior objects which here surround him should be to him only so many ties and obstacles, which, retarding his course and prolonging his banishment, ought to increase and inflame his desire after his country: all the temptations which the world offers or throws his way, all his secret conflicts with his passions—all these should lead him to lift up his eyes continually to heaven; there to send up his sighs and prayers, and to address himself in secret, and in every place, to that faithful, heavenly, invisible witness of all his dangers, and all his troubles, from whose protection alone he expects his consolation and his strength. Every Christian, then, is a man of prayer; and he who lives not in the exercise and spirit of prayer, is a man without God, without divine worship, without religion, without hope; and if this be an incontestable truth, what instructions are not due to the people, to animate them to the love and exercise of prayer. [1] ◄

All Are Called

One of the most amazing things about the call to make disciples is that it isn't restricted to clergy. Jesus' call was as nonelitist as they come. He called all men and women who were His disciples to be involved in the ongoing work of ministry.

God does not comfort us to make us comfortable, but to make us comforters.

⮜JOHN HENRY JOWETT

Waldron Scott, a former leader of the American Leprosy Missions and the former general secretary of World Evangelical Fellowship, commented on the sense of frustration some believers experience when they realize the immensity of the challenge:

▶ When we as individuals are confronted by the enormity of the task before us, the multitudes of people still unreached by the gospel, the moral apathy of the Christian community, and the appalling poverty and violation of human rights in the global order—we are tempted to see the task as hopeless.

What can one individual do in the face of such massive problems? What possible good can be achieved by eating one less hamburger or bowl of rice per week, or by contributing a few more dollars to world evangelization? What is my pittance worth in the face of such incredible need? What can my small efforts achieve against principalities and powers?

Any plan of action can fall prey to two pitfalls: thinking that the problems are so enormous that there is little we can do, or that the achievement of global justice rests on our shoulders alone. As Dennis Shoemaker has pointed out, the first is defeatism and the second is rank arrogance.

These, of course, are the same pitfalls the Lord Jesus faced as he began his ministry in a land occupied by foreign troops and governed by corrupt leaders. What did Jesus do? He did what he could. Perhaps that seems trite; nevertheless, it accurately describes Jesus' response.

He did what he could, starting where he was in the hill country of Galilee and utilizing the limited resources at his disposal. He could preach and teach, so he did. He could heal, so he healed thousands of people oppressed by the devil. He was also aware of what he could not do, either because it would be futile in the face of ruthless Roman legions, or because it would be contrary to the

**Looking
Beyond the
Walls of the
Church**
The Church is
never true to itself
when it is living
for itself, for if it is
chiefly concerned
with saving its
own life, it will
lose it. The nature
of the Church is
such that it must
always be
engaged in find-
ing new ways by
which to tran-
scend itself. Its
main responsibil-
ity is always out-
side its own walls
in the redemption
of common life.
That is why we
call it a redemp-
tive society.

The outgoing
character of the
Christian move-
ment is of such
crucial impor-
tance that when
it is understood,
many of our reli-
gious presupposi-
tions are thereby
altered or
rejected. Chris-
tians may indeed
come in [to the
church], but they
do so only that
they may, in con-
sequence, go out,
and furthermore,
that they may go
out with greater
effectiveness.

The preposition
used in describ-
ing Christ's own
strategy is highly
significant. "He
called to him the
Twelve, and
began to send
them out" (Mark
6:7). The point is
almost equally
clear in the dis-
patch of the
Seventy, whom

*continued on the
next page*

ethics of the kingdom. So he set aside the Zealot option and refused
to ally himself with the religious leadership of his day.

He knew full well his limitations, predetermined by his incarnation as a mere Jew, a member of a scorned and insignificant race
within a mighty world empire. To feed five thousand, he knew, was
not the same as eliminating world hunger. To heal a few sick and
lame persons was not synonymous with eradicating disease. Yet he
did what he could, because to do so was right and in line with the
kingdom of God. [3] ◄

Go for souls, and go for the worst.

 ～WILLIAM BOOTH

Gottfried Osei-Mensah, a native of Ghana and former executive
director of the Lausanne Continuation Committee, an organization
involved in world evangelization, believes it is only a profound sense
of God-given compassion that will enable believers to do their part
in the work set before them:

▶ The Lord wants to open our eyes to the enormity of the task.
He wants us to feel the same compassion for the lost that caused him
to weep over Jerusalem and die on a cross.

Such compassion will then drive us to pray to the Lord of the harvest, to the One who has the power to do something about the
harassed and lost condition of man. Prayer is aligning ourselves with
the will of God, the giving of ourselves to his unswerving purpose to
save men through faith in him.

Such prayer will lead us into action. We are God's hands and his
feet. We are his heart. To those concerned enough to pray, God gives
guidance into the particular ministry most directly tied to world
evangelization.

World evangelization therefore becomes not a matter of every
person being converted, but a matter of every person being in a
place where he or she can see Jesus incarnated in the lives of people. So there must be in every community of every cultural and language group a body of believers whose actions and words are a
powerful witness to Christ. When this happens, no person on earth

is out of range of the gospel. Every interested person can easily see Jesus and learn about him from someone of his own kind.

The task given to us by our Lord is an immense one. But we do not lose heart, for it is not an impossible one. As more and more believers are driven by compassion for the lost, as we commit ourselves to prayer and in turn become part of the answer to our prayers, and as we work together to see gatherings of believers that can be known and read by all men in every community on earth, we can work in hope that the task of world evangelization will be accomplished. 4 ◄

He sent "on ahead of him" (Luke 10). Though it is discouraging to find how few of the millions of nominal Christians have even a slight comprehension of this, it is heartening to find it understood in some places. 5

—*Elton Trueblood*

A New Commandment

In Jesus' day—as in our own—there was no lack of competing social, political, or religious movements, all of them with leaders who were promoting their philosophies and programs in the marketplace of ideas and trying enlist others to join their particular crusades.

He alone loves the Creator perfectly who manifests a pure love for his neighbor.

≈BEDE

To many observers, Jesus appeared to be just another in a seemingly endless succession of Middle Eastern spiritual teachers or cultural rebels, all of whom sought to recruit their own disciples.

One of the major differences, though, between Jesus and the other teachers was that He preached a radical and life-transforming message based on love, and He backed up His message with His life. "My command is this," He said, "love each other as I have loved you" (John 15:12).

This message had been expressed in Jewish law, as an expert in that law demonstrated one day when he attempted to interrogate Jesus:

"'Teacher,' he asked, 'what must I do to inherit eternal life?'

"'What is written in the Law?' he replied. 'How do you read it?'

"He answered: 'Love the Lord your God with all your heart and with all your soul and with all your strength and with all your mind';

continued on the next page

and, 'Love your neighbor as yourself.'

"'You have answered correctly,' Jesus replied. 'Do this and you will live'" (Luke 10:25-28).

On another occasion, it was a rich young man who approached Jesus and asked the identical question about inheriting eternal life. "You know the commandments," Jesus told him, giving the young man a brief lesson on teachings in the Mosaic law about murder, adultery, and other issues.

"'Teacher' [declared the young man], 'all these I have kept since I was a boy.'

"Jesus looked at him and loved him. 'One thing you lack,' he said. 'Go, sell everything you have and give to the poor, and you will have treasure in heaven. Then come, follow me.'

"At this the man's face fell. He went away sad, because he had great wealth.

"Jesus looked around and said to his disciples, 'How hard it is for the rich to enter the kingdom of God!'

"The disciples were amazed at his words. But Jesus said again, 'Children, how hard it is to enter the kingdom of God! It is easier for a camel to go through the eye of a needle than for a rich man to enter the kingdom of God'" (Mark 10:20-25).

Love of God is the root, love of our neighbor the fruit of the Tree of Life. Neither can exist without the other, but the one is cause and the other effect.

—WILLIAM TEMPLE

The point of this passage isn't that money or rich people are inherently bad. Rather, Jesus was trying to demonstrate that the kingdom of God was about love, not mere legalism.

"A new command I give you: Love one another. As I have loved you, so you must love one another. By this all men will know that you are my disciples, if you love one another" (John 13:34-35).

A Life of Service

It took a while for Jesus' disciples to understand what their master was teaching them. For some of them, the picture didn't really come into focus until after His resurrection.

But some things were clear from the very beginning. For one, the disciples knew they needed to listen to Jesus' words, allowing them to seep down into the core of their lives, changing their thoughts, their attitudes, and their deepest beliefs. For another, they knew they had to put these ideas into action.

Christianity has taught us to care. Caring is the greatest thing, caring matters most.

      ~FRIEDRICH VON HUGEL

As we will see throughout the following pages, hearing and doing were inextricably linked. There was no such thing as discipleship without doing.

While some Christians have felt that this obligation to "do" was a terrible burden, others, like 13th-century contemplative writer Hadewijch of Brabant, found service was a natural response to the overwhelming love of God:

▶ Do good under all circumstances, but with no care for any profit, or any blessedness, or any damnation, or any salvation, or any martyrdom; but all you do or omit should be for the honor of Love. If you behave like this, you will soon rise up again. And let people take you for a fool; there is much truth in that. Be docile and prompt toward all who have need of you, and satisfy everyone as far as you can manage it without debasing yourself. Be joyful with those who rejoice, and weep with those who weep (Romans 12:13). Be good toward those who have need of you, devoted toward the sick, generous with the poor, and recollected in spirit beyond the reach of all creatures.

And even if you do the best you can in all things, your human nature must often fall short; so entrust yourself to God's goodness, for his goodness is greater than your failures. And always practice true virtues, with confidence, and be diligent and constant in always following unconditionally our Lord's guiding and his dearest will wherever you can discern it, taking trouble and doing your utmost to examine your thoughts strictly, in order to know yourself in all things.

And live for God in such a way, this I implore you, that you be not wanting in the great works to which he has called you. Never

> but after his own; or rather, not even after his own, since he is thus making his heart a divided heart and so preventing himself from seeing God, in the vision of whom alone is certain and lasting blessedness. [6]
>
> —*St. Augustine*

A Matter of
Motives

Without charity external work is of no value, but anything done in charity, be it ever so small and trivial, is entirely fruitful inasmuch as God weighs the love with which a man acts rather than the deed itself. He does much who loves much. He does much who does a thing well. He does well who serves the common good rather than his own interests.

Now, that which seems to be charity is oftentimes really sensuality, for man's own inclination, his own will, his hope of reward, and his self-interest, are motives seldom absent. On the contrary, he who has true and perfect charity seeks self in nothing, but searches all things for the glory of God. Moreover, he envies no man, because he desires no personal pleasure nor does he wish to rejoice in himself; rather he desires the greater glory of God above all things. He ascribes to man nothing that is good but attributes it wholly to God from whom all things proceed as from a fountain, and in whom all the blessed

continued on the
next page

neglect them for any less important work, this I implore and counsel you. For you have great motives impelling you to take trouble in God's service. He has protected you from all trouble, if you yourself will but take heed; so that your way is smoothed by grace, if you will but recognize it. And all things considered, you have suffered too little to grow up, as in justice you owed it to God to do—although, now and then, you willingly comply in this.

---

*You can give without loving, but you
cannot love without giving.*

—AMY CARMICHAEL

Although, too, you sometimes feel such affliction in your heart that it seems to you you are forsaken by God, do not be discouraged by it. For verily I say to you: Whatever misery we endure with good will and for God is pleasing to God in every respect. [7] ◀

And for Quaker philanthropist and author Hannah Whitall Smith (1832–1911), service was one of the keys to unlocking the deeper joys of the Christian life. As she wrote in her classic work, *The Christian's Secret to a Happy Life:*

▶ There is, perhaps, no part of Christian experience where a greater change is known upon entering into the life hid with Christ in God, than in the matter of service.

What we need in the Christian life is to get believers to want to do God's will, as much as other people want to do their own will. And this is the idea of the Gospel. It is what God intended for us; and it is what He has promised.

God's plan for us therefore is to get possession of the inside of a man, to take the control and management of his will, and to work it for him; and then obedience is easy and a delight, and service becomes perfect freedom, until the Christian is forced to exclaim, "This happy service! Who could dream earth had such liberty?"

Surrender Your Will. What you need to do then, dear Christian, if you are in bondage, is to put your will over completely into the hands of your Lord, surrendering to Him the entire control of it. Say,

"Yes, Lord, YES!" to everything; and trust Him so to work in you to will, as to bring your whole wishes and affections into conformity with His own sweet and lovable and most lovely will. I have seen this done over and over, in cases where it looked beforehand an utterly impossible thing. In one case, where a lady had been for years rebelling fearfully against a thing which she knew was right, but which she hated, I saw her, out of the depths of despair and without any feeling, give her will in that matter up into the hands of her Lord, and begin to say to Him, "Thy will be done; thy will be done!" And in one short hour that very thing began to look sweet and precious to her. It is wonderful what miracles God works in wills that are utterly surrendered to Him. He turns hard things into easy, and bitter things into sweet. It is not that He puts easy things in the place of the hard, but He actually changes the hard thing into an easy one. And this is salvation. It is grand. Do try it, you who are going about your daily Christian living as to a hard and weary task, and see if your divine Master will not transform the very life you live now as a bondage, into the most delicious liberty!

I have found the paradox that if I love until it hurts,
then there is no hurt, but only more love.

—MOTHER TERESA

Or again, if you do love His will in the abstract, but find the doing of it hard and burdensome, from this also there is deliverance in the wonderful life of faith. For in this life no burdens are carried, nor anxieties felt. The Lord is our burden-bearer, and upon Him we must lay off every care. He says, in effect, Be careful for nothing, but just make your requests known to Me, and I will attend to them all. Be careful for nothing, He says, not even your service. Above all, I should think, our service, because we know ourselves to be so utterly helpless in this, that even if we were careful, it would not amount to anything. What have we to do with thinking whether we are fit or not! The Master-workman surely has a right to use any tool He pleases for His own work, and it is plainly not the business of the tool to decide whether it is the right one to be used or not. He knows; and if He chooses to use us, of course we must be fit. And

shall rest as their last end and fruition.

If man had but a spark of true charity he would surely sense that all the things of earth are full of vanity! [8]

—*Thomas à Kempis*

77

in truth, if we only knew it, our chiefest fitness is in our utter help-lessness. His strength can only be made perfect in our weakness. I can give you a convincing illustration of this.

To sum it all up then, what is needed for happy and effectual service is simply to put your work into the Lord's hands, and leave it there. Do not take it to Him in prayer, saying, "Lord, guide me; Lord, give me wisdom; Lord, arrange for me," and then arise from your knees, and take the burden all back, and try to guide and arrange for yourself. Leave it with the Lord, and remember that what you trust to Him, you must not worry over nor feel anxious about. Trust and worry cannot go together. If your work is a burden, it is because you are not trusting it to Him. But if you do trust it to Him, you will surely find that the yoke He puts upon you is easy, and the burden He gives you to carry is light, and even in the midst of a life of ceaseless activity you shall find rest to your soul. [9] ◄

The Great Discipler

T he Gospels don't give us a manual on the discipleship methods of Jesus, but the accounts of Jesus' earthly ministry do give the careful reader numerous examples of the ways Jesus instructed the 12 excited but very human disciples who followed Him.

Walking on the water is easy to impulsive pluck, but walking on dry land as a disciple of Jesus Christ is a different thing.

≈OSWALD CHAMBERS

Clearly, some of the portraits that emerge from the Gospel writers reveal Jesus as an unquestionably divine Savior whose unique meth-ods could never be duplicated by any of His disciples, then or now.

"Do not let your hearts be troubled," He tells His followers at one point. "Trust in God; trust also in me" (John 14:1). It would be blas-phemy for anyone but Jesus to make such a claim.

Likewise, Jesus had a unique ability to control forces of nature, leading His terrified disciples to ask, "Who is this? Even the wind and the waves obey him!" (Mark 4:41).

Jesus also initiated new sacraments of worship that were based on His singular calling as the Son of God:

"After taking the cup, he gave thanks and said, 'Take this and divide it among you. For I tell you I will not drink again of the fruit of the vine until the kingdom of God comes.'

"And he took bread, gave thanks and broke it, and gave it to them, saying, 'This is my body given for you; do this in remembrance of me.'

"In the same way, after the supper he took the cup, saying, 'This cup is the new covenant in my blood, which is poured out for you'" (Luke 22:17-20).

And even though today's Christian leaders would like to find a way to relieve believers' doubts, none can do so as effectively or convincingly as Jesus did soon after His resurrection:

"A week later his disciples were in the house again, and Thomas was with them. Though the doors were locked, Jesus came and stood among them and said, 'Peace be with you!' Then he said to Thomas, 'Put your finger here; see my hands. Reach out your hand and put it into my side. Stop doubting and believe'" (John 20:26-27).

The Lord called his disciples the salt of the earth because they seasoned with heavenly wisdom the hearts of men that were rendered insipid by the devil.

≈CHROMATIUS OF AQUILEIA

Still, many other passages of Scripture reveal that Jesus utilized rather mundane human techniques to train His disciples.

One can clearly see Jesus' humanness and vulnerability in the hours before His crucifixion, as He takes His disciples along with Him for companionship and says to them, "Sit here while I go over there and pray" (Matthew 26:36).

Jesus also apparently engaged in lengthy teaching sessions during which He separated His disciples from the crowds:

"They left that place and passed through Galilee. Jesus did not want anyone to know where they were, because he was teaching his disciples" (Mark 9:30-31a).

Other passages repeatedly reveal that even when surrounded by crowds, Jesus would find ways to provide instruction to His disciples:

"Meanwhile, when a crowd of many thousands had gathered, so that they were trampling on one another, Jesus began to speak first to His disciples, saying: 'Be on your guard against the yeast of the Pharisees, which is hypocrisy' (Luke 12:1).

But as many expert teachers argue, some things are "caught" better than they are taught. Knowing this to be the case, Jesus taught some of the most important lessons through His actions and His life:

"Jesus called his disciples to him and said, 'I have compassion for these people; they have already been with me three days and have nothing to eat. I do not want to send them away hungry, or they may collapse on the way'" (Matthew 15:32).

Jesus demonstrated His compassion in a most powerful way in the hours before His crucifixion:

"He came to Simon Peter, who said to him, 'Lord, are you going to wash my feet?' Jesus replied, 'You do not realize now what I am doing, but later you will understand'" (John 13:6-7).

Lessons from the Master

Few biblical scholars have given more attention to the ways Jesus discipled His followers than 19th-century Scottish writer A.B. Bruce, whose *The Training of the Twelve* first appeared in 1871.

What other people think of me is becoming less and less important; what they think of Jesus because of me is critical.

—CLIFF RICHARD

One of the first questions is why Jesus chose these particular 12 disciples:

▶ Was He guided by feelings of antagonism to those possessing social advantages, or of partiality for men of His own class? No; His choice was made in true wisdom. If He chose Galileans mainly, it was not from provincial prejudice against those of the south; if, as some think, He chose two or even four of his own kindred, it was not from nepotism; if He chose rude, unlearned, humble men, it was not because He was animated by any petty jealousy of knowledge, culture, or good birth. If any rabbi, rich man, or ruler had been willing to yield himself unreservedly to the service of the kingdom, no objection would have been taken to him on account of his acquirements, possessions, or titles. The case of Saul of Tarsus, the pupil of Gamaliel, proves the truth of this statement. Even Gamaliel himself would not have been objected to, could he have stooped to become a disciple of the unlearned Nazarene. But, alas! neither he nor any of his order would condescend so far, and therefore the despised One did not get an opportunity of showing His willingness to accept as disciples and choose for apostles such as they were.

When once the day comes when I have to appear
before my Lord, then I will not come with my deeds,
with the volumes of my Dogmatics on my back.
All the angels there would have to laugh. But then
I shall also not say, "I have meant well; I had
good faith." No, then I will only say one thing;
"Lord, be merciful to me, a poor sinner!"

—Karl Barth

The truth is, that Jesus was obliged to be content with fishermen, and publicans, and quondam zealots, for apostles. They were the best that could be had. Those who deemed themselves better were too proud to become disciples, and thereby they excluded themselves from what all the world now sees to be the high honor of being the chosen princes of the kingdom. The civil and religious aristocracy boasted of their unbelief. The citizens of Jerusalem did feel for a moment interested in the zealous youth who had purged the temple with a whip of small cords; but their faith was superficial, and their attitude patronizing, and therefore Jesus did not commit Himself unto them, because He knew what was in them. A few of good position were sincere sympathizers, but they were not so decided in their attachment as to be eligible for apostles. Nicodemus was barely able to speak a timid apologetic word in Christ's behalf, and Joseph of Arimathea was a disciple "secretly," for fear of the Jews. These were hardly the persons to send forth as missionaries of the cross—men so fettered by social ties and party connections, and so enslaved by the fear of man. The apostles of Christianity must be made of sterner stuff.

And so Jesus was obliged to fall back on the rustic, but simple, sincere, and energetic men of Galilee. And He was quite content with His choice, and devoutly thanked His Father for giving Him even such as they. Learning, rank, wealth, refinement, freely given up to His service, He would not have despised; but He preferred devoted men who had none of these advantages to undevoted men who had them all. And with good reason; for it mattered little, except in the eyes of contemporary prejudice, what the social position or even the previous history of the twelve had been, provided they were spiritually qualified for the work to which they were called. 10 ◀

When you follow the Lord with burning love, it may
happen that on the road of life you strike your foot
against the stone of some passion and fall unexpect-
edly into sin; or else, finding yourself in a muddy
place, you may slip involuntarily and fall headlong.
Each time you fall and in this way injure your body,
you should get up again with the same eagerness as
before, and continue to follow after your Lord
until you reach him.

~JOHN OF CARPATHOS

Bruce also answers another important question: Why did the disciples stay with Jesus, even though there were times when following Him was difficult and disappointing? Bruce offers three answers:

▶ 1. The twelve, as a body, were sincere and thoroughly in earnest in religion. Their supreme desire was to know "the words of eternal life," and actually gain possession of that life.

2. The second anchor by which the disciples were kept from shipwreck at this season was a clear perception of the alternatives. "To whom shall we go?" asked Peter, as one who saw that, for men having in view the aim pursued by himself and his brethren, there

was no course open but to remain where they were. He had gone over rapidly in his mind all the possible alternatives, and this was the conclusion at which he had arrived.

3. The third anchor whereby the twelve were enabled to ride out the storm, was confidence in the character of their Master. They believed, yea, they knew, that He was the Holy One of God. [11] ◄

Knowing God without knowing our own wretchedness makes for pride. Knowing our wretchedness without knowing God makes for despair. Knowing Jesus Christ strikes the balance because he shows us both God and our own wretchedness.

◄BLAISE PASCAL

Teaching and Showing

One of the most important observations Bruce makes about the methods of Jesus was that the Master trained His disciples through a combination of teaching and showing. Jesus both articulated the truths of God and demonstrated them in His daily life, which was almost always under the closest scrutiny from the disciples:

► In the training of the twelve for the work of the apostleship, hearing and seeing the words and works of Christ necessarily occupied an important place. Eye and ear witnessing of the facts of an unparalleled life was an indispensable preparation for future witness-bearing. The apostles could secure credence for their wondrous tale only by being able to preface it with the protestation: "That which we have seen and heard declare we unto you." None would believe their report, save those who, at the very least, were satisfied that it emanated from men who had been with Jesus. Hence the third evangelist, himself not an apostle, but only a companion of apostles, presents his Gospel with all confidence to his friend Theophilus as a genuine history, and no mere collection of fables, because its contents were attested by men who "from the beginning were eye-witnesses and ministers of the Word."

In the early period of their discipleship hearing and seeing seem

Being Patient with Imperfection

Try to bear patiently with the defects and infirmities of others, whatever they may be, because you also have many a fault which others must endure. If you cannot make yourself what you would wish to be, how can you bend others to your will?

We want them to be perfect, yet we do not correct our own faults. We wish them to be severely corrected, yet we will not correct ourselves. Their great liberty displeases us, yet we would not be denied what we ask. We would have them bound by laws, yet we will allow ourselves to be restrained in nothing. Hence, it is clear how seldom we think of others as we do of ourselves.

If all were perfect, what should we have to suffer from others for God's sake? But God has so ordained, that we may learn to bear with one another's burdens, for there is no man without fault, no man without burden, no man sufficient to himself nor wise enough. Hence we must support one another, console one another, mutually help,

continued on the next page

to have been the main occupation of the twelve. They were then like children born into a new world, whose first and by no means least important course of lessons consists in the use of their senses in observing the wonderful objects by which they are surrounded. [12] ◀

Working with Flawed, Fallen People

People can be forgiven for periodically thinking that Jesus would have had greater success if He had chosen 12 more qualified candidates as His first disciples. Story after story from the Gospels confirms the conviction that the 12 men Jesus chose were flawed and fallen creatures.

The defections of Peter and the other disciples at the end of the Gospels are only a continuation of years' worth of failings:

"Peter replied, 'Even if all fall away on account of you, I never will.'

"'I tell you the truth,' Jesus answered, 'this very night, before the rooster crows, you will disown me three times.'

"But Peter declared, 'Even if I have to die with you, I will never disown you.' And all the other disciples said the same" (Matthew 26:33-34).

Later, Matthew 26:56 tells us: "Then all the disciples deserted him and fled."

Wouldn't it have been better if Christ had chosen men who were more stable, more emotionally balanced, or more capable of carrying His burdens on their shoulders?

Regardless of how we might like to rewrite the biblical story, the way Jesus chose His disciples was consistent with His entire ministry: He reached out to flawed and fallen people and offered the way for them to receive redemption.

"It is not the healthy who need a doctor, but the sick," said Jesus, who was teaching the crowds one day alongside a lake. "I have not come to call the righteous, but sinners" (Mark 2:17).

Jesus' deep love for sinners was a source of constant curiosity

84

among His disciples and the cause of continual criticism from Jewish leaders:

"Now the tax collectors and 'sinners' were all gathering around to hear him. But the Pharisees and the teachers of the law muttered, 'This man welcomes sinners and eats with them'" (Luke 15:1-2).

Even today, many believers might prefer to steer clear of soiled souls, but that was not the way of Jesus.

Not all of us have a history of sinful behavior that is as bold and colorful as that of the Apostle Paul, but regardless, we can certainly share his joy:

"I thank Christ Jesus our Lord, who has given me strength, that he considered me faithful, appointing me to his service. Even though I was once a blasphemer and a persecutor and a violent man, I was shown mercy because I acted in ignorance and unbelief. The grace of our Lord was poured out on me abundantly, along with the faith and love that are in Christ Jesus. Here is a trustworthy saying that deserves full acceptance: Christ Jesus came into the world to save sinners—of whom I am the worst" (1 Timothy 1:12-15).

Paul wrote many eloquent passages about his ongoing battles with his sinful nature. In Romans, he expands on the Hebrew law, which states: "There is no one righteous, not even one" (3:9-20); and he also describes his own inner struggles: "I do not understand what I do. For what I want to do I do not do, but what I hate I do" (7:14-25).

The Gentleness of Grace

The only way out of such a distressing dilemma is through something writer Michael Yaconelli calls "reckless grace." In the following lengthy article Yaconelli, the cofounder of Youth Specialties, describes his own relief at receiving God's overflowing grace.

► I want to introduce a new sociological category: failers. That is, people who fail on a regular basis. People like me.

I am a lay pastor of a small, not-growing church. I am not ordained. I am not seminary trained. I was asked to leave both Bible colleges I attended. I am divorced and remarried. On any given day

counsel, and advise, for the measure of every man's virtue is best revealed in time of adversity—adversity that does not weaken a man but rather shows what he is. [13]

—*Thomas à Kempis*

Face the Facts about Sin
If we claim to be without sin, we deceive ourselves and the truth is not in us. If we confess our sins, he is faithful and just and will forgive us our sins and purify us from all unrighteousness. If we claim we have not sinned, we make him out to be a liar and his word has no place in our lives (1 John 1:8-10).

Seeing the Child Within

The gentleness of Jesus with sinners flowed from His ability to read their hearts and to detect the sincerity and goodness there. Behind men's grumpiest poses and most puzzling defense mechanisms, behind their arrogance and airs, behind their silence, sneers, and curses, Jesus saw little children who hadn't been loved enough and who had ceased growing because someone had ceased believing in them. His extraordinary sensitivity and compassion caused Jesus (and later the apostles) to speak of the faithful as children no matter how tall, rich, clever, and successful they might be. [14]

—Brennan Manning

I am capable of being a jerk with my wife and family. I am terminally insecure, which causes me to compensate with bouts of arrogance. At times people irritate me, and I hide from them. I am impulsive, which causes me to say things I shouldn't and make promises I cannot keep. I am inconsistent.

Every man should keep a fair-sized cemetery in which to bury the faults of his friends.

—HENRY WARD BEECHER

My walk with Christ is a stuttering, stumbling, bumbling attempt to follow Him. At times His presence is so real I can't stop the tears, and then, without warning, I can't find Him. Some days my faith is strong, impenetrable, immovable—and some days my faith is weak, pathetic, helpless, knocked about like a paper cup floating on the ocean in the middle of a hurricane.

I have been a Christian for 45 years. I am familiar with the vocabulary of faith, and I am often asked to give advice about matters of faith. But I am still a mess. I am light-years away from being able to say with Paul, "Copy me." I am 56 years old and still struggling—a flawed, clumsy, unstable follower of Jesus. A bona fide failer.

That bothers a lot of people. Over the years they have expressed their displeasure with my failings. Some have abandoned me. Some have even written me out of the kingdom.

Not Jesus.

He refuses to give up on me. Sometimes, late at night, when I am just about to give in to sleep, I know I have heard Him weeping for me.

A Lover of Losers. You see, Jesus has a fatal flaw: He can't stay away from failers. He is a friend of failers, a lover of failers. When everyone else has given up, He seeks them out—the woman who failed at five marriages; the blind man by the pool, who had failed to get his timing down for 38 years in a row; the woman with the blood disease, who failed at giving up; the disciple who failed at following; the fisherman who failed at fishing; the thief who failed at keeping the law; the adulterous woman who failed at moral purity; the doubting disciple who failed to believe.

In Luke 14:15-24, Jesus told a parable about failers. A wealthy man prepared a party for his successful friends. When the day of the party arrived, all of his "friends" decided they couldn't come. So the host told his servants, "Go out and invite all the losers you can find— the drunks, the prostitutes, the homeless, the lame." The host threw a party for all the failers. Jesus was defining His church. He was making it very clear that the church is more than a safe place for losers; its membership is made up of losers—failers like you and me.

God loves to look at us, and loves it when we will look back at him. Even when we try to run away from our troubles, as Jacob did, God will find us, and bless us, even when we feel most alone, unsure if we'll survive the night. God will find a way to let us know that he is with us in this place, wherever we are, however far we think we've run. And maybe that's one reason we worship—to respond to grace.

⮾KATHLEEN NORRIS

Frugal with Forgiveness. Why is it, then, that so many Christians don't like failers very much—unless they are reformed long-ago failers? Ex-failers. Practicing failers seem to be an embarrassment to today's upwardly mobile Christianity.

I don't understand why.

As Henri Nouwen points out, Christians have always been downwardly mobile. We are unified by our common weaknesses—our common failures, our common disappointments, our common disillusionment, and our common inconsistencies. It is while we are yet sinners (Romans 5:8) that Jesus is attracted to us. It is our common failure that makes us desperate enough to look, finally, to the cross, to the body of Jesus, whose blood flows and mingles with ours and graces us with His forgiveness.

That is why I love Jesus so much. He was so . . . well . . . well . . . irresponsible with grace. He was so indiscriminate and reckless with forgiveness. Even more shocking, Jesus encouraged irresponsible grace by telling stories that suggested such acts of recklessness be followed by a party.

In contrast, modern Christianity is so responsible with grace. It is almost as though Christ's church is afraid to squander grace, as though it were a limited resource that must be protected and dispensed cautiously. The Grace Dispensers worry that grace might be wasted or misused. Sure, go ahead, the church can forgive one divorce, maybe two, but five? OK, Christians can forgive adultery, but . . . uh . . . we can't have sinners running wild in our churches, can we?

And then there is the prodigal son.

He dishonored his father, wasted his inheritance, partied until he ended up a disgusting, homeless, mud-covered, foul-smelling loser. And he is supposed to be treated with a party? Jesus responds to the Grace Dispensers with reckless forgiveness and lavish celebration.

Anyone who thinks himself a perfect follower of Christ's teaching and way of life. . . but who cannot follow Christ in having love and charity towards all, both good and bad, friends and foes, without pretense or flattery, contempt, anger, or spiteful criticism, is indeed deceiving himself.

~WALTER HILTON

A Community of Celebration. When we as failers fail and then come to our senses, we should be eager to return home to our Christian community because we know what to expect.

We do not expect a chorus of "I told you so's."

We do not expect a group of accusers and theology monitors.

We do not expect to jump through hoops to prove we're repentant. No.

We expect a party.

That is what Christians do with failers. We are irresponsible just like Jesus. We do more than instruct, we surprise. We do more than pray, we party. We do more than correct, we dance. And we do more than love, we celebrate.

Just like Jesus. [15] ◀

Incarnational Living

Every Christmas, millions of believers celebrate the incarnation of Christ by singing carols, reading the Nativity passages from the Gospels, and hearing sermons on biblical texts like John 1:14: "The Word became flesh and made his dwelling among us."

The Christian life is not a way "out,"
but a way "through" life.
~Billy Graham

Too frequently, though, all such thoughts about the Incarnation are put aside until the next Christmas, and the next. In such cases, disciples of Jesus are missing a crucial point: If we are to model our lives around His, we should daily reenact the Incarnation.

Of course, unlike Jesus, we are not God taking on humanity. But each of us can take on aspects of the humanity all around us, seeking to redeem and transform it. François Fénelon (1651–1715), a French priest, mystic, and writer who worked with the poor, continually sought ways to offer the seemingly mundane details of daily life to God's use:

▶ How can I offer my common daily actions to God . . . visits received and paid, dressing . . . reading . . . the business which comes upon me on behalf of friends and relations, amusements, shopping . . . and the like? I want to learn how, by some kind of prayer, to offer all these things to God.

The most unimportant acts cease to be so, and become important, [as soon as] they are done with the intention of conformity to God's will. Indeed, they are often better and purer than what may seem more religious acts; first because they are less self-chosen, and more according to the order of God's providence; secondly, because they are simpler, and less exposed to self-complacency; thirdly, because if performed in moderation, and with a right intention of heart, we may find more means of self-abnegation than in actions where excitement or self have a larger part; and lastly, because these trifling matters are continually recurring, and furnish a constant opportunity for unobtrusively serving God.

Breaking the Bread of Life

In setting Himself forth as the bread which came down from heaven, Jesus virtually taught the doctrine of the incarnation. The solemn assertion, "I am the bread of life," is equivalent in import to that made by the evangelist respecting Him who spoke these words: "The Word became flesh, and dwelt among us, full of grace and truth."

It is, however, not merely as incarnate that the Son of God is the bread of eternal life. Bread must be broken in order to be eaten. The Incarnate One must die as a sacrificial victim that men may truly feed upon Him. The Word become flesh, and crucified in the flesh, is the life of the world. [16]

—A.B. Bruce

Offer the Ordinary to Him. We do not need great efforts, or much thought, to offer these actions which we call unimportant. The offering may be made with a momentary uplifting of the heart to God. Whatever He wills us to do, whatever belongs to the ordinary course of duties appertaining to our state of life, may, and ought to be, offered to God; nothing is unworthy of Him save what is wrong. When you feel that any given action cannot be offered to God, you may conclude that it is not suitable to a Christian; at all events, it is suspicious, and you should investigate the matter.

I [would] not make a formal act of prayer about each separate thing; an uplifting of the heart at the moment will suffice. The practice may be easy and simple if it is to become habitual. As to visits, shopping and the like, as these are liable to be pursued with self-indulgence, I [would] add a petition for grace to be moderate as a caution.

Be Diligent in Your Faithfulness. We are bound to seek our sanctification in that state wherein Providence has placed us, rather than to build castles in the air concerning great possible virtue in positions we do not fill. . . . We need very diligent faithfulness to God in the smallest things.

Most people spend the best part of their life in avowing and regretting their habits, in talking about changing them; in making rules for a future time which they look for, but which is not given them; and in thereby losing time which ought to be spent in good works and in setting forward their salvation.

Through him [Christ] we see as in a mirror the
spotless and excellent face of God.

—St. Clement

You should treat all such notions as very dangerous. Our salvation ought to be the work of every day and every hour. No time is fitter for it than that which God in His mercy accords to us now; and that because today is ours, but we know not what tomorrow may bring forth. . . . The uncertainty of life ought to make us realize that we should prosecute this undertaking with all our energies, and that all other pursuits are worthless, since they do not bring us nearer to God, the rightful End of all we do—the God of our salvation, as

David continually calls Him in the Psalms.

Make Obedience an Everyday Habit. Make a habit of frequently adoring His holy will by humbly submitting yourself to the order of His good providence. Ask Him to uphold you, lest you fall. Entreat Him to perfect His work in you, so that, having inspired you in your present state of life with the desire to be saved, you may actually work out your salvation therein.

There is only one physician, a physician who is at once fleshly and spiritual, generate and ingenerate, God in man, true life in death, born of Mary and of God, first passible then impassible, Jesus Christ our Lord.

~IGNATIUS OF ANTIOCH

He does not require great things for success. Our Lord Himself has said, "The kingdom of God is within you" [see Luke 17:21]; we can find it there when we will. Let us do what we know He requires of us, and [as] soon as we perceive His will in anything, let there be no drawing back, only absolute faithfulness.

Such faithfulness ought not merely to lead us to do great things for His service and for our salvation, but whatever our hands find to do, or which appertains to our state of life. If one could only be saved by means of great deeds, [only a] few could hope for salvation. It depends, however, in fulfilling God's will. The smallest things become great when God requires them of us. They are only small as regards themselves; but they forthwith become great when done for Him, when they lead to Him, and serve to unite [us] with Him eternally.

God clothed himself in vile man's flesh so he might be weak enough to suffer woe.

~JOHN DONNE

Be Faithful in the Small Things. Remember how He has said, "He that is faithful in that which is least is faithful also in much, and he that is unjust in the least is unjust also in much" [see Luke 16:10]. I [would] say that a soul which sincerely longs after God never considers whether a thing be small or great; it is enough to know that He for whom it is done is infinitely great, that it is His due to have all creation solely devoted to His glory, which can only be by fulfilling His will. [17] ◄

Christianity is not primarily a theological system, an ethical system, a ritual system, a social system or an ecclesiastical system—it is a person: it's Jesus Christ, and to be a Christian is to know Him and to follow Him and believe in Him.

—JOHN STOTT

A Picture of Incarnational Love

The incarnational love of Jesus is a powerful concept, but it can be difficult for some people to grasp. Pastor and award-winning writer Walter Wangerin, Jr. helps us understand it with the following story taken from his own life:

► The coming of the kingdom is like the coming of my father to my brothers and me when we sat fishing, blithely fishing, from a ledge twelve feet above the water in a stony cove in Glacier National Park.

In that year of sudden awakening, 1954, I was ten. My brothers, grinning idiots all (for that they followed a fool) were, in descending order, nine, seven, and six.

Before our trip from Grand Forks west, I had furnished myself with fishing equipment. With a Cheerios box top and my personal dime, I sent away for ten small hooks, three flies, leader, line, a red-and-white bobber, and three thin pieces of bamboo that fit snugly into one pole. Such a deal! Such a shrewd fellow I felt myself to be.

On a bright, blue morning we chopped bits of bacon into a pouch and went forth to fish. We sought a mountain stream, though we ourselves did not depart the trail down from the campground. Fortunately, that same trail turned into a wooden bridge that crossed furious roaring waters, the crashing of a falls from the slower bed of a stream.

A mountain stream! There, to our right, before it dived down into the rocky chasm immediately below this bridge, was a mountain stream. Filled with fishes, certainly. We had found it.

But the bridge joined two walls of stone, and even the slower stream came through a high defile.

But I was a shrewd fellow in those days, a leader indeed. I noticed that a narrow ledge snaked away from the far end of the bridge, that it was over-bellied by an enormous boulder and there-fore hidden from the view of lesser scouts. If we could crawl that ledge on hands and knees through its narrowest part, ducking low the boulder, why, we'd come to a widening, a hemisphere of stone big enough to sit on, from which to dangle our legs, a sort of fortress of stone since the wall went up from that ledge a flat twelve feet and down again from that ledge another direct twelve feet. Perfect. Safe from attacks. Good for fishing.

"The Word became flesh," wrote John, "and dwelt among us, full of grace and truth" (John 1:14). That is what incarnation means. It is untheological. It is unsophisticated. It is undignified. But according to Christianity it is the way things are.

FREDERICK BUECHNER

I led my blinking brothers thither. None questioned me. I was the oldest. Besides, I was the one with foresight enough to have pur-chased a fishing pole.

"You got to flatten out here," I called back, grunting in order to fit beneath the out-cropping boulder. They did. One by one they arrived with me in a fine, round hideout. Above the sheer rock some trees leaned over and looked down upon us. Below our feet there turned a lucid pool of water, itself some twelve feet deep.

And so the Brothers Wangerin began to spend a fine day fishing. We took turns with the pole.

The bacon didn't work, but—as a sign of our favor with all the world—the trees dropped down on silken threads some tiny green worms, exactly the size of our tiny hooks. We reached out and plucked worms from the air, baited the hooks, and caught (truly, truly) several fingerling fish. Oh, it was a good day! All that we needed we had.

Then came my father.

We didn't see him at first. We weren't thinking about him, so filled with ourselves were we, our chatting and our various successes. But I heard through the water's roar a cry. Distant, distant: "Wally!"

I glanced up and to my right—where the water disappeared over stone, where the bridge arched it—and I almost glanced away again, but a wild waving caught my eye.

"WALLY! WALLY! WALLY!"

"Dad?" Yes!—it was Dad. "Hey, look, you guys. There's Dad leaning over the bridge."

They all looked, and straightway Philip started to cry, and then Mike, too. Paul dropped my pole into the water twelve feet below. And I saw in our father's eyes a terror I had never seen before.

"WALLY, HOW DID YOU GET OVER THERE?"

Over here? I looked around.

Suddenly here was no fortress at all. It was a precipice, a sheer stone drop to a drowning water, and that water rushed toward a thundering falls far, far below my father. With his eyes I saw what I had not seen before. In his seeing (which loved us terribly) I saw our peril.

He was crying out as loud as he could: "WALLY, COME HERE! COME HERE!"

But the ledge by which we'd come had shrunk. It was thin as a lip now. The hairs on my neck had started to tingle, and my butt grew roots. I couldn't move. Neither did my brothers. I didn't even shake my head. I was afraid that any motion at all would pitch me headlong into the pool below. I gaped at my father, speechless.

He stopped waving. He lowered his arms and stopped shouting. He stood for an eternal moment looking at us from the bridge, and then his mouth formed the word Wait. We couldn't hear it. He didn't lift his voice. Quietly under the booming waters he whispered, "Wait."

Then he bent down and removed his shoes. At the near end of the bridge, he bent down farther, farther, until he was on his stomach, worming forward, knocking dust and pebbles by his body into the stream, bowing beneath the enormous boulder that blocked our freedom.

"Dad's coming. See him?"

"Yep, Dad's coming."

"I knew he would."

He pulled himself ahead on the points of his elbows, like the infantry beneath barbed wire, his face drawn and anxious. He was wearing shorts and a long-sleeved flannel shirt. Red with darker red squares. I remember.

When he came into our tiny cove, he turned on his belly and hissed to the youngest of us, "Mike, take my heel." Mike was six. He didn't.

"Mike, now!" Dad shouted above the waterfall with real anger. "Grab my heel in your hand and follow me."

You should know that my father is by nature and breeding and profession a formal man. I don't recall him often to go into public wearing short-sleeved shirts. Nor would he permit people to call him by his first name, asking rather that they address him according to his position, his title, and degree. Even today the most familiar name he will respond to is "Doc." Dad is two-legged and upright. Dad is organized, controlled, clean, precise, dignified, decorous, civil—and formal.

What a descent it was, therefore, what a sweet humiliation, that he should on his stomach scrabble this way and that, coming on stone then going again, pulling after him one son after the other: Michael, Philip, Paul.

And then me.

"Wally, grab my heel. Follow me."

It wasn't he who had put us in these straits. Nevertheless, he chose to enter them with us, in order to take us out with him. It was foolishness that put us here. It was love that brought him.

Blood includes us in the Incarnation—not so crazy,
after all, but an ancient thing, and wise. The rhythm
of life that we carry in our veins is not only for us,
but for others, as Christ's Incarnation was
for the sake of all.
—KATHLEEN NORRIS

So he measured the motion of his long leg by the length of my small arm, and he never pulled farther than I could reach. The waters roared and were troubled; the granite shook with the swelling thereof. But my father was present, and very present. I felt the flesh of his heel in my hand, leading me; and I was still in my soul. I ceased to be afraid.

That stony cove had not been a refuge at all but a danger. Rather, my father in love bore refuge unto me; my father bore me back to safety again. So I did not die in the day of my great stupidity. I lived.

Thus is the kingdom of heaven likened unto a certain man whose eldest son was a nincompoop. [18] ◄

Giving All, or Just a Little

Time after time, the Gospels tell us that Jesus was often surrounded by crowds, and that flocks of people would follow Him to hear His teaching or see His miracles. "Great crowds came to him," wrote Matthew, "bringing the lame, the blind, the crippled, the mute and many others, and laid them at his feet; and he healed them" (Matthew 15:30).

> *Gifts excite and stir up grace unto its proper exercise and operation.*
>
> ＪOHN OWEN

But somehow, at the end of the day, relatively few members of these huge throngs totally devoted their lives to following Jesus. His flock of disciples was much smaller. "My sheep listen to my voice," He said. "I know them, and they follow me" (John 10:27).

Each person who declines the offer of Jesus has what seems like good reasons. Some are burdened by matters of work or possessions. Others are preoccupied by family matters.

Today, it seems that people have more and more persistent distractions from the call of Jesus, but the human motives for neglecting the call have changed little over the ages of human history.

Georg Strumpf and J. Stephen Lang, two American writers who have traveled through many areas of the globe, explain how the contemporary problem of excessive busyness has paralyzed many of their fellow Americans and prevented them from seeing and seizing spiritual opportunities that present themselves. The cross-cultural lessons they explore in the following essay should be helpful to residents of any of the world's developed or rapidly developing countries:

▶ "Datsun—we are driven!" That old advertising slogan could easily be reworded "Americans—we are driven!" Of course, not all Americans feel the strong drive to produce, to achieve, to be constantly busy (even with leisure), constantly changing and improving, exploring as many of life's options as possible. But the air we breathe in America is the air of busyness. Most of us feel we must be doing something. Busyness has become such an American ideal that we often feel guilty when we aren't busy.

I [Georg] know about drivenness, having seen it (or the lack of it) in several cultures. I have lived in the United States since 1966, but was born and reared in Germany, with schooling and work in France, England, and Italy, and I spent several years in Algeria as a translator.

The positive side of busyness and hard work is that Americans and Europeans have made great contributions to human life—in medicine, technology, entertainment. Most of us are (or should be) grateful for the ingenuity and hard work that gave us antibiotics, cars, air conditioners, VCRs, etc. Drive and busyness have made life more comfortable. Spiritually speaking, busy saints have fulfilled Jesus' mandates in Matthew 25:31-46 and Matthew 28:19-20 by aiding the needy and spreading the gospel.

But the negative side of busyness is that our obsession with it can keep us from enjoying life—even during our leisure hours. Many Americans find it hard to "mellow out" and relax. There is a "Friday afternoon fever" that sends families rushing out of town, fighting traffic to get to the beach or the mountains or the theme park. Some people enjoy this, despite the hassles. But many people return to work on Monday morning feeling relieved that the busy weekend is over. Can we call a frantic weekend "leisure"? Have we lost sight of the Sabbath as a day of rest? And has anyone noticed that the Bible has a lot to say about peace and joy and contentment, but nothing about constantly seeking new ways of amusing ourselves?

Our culture also influences us to buy the latest clothing styles for ourselves and our children. It insists that instead of simple cable TV

Run Without Hindrance

Therefore, since we are surrounded by such a great cloud of witnesses, let us throw off everything that hinders and the sin that so easily entangles, and let us run with perseverance the race marked out for us. Let us fix our eyes on Jesus, the author and perfecter of our faith, who for the joy set before him endured the cross, scorning its shame, and sat down at the right hand of the throne of God. Consider him who endured such opposition from sinful men, so that you will not grow weary and lose heart (Hebrews 12:1-3).

we need a satellite dish that brings in 200 channels. We need to find better jobs, ones that usually demand more of our time, and both parents need to go to work to support our materialistic needs. Christians in America are part of our culture, for better or worse, and we seldom ask, "Is my busyness rooted in my desire to possess more things and display those things?" If the answer is yes, then maybe we've made things into a god we worship. That's idolatry.

Busyness and Church. Materialism isn't the only drive behind busyness. Christians in America often pride ourselves on being busy with church activities. It is a compliment to say that So-and-so is "active in church." In some suburban megachurches it is almost possible to spend all one's nonworking, nonsleeping hours at church.

That isn't necessarily bad. We need fellowship with other Christians, and church activities are better than many of the secular alternatives. But it might be healthy to consider our motives for remaining busy with church activities. According to 1 Corinthians 13, doing a lot of things is no substitute for genuine Christian love—even though a loving Christian will, of course, do good works.

Sow everywhere the good seed given to you.
≈SERAPHIM OF SAROV

In my youth in Germany, my impression was that churches are places of worship, not activity centers. Europeans (whose rates of church attendance are much lower than Americans) still puzzle that American churches schedule so many activities outside the worship times. Personally, I like the busyness, since it dispels the notion that Christianity is strictly a Sunday morning affair. Bible studies, fellowship times, etc., are wonderful things. My chief criticism of church busyness is this: We can bury ourselves in activities and withdraw from a world that needs to hear the gospel. Busy churches can be like monasteries—beehives of activity, but forgetful of Jesus' mandate to "go and make disciples" (Matthew 28:19). We can't "let [our] light shine before men" (Matthew 5:16) if our lights only shine within the church fellowship hall.

Busyness and Fatalism. Doris Day sang, "*Que sera, sera*, whatever will be, will be." When one's options in life are limited, that is a sensible creed. "I'm not rich, my parents were not rich, and odds are that my children won't ever be rich. Busyness won't change this. So be it."

I observed this attitude among Algerians, who tended to be content with what they had. To a large extent, this was the influence of Islam, a fatalistic faith that makes people resign themselves to whatever happens. Yet it was the Apostle Paul who said, "I know what it is to be in need, and I know what it is to have plenty. I have learned the secret of being content in any and every situation" (Philippians 4:12). He also said, "Godliness with contentment is great gain" (1 Timothy 6:6).

Sometimes it appears that people (of whatever religion) in poor nations accept this truth more readily than do Christians in wealthy nations. This doesn't mean that resignation is the same as faith. But perhaps Christians should focus occasionally on the biblical theme of contentment in any circumstance. Godly contentment can lead us to make "keeping up with the Joneses" a low priority.

If we use God's talents, we shall find that they become
multiplied in the use. We thought
we had two; we find we have five.
∼RICHARD MEUX BENSON

Many Muslims—perhaps by necessity—seem more able to accept life as the will of Allah than Christians are able to accept life as the will of God. They seem more able to "be still, and know that I am God" (Psalm 46:10). In America, the "land of opportunity," the land of "the pursuit of happiness," even Christians have difficulty in being still, being content, just accepting life. So many options are open to us, and we run ourselves ragged, cramming our days full.

Busyness and Companionship. Busyness robs us Americans of enjoying human companionship. Our spin on companionship makes us feel obligated to "do" things together—rent a movie, play a video game, anything so that we don't just "sit around and stare at each other."

I never found that Algerians "sit around and stare." When they visit (usually involving a carload of relatives visiting a houseful of relatives), things are never quiet. Talk fills up the time—very nicely, as anyone from a large family will tell you. There is no feeling that you need to plan an activity or spend a lot of money. Throw a large group of people together and, no, they will not get bored. "Doing nothing" can be jolly fun in a large family. But most Americans, Christians included, don't want to admit that they did nothing over the weekend. Admitting you did nothing is admitting you and the family didn't spend much money.

Of course, many Muslims are attracted to American and European ways. Algerians who can afford the "toys" produced abroad will buy them, and many young Algerians hanker for the American lifestyle. But for most people these goals are unattainable. So they accept life as it is: unpredictable, with many matters beyond one's control, but with stability found in one's spiritual heritage and one's family.

Wouldn't all Christians benefit from such acceptance? [19] ◄

Go and Teach

When Jesus issued His Great Commission, He told His disciples to "go and make disciples of all nations." He included this specific command: "teaching them to obey everything I have commanded you."

Going out and teaching people the message of the Gospel has been a fundamental part of evangelism for the past 20 centuries, but Jim Petersen, an executive with The Navigators ministry, discovered to his chagrin that many Christians either don't feel called to go and teach, or they simply don't know how to do so.

Petersen's experiences on a boat full of missionaries would have been hilarious if it hadn't been so sad. But from that experience he emerged with a renewed appreciation of the importance of something he would later call "lifestyle evangelism."

► In 1963 my family traveled by ship from the United States to Brazil. The trip marked a new beginning. We expected that. We did not expect that the sixteen days aboard the ship would, in themselves, mark the beginning of discoveries that are still going on.

There were 120 people on the ship. Half were tourists and half were missionaries—including us. Sixty missionaries and sixty tourists! A one-to-one ratio for sixteen days. Since there isn't much more to do aboard ship than to walk, read, or converse, I couldn't imagine how any of those tourists could get through the trip without receiving a thorough exposure to the Christian message. More ideal conditions for evangelism couldn't exist.

During the first three days my wife and I spent our time relating to the other passengers. Conversations were unhurried and soon we found ourselves deeply involved in discussing Christ with our new acquaintances.

On the third day I thought that if the other fifty-eight missionaries were doing what we were, we would have a serious case of overkill. I decided to check with the others about coordinating our efforts. My first opportunity came when I encountered six missionaries sitting together on the deck. I joined them and expressed my concern that we get our signals straight so we wouldn't overwhelm the passengers.

I had totally misjudged the problem. When I explained what was on my mind, the six just looked at one another. Apparently, it hadn't occurred to them to talk to the other sixty passengers about Christ. Finally one said, "We just graduated from seminary and didn't learn how to do that sort of thing there." Another said, "I don't know. I have sort of a built-in reservation against the idea of conversion." A third said, "I've been a pastor for three years, but I've never personally evangelized anyone. I don't think I know how either."

I remember saying that if we, in sixteen days and with a one-to-one ratio, couldn't evangelize sixty people, we might as well forget about ninety-five million Brazilians. Perhaps it would be just as well if we would all catch the next boat north.

A few hours later there was a knock on our cabin door. I opened it to find three of the six I had just been talking to. They had come to tell me they had obtained permission from the captain to conduct a Sunday service for the ship's crew and that they wanted me to preach the sermon.

As they elaborated their plan, I was reminded of a conversation I had three weeks before with a friend's pastor. The pastor told me his congregation had recently begun witnessing. He said the young people were going to the old folks' home each Sunday to conduct a service. Some of his men were holding weekly jail services after which they would counsel prisoners individually.

The creature is like a mighty trumpet
that speaks to us of God.
—GREGORY OF NYSSA

Carrying the Message. Obviously, there is nothing wrong with conducting services in jails and rest homes, but if such things alone constitute the main evangelistic thrust of a body of Christians it raises a problem. I asked the pastor, "Aren't you running the risk of teaching your congregation that the gospel is only for those in unfortunate circumstances—for those who are relatively unthreatening to us? Shouldn't Christians learn to carry the message to their peers, to go after people on their own level?"

I expressed the same concern to the three missionaries in my cabin. We could slip into the same mental trap aboard ship. I said, "Your consciences were pricked by what we talked about. So now you've spotted the unfortunate sailors who never go to church and have planned a service for them. That is good, but I don't think we can escape from our responsibility to the passengers."

They got the point, but they had already committed themselves to conducting a service for the crew. The captain posted a notice in the crew's quarters, and arrangements had been made to use the galley. I agreed to attend, but not to speak.

The four of us arrived in the galley on schedule. It was empty. Occasionally a sailor would have to go through the room in the course of his duties. He would dart through quickly, obviously intent on not getting caught. Finally, one sailor came in and sat down. He was a Baptist. So we had the service: four missionaries and one Baptist sailor!

After that, my three friends began to think in terms of going to the tourists.

There was an elderly Christian couple among the passengers. It was the husband's birthday so the three missionaries organized an old-fashioned sing to commemorate the occasion. Sensing what was coming and not wanting to jeopardize my relationship with the people I was evangelizing, I felt it wiser to stay away. When the time came for the program, I was up on the third deck. One other passenger was up there enjoying the night air. We began discussing the New Testament I had taken along to read.

Down below we could hear the old songs: "Suwanee River," "My Old Kentucky Home"; then it was "Rock of Ages," another hymn, a pause. And so it went: hymns, testimonies, and a message.

When it was over my three friends were euphoric. They had succeeded in "preaching" to virtually all the passengers. Naturally, they called another sing for two nights later. Once again I went to the third deck, but this time there were sixty others up there with me. They weren't about to get caught twice!

As I later reflected on those sixteen days aboard ship, it occurred to me that this situation represented a microcosm of the church in the world. That realization, combined with the subsequent years of adapting to a new culture and language for the sake of the gospel, has raised scores of questions and set me on a quest that continues to this day. This search has to do with what it really means to take the gospel into the world.

Jesus gave us our "marching orders"
in the great Commission.
<small>≈BILLY GRAHAM</small>

Closing the Communication Gap. Closing the communication gap between Christians and the secularized must become a primary concern if we are to go beyond evangelizing our own kind.

A short passage by Paul in 1 Corinthians 9 synthesizes this as a single principle. The subject of the passage is clearly evangelism. Paul wrote:

"Though I am free and belong to no man, I make myself a slave to everyone, to win as many as possible. To the Jews I became like a Jew, to win the Jews. To those under the law I became like one under the law (though I myself am not under the law), so as to win those under the law. To those not having the law I became like one not having the law . . . so as to win those not having the law. To the weak I became weak, to win the weak. I have become all things to all men so that by all possible means I might save some. I do all this for the sake of the gospel, that I may share in its blessings (vv. 19-23).

Paul said that as a witness he recognized it was up to him to adapt to the unevangelized. The witness adjusts to those he evangelizes, and not vice versa. Paul defended his freedom to be all things to all men because he knew this was the balance between being "in the world" and being "separate" from it. To be in the world one has to be free to participate in the lives of those around him. Being separate means we do this without compromising the sovereign rule of God in our heart—without sinning, in other words.

What does being "all things to all men" mean in practice? What did it mean for Paul to live like a Jew while among Jews, and then change and live like one without the law when he was among the Gentiles? It meant he would respect the scruples and traditions of whomever he was with, and have the flexibility to set one group's practices aside as he entered the world of persons with different customs.

This struck many as a scandalous thought, but Paul was willing to pay a price for his position. He was a controversial figure among Christians and non-Christians until the day he died. It takes maturity and courage to "go to the Gentiles."

As we discussed why a team of missionaries in his country was having difficulty establishing a solid ministry, a South American said, "Their sanctification is American. I get the impression they are afraid to adapt to the culture because in so doing they would become soiled by the world. They fear they would be 'going pagan.'"

When the bread is broken and the wine is poured into the cup at the eucharist, we are brought face to face with our own need for evangelism, with our own brokenness and the call for our lives to be outpoured. . . .

—ERICE FAIRBROTHER

The Incarnation as a Model. Change is hard to face, especially in areas of behavior. Going into the world requires change. It implies participation in people's lives. It means to think, to feel, to understand, and to take seriously the values of those we seek to win.

The incarnation is our prototype. Jesus set his glory aside, "made himself nothing," and "humbled himself" (Philippians 2:7-8). Consequently, "we have one who has been tempted in every way, just as we are—yet was without sin" (Hebrews 4:15). He came into the world, lived life in our presence, and participated with us in life as we live it. He drew the line only at sin. To what degree could we identify with God if there had been no incarnation?

The Apostle Paul followed the same principle. He went to non-Christians in order to bring them to God, but he knew their route to God had to pass through his own life. "You are witnesses," he reminded the Thessalonians, "of how holy, righteous and blameless we were among you" (1 Thessalonians 2:10).

For better or for worse, the life a Christian lives in the presence of those he seeks to win is a preview of what the non-Christian's life will become if he accepts what he is hearing. Generally, he will decide either to accept or reject Christianity according to what he has seen. I stumbled onto this rather unnerving truth unwittingly.

Our family was unaware of our influence on Mario. God had done this work through our family without our knowing it. Most Christians are probably unaware of most of the improvements God makes on us in the sanctification process. We tend to see the weaknesses and incongruities in our lives, and our reaction is to recoil at the thought of letting outsiders get close enough to see us as we really are.

Ultimately, evangelism is not a technique. It is the Lord of the Church who reserves to Himself His sovereign right to add to His Church.

—John Stott

Even if our assessment is accurate, it is my observation that any Christian who is sincerely seeking to walk with God, in spite of all his flaws, reflects something of Christ. It seems that the better we think we are doing, the worse we come across.

It is not enough, then, to occasionally drop into another individual's world, preach to him, and go our way. Somehow, he needs to be brought into our world as well. If he isn't, the view he gets of us is so fragmented he could miss the total picture. He doesn't see the effects the grace of God has had in our day-to-day lives.

But this two-way interaction will never happen unless we Christians learn how to become "all things to all men. [20] ◄

Evangelism for Everyone

One gets the distinct impression that for Jesus, sharing the good news of the kingdom of God was never drudgery or something He did out of a sense of obligation. Rather, the message of redemption flowed effortlessly from His mouth and His life.

But somewhere along the way, followers of Jesus have adopted approaches to evangelism that make it seem difficult and demanding to many.

Then [Jesus said] to his disciples, "The harvest is plentiful but the workers are few. Ask the Lord of the harvest, therefore, to send out workers into his harvest field."
≈ MATTHEW 9:37-38

Rebecca Manley Pippert has spent much of her life trying to change that. Her 1979 book, *Out of the Saltshaker and Into the World: Evangelism as a Way of Life* (InterVarsity Press), was a major best-seller during the 1980s. In an interview with journalist Beth Spring, printed in *Discipleship Journal*, Pippert encouraged people to return to a "natural" style of evangelism like that used by Jesus, and she argued that "Christian realism" should replace put-on piety.

▶ **DJ:** The concept of "sharing our faith" presumes that Christians have something that non-Christians need. Yet a nonbeliever might not perceive any spiritual need. How can a Christian establish common ground?

Pippert: Just because a person is not aware of a need for Christ, it doesn't mean he or she does not have some need. So we must consider, "What are their needs?" I've found it helpful to examine where the person is in his or her life cycle. Even finding out how old a person is gives me some clues.

A friend and I have just started a Bible study for some high-flying professional women. There is one woman in it for whom I've been praying for twelve years. When I first met her, she was on the fast track professionally; she had no time for reflection, but she seemed spiritually open. Now, with her children in their teenage years, she told me she can barely look at their baby pictures because those years are gone; they are a blur, and she can't get them back.

Agonized, she told me, "I want to keep my children from the perils of their adolescent culture; I want to give them strong moral values; but first I've got to find them myself." This woman jumped at the chance to be in a Bible study. Where she is in her life as a mother made her very open to recognizing her need, but it took time and prayer.

DJ: If we've been transformed by the Holy Spirit, made new creatures in Christ, is it possible for us to identify genuinely with the life of a nonbeliever?

Pippert: What is new is that God's Spirit lives in us, and His Spirit will enable us to overcome. But His Spirit is still housed in our humanity, and it's our humanity that we share with the world. We will laugh and weep over the same things the world laughs and weeps over. We will long for children to be secure and happy. We will experience temptation and failure.

If the world can write us off as super-spiritual people who don't have needs and problems like theirs, they'll write off God as irrelevant. But once they see and know that we are alike, and that we have common needs and problems and interests, they'll be far more curious when we say, "God makes a difference."

DJ: So is it up to us to find that common ground? Do we make it known that we have needs and problems?

Pippert: That's right. We shouldn't be afraid to share our humanity. This allows people to see the difference that God makes. This is revealed in how we handle problems and personal failings—not in freedom from them. I have seen that there is nothing I do that does not contain some corruption, that does not have some self-serving motive. God shows us the problem of human nature and He gives us a diagnosis for the condition: sin.

DJ: So you are open about your own sinfulness—your own mixed motives, for instance. Is that what you mean by "Christian realism"?

Pippert: Yes. Christian realism begins with the fact that we are not who we were created to be. G.K. Chesterton wrote, "I find it amazing that moderns have rejected the doctrine of original sin when it's the only Christian doctrine that can be empirically verified." There is plenty of evidence to convince us of the reality of the Christian view of human nature, meaning the presence of sin in our lives.

But Christian realism is not only negative—it's extraordinarily positive. Christian realism requires us to face the mess so that we can experience the mystery and the miracle that Jesus Christ can change human beings. But to experience this miracle, we have to face the mess: the human heart. To be a Christian realist is to know the problem of the human heart and the solution that Jesus offers.

For we cannot help speaking about what
we have seen and heard.
~ACTS 4:20

Spiritual growth does not come from insisting that I have no problems. Rather, it means recognizing who it is that God calls me to be, the reality of who I presently am, learning how to overcome through the power of the Holy Spirit. That is a different kind of model from either excusing sin or being falsely spiritual.

DJ: Have you seen God use a new Christian or a very unlikely Christian as an effective agent for sharing the gospel?

Pippert: When I was on InterVarsity staff, there was a young woman in the dorm with a real heart for evangelism. She said to me, "I want you to meet somebody I've been sharing my faith with. She's got so many problems. If you would just meet her, maybe you could keep on seeing her."

So I went to meet her. And the student, to my absolute horror, introduced us with, "Becky, this is Pat. And Pat, I've told Becky all about what a mess you are, and how if you don't give your life to Jesus it's just going to be curtains for you. Maybe Becky can help you."

Well, I felt like dying of embarrassment. I was sure the woman was going to be furious. But she turned around and said, "You know, she loves me so much and it always shows."

You can break every rule of communication, but if people know that you love them, and that Jesus loves them, you're home free. Love is the soil of evangelism.

DJ: What is the basic message of the gospel?

Pippert: God is alive, He is real, He is a person, and He is here. He loves us and seeks us, but we have a problem. We were meant to be God-centered people, and instead we are thoroughly self-centered. The hope for us is that our self-centeredness is not making us happy, because that is not how we were created to be. We were created to be centered in God.

DJ: Is a suffering Messiah one that nonbelievers today can understand? Aren't they focused on fitness and wellness—on the avoidance of suffering?

Pippert: Exactly. But that in itself is a clue. Why are we so frantic to stay fit, to look perfect, to pursue wealth? Isn't it because we have an uneasy sense that something is wrong, so we try all the harder to control the externals of our lives?

I've often discovered that the most insecure people are those who so feverishly pursue health and wealth.

DJ: Can evangelism be taught or learned?

Pippert: Sure it can. Part of evangelism consists of content skills. That's the easy part, and that's what American Christians specialize in. We are so good at explaining the gospel in four steps, or fifteen steps, or whatever.

But we also need communication skills. That's more complicated—learning how to listen, for instance. Beyond getting the story straight and getting the story out, we also need to take the story in.

DJ: What motivates us to do evangelism?

Pippert: I hope our primary motivation comes from being set on fire

Love Fulfills the Law

Let no debt remain outstanding, except the continuing debt to love one another, for he who loves his fellowman has fulfilled the law. The commandments, "Do not commit adultery," "Do not murder," "Do not steal," "Do not covet," and whatever other commandment there may be, are summed up in this one rule: "Love your neighbor as yourself." Love does no harm to its neighbor. Therefore love is the fulfillment of the law (Romans 13:8-10).

with love for Jesus. Charles Wesley was asked, "Why are people drawn to you as if to a magnet?" He responded, "When you set yourself on fire, people just love to come and watch you burn."

That is the key to evangelism. It's not a technique, it's not a format, it's not communication skills. It is first of all a fire that burns in us.

Preach not because you have to say something
but because you have something to say.

      ~RICHARD WHATELY

So the question is, "Have we been set on fire?" That's the motivation. [21] ◀

Combining Words with Action

If all Jesus wanted to give the world was a message, He could have blanketed the earth with leaflets or spoken to residents of our planet through a huge, cosmic loudspeaker.

Every man is a priest, even involuntarily; his conduct is an unspoken sermon, which is forever preaching to others.

      ~H.F. AMIEL

But Jesus had more than words for humanity. He wanted to show us a way, which required that He demonstrate it with His life.

Often, though, followers of Jesus fail to demonstrate the full breadth and depth of the Gospels through their own lives. Rebecca Manley Pippert once attempted to explain the large gulf separating Christians' perceptions of themselves from the perceptions non-Christians often have of us. Here's how she explained it:

▶ If you asked non-Christians what they felt made a Christian different their answer probably would be frightfully inadequate. Recently in an evangelistic talk I asked the non-Christians what they thought the big issues were for Christians, what we truly fight for.

110

In utter seriousness a boy answered, "Judging from what I've seen, you stand against swearing, dirty jokes, and rowdy parties. Isn't that right?"

"I think there are larger issues than that for Christians," I said. "For example, I'm against murder."

Everyone laughed, and he said, "I hardly think anyone wouldn't be, but that issue doesn't come up very often."

"Oh? Do you know how Jesus defines murder? He says it's murder when we destroy people with our words. It's murder when we put people down and treat them as insignificant. If I saw that happening, which I do frequently, as a Christian I would have to stand against it." I was referring here to Jesus' Sermon on the Mount, especially Matthew 5:21-22.

Christ's lore and His apostles twelve,
He taught, but first he practised it himself.
∾GEOFFREY CHAUCER, *THE CANTERBURY TALES*

There was an instant hush in the audience. He said, "I had no idea that Christianity had anything to do with how you treat people. I thought it was merely do's and don'ts." 22 ◄

Following Jesus' Example

Over the centuries, many disciples of Jesus have sought to follow His example by living their lives in such a way that others will see love and be drawn to God.

When Christ said, "I was in prison and you visited
me," he did not draw a distinction between
the guilty and the innocent.
∾POPE JOHN PAUL II

Dorothy Day (1897–1980) was one such disciple. Raised an Episcopalian, she rejected the bourgeois conventionality of religion for the radical egalitarianism of socialism before converting to Catholicism. As a Christian, Day made concern for the poor and crusading against social injustice constants in her life, cofounding the Catholic

Looking for Love

The greatest disease in the West today is not TB or leprosy; it is being unwanted, unloved, and uncared for. We can cure physical diseases with medicine, but the only cure for loneliness, despair, and hopelessness is love. There are many in the world who are dying for a piece of bread but there are many more dying for a little love. The poverty in the West is a different kind of poverty— it is not only a poverty of loneliness but also of spirituality. There's a hunger for love, as there is a hunger for God.

—*Mother Teresa*

Worker movement in the process.

Jesus once said, "I tell you the truth, whatever you did for the least of these brothers of mine, you did for me" (see Matthew 25:31-46). As Dorothy Day saw it, caring for others was an expression of caring for Jesus:

▶ It is no use saying that we are born two thousand years too late to give room to Christ. Nor will those who live at the end of the world be born too late. Christ is always with us, always asking for room in our hearts.

But now it is with the voice of our contemporaries that He speaks, with the eyes of store clerks, factory workers, and children that He gazes; with the hands of office workers, slum dwellers, and suburban housewives that He gives. It is with the feet of soldiers and tramps that He walks, and with the heart of anyone in need that He longs for shelter. And giving shelter or food to anyone who asks for it, or needs it, is giving it to Christ. . . .

All that the friends of Christ did for Him in His lifetime, we can do. Peter's mother-in-law hastened to cook a meal for Him, and if anything in the gospels can be inferred, it surely is that she gave the very best she had, with no thought of extravagance. Matthew made a feast for Him, inviting the whole town, so that the house was in an uproar of enjoyment, and the strait-laced Pharisees—the good people—were scandalized.

The people of Samaria, despised and isolated, were overjoyed to give Him hospitality, and for days He walked and ate and slept among them. And the loveliest of all relationships in Christ's life, after His relationship with His mother, is His friendship with Martha, Mary, and Lazarus and the continual hospitality He found with them. It is a staggering thought that there were once two sisters and a brother whom Jesus looked on almost as His family and where He found a second home, where Martha got on with her work, bustling around in her house-proud way, and Mary simply sat in silence with Him.

No Visible Halos. If we hadn't got Christ's own words for it, it would seem raving lunacy to believe that if I offer a bed and food and hospitality to some man or woman or child, I am replaying the part of Lazarus or Martha or Mary, and that my guest is Christ. There is nothing to show it, perhaps. There are no halos already glowing round their heads—at least none that human eyes can see. . . . To see how far one realizes this [reality], it is a good thing to ask honestly what you would do, or have done, when a beggar asked at your house for food. Would you—or did you—give it on an old, cracked plate, thinking that was good enough? Do you think that Martha and Mary thought that the old and chipped dish was good enough for their guest?

In Christ's human life, there were always a few who made up for the neglect of the crowd. The shepherds did it; their hurrying to the crib atoned for the people who would flee from Christ. The wise men did it; their journey across the world made up for those who refused to stir one hand's breadth from the routine of their lives to go to Christ. Even the gifts the wise men brought have in themselves an obscure recompense and atonement for what would follow later in this Child's life. For they brought gold, the king's emblem, to make up for the crown of thorns that He would wear; they offered incense, the symbol of praise, to make up for the mockery and the spitting; they gave Him myrrh, to heal and soothe, and He was wounded from head to foot and no one bathed His wounds. The women at the foot of the Cross did it too, making up for the crowd who stood by and sneered.

We can do it too, exactly as they did. We are not born too late. We do it by seeing Christ and serving Christ in friends and strangers, in everyone we come in contact with. . . . For He said that a glass of water given to a beggar was given to Him. . . .

We ought not to dwell upon the vices of men, but
rather contemplate in them the image of God,
which by his excellence and dignity can and
should move us to love them and forget all their
vices which might turn us therefrom.

JOHN CALVIN

The Least of His Brothers and Sisters. [One day Jesus will ask:] Did you give Me food when I was hungry? Did you give Me to drink when I was thirsty? Did you give Me clothes when My own were all rags? Did you come to see Me when I was sick, or in prison or in trouble?

And to those who say, aghast, that they never had a chance to do such a thing, that they lived two thousand years too late, He will say again what they had the chance of knowing all their lives, that if these things were done for the very least of His brethren they were done to Him.

To say that love is God is romantic idealism.
To say that God is love is either the last
straw or the ultimate truth.

≈FREDERICK BUECHNER

For a total Christian, the goad of duty is not needed—always prodding one to perform this or that good deed. It is not a duty to help Christ; it is a privilege. Is it likely that Martha and Mary sat back and considered that they had done all that was expected of them— is it likely that Peter's mother-in-law grudgingly served the chicken she had meant to keep till Sunday because she thought it was her "duty"? She did it gladly; she would have served ten chickens if she had had them.

If that is the way they gave hospitality to Christ, it is certain that that is the way it should still be given. 23 ◀

Loving Neighbor and Self

Paul once demonstrated that he was the master of the sound bite by summing up the entire law in a single command: "Love your neighbor as yourself" (Galatians 5:14).

He alone loves the Creator perfectly who manifests a
pure love for his neighbor.

≈BEDE

Many sermons have been preached on the first three words of

this summary: "Love your neighbor." But much less is said about the last two words: "as yourself." Ted W. Engstrom and Ron Wilson set out to correct that omission:

▶ It may sound contradictory at first, but loving others begins with respecting ourselves. In recent years psychologists have written volumes on the need for a healthy self-image. That's probably a good thing. Low self-respect may lead to depression, shyness, excess drinking, drugs, and many other forms of destructive behavior, including the ultimate form, suicide.

A healthy self-image means feeling comfortable with ourselves, accepting ourselves, knowing who we are. "Having a healthy estimate of ourselves" is really a good paraphrase of that part of Romans 12:3 which tells us, "Do not think of yourself more highly than you ought, but rather think of yourself with sober judgment. . . ."

When we have a good sense of who we are and accept ourselves, it frees us to think about others. We don't have to prove ourselves. We don't have to compete and win to reinforce our feelings of self-worth. We don't need to play that old game of one-upmanship. We're free to focus on the person closest to us and try to bring him closer to the Lord.

But love isn't selfish. Paul had this in mind when he told the Philippians, "Do nothing out of selfish ambition or vain conceit, but in humility consider others better than yourselves" (Philippians 2:3). The goal of our love should be simply to minister to someone. The purpose of our caring should be nothing more than seeing something positive happen in that person's life.

This means, of course, that very often we have to put aside our own needs and concentrate on the needs of others. We'll still want someone to meet our needs, and we can't completely ignore them. We can't convince ourselves that we don't have what we really have. That's decidedly unhealthy. We can, of course, ask the Lord for someone to meet our needs. Meanwhile, however, we have to make up our minds that to live the caring life, our particular hurts and longings will have to wait a little longer.

Obstacles to Love. It's easy for all of us to let a number of otherwise good works substitute for taking time to encourage and care for those close by. Check your church bulletin for a list of activities, or check your engagement calendar for a free hour, and you'll see what I mean. Covenant groups, board meetings, church suppers, training classes, missionary conventions, baseball practice, choir rehearsal, clean-up day, ad infinitum! We can recite the creed, chant the anthem, play church, and burn out for Jesus, but never penetrate the protective armor of our friends and neighbors and apply a little balm to their wounds.

Having said all this, I don't believe that you or I will suddenly turn about face and practice a kind of loving, caring behavior we haven't practiced before. Turning on the light by itself doesn't get the sleepy-head out of bed. It will take some pushing and prodding and a determined effort to make it happen. We'll have to go after it, develop new habits, build new muscles. We'll have to approach improvement in this matter of caring the way we work on our backswing.

I've found, for example, that the simple act of touching not only conveys a deep dimension of feeling, but it frees me to forget myself and attend to the person beside me. An arm around the shoulder or an extra warm handshake or even an embrace is redemptive both to the one to whom I offer it and to me.

But until about ten years ago, I carefully avoided that kind of contact. Once I learned the benefits and became convinced of the value, I had to practice it. I worked at it purposefully until it happened spontaneously.

I pray that since we are all made of the same substance, which has a beginning but no end, we may love one another with a single love.

~ANTONY OF EGYPT

You Grow as You Serve. The determination to minister in love to anyone who enters our workaday world produces an unexpected by-product. Throughout the New Testament, we find a principle of gain through loss, of life through death. "In seeking the glory of God and the good of your fellow-creatures," Jonathan Edwards put it, "you take the surest way to have God seek your interests, and promote your welfare."

"I tell you the truth," Jesus said, "unless a kernel of wheat falls to the ground and dies, it remains only a single seed. But if it dies, it produces many seeds. The man who loves his life will lose it, while the man who hates his life in this world will keep it for eternal life" (John 12:24-25).

The caring soul can't lose. Make your priority other people's and you'll add a foot to your own spiritual stature. Learn to feel the throb of another's heart and your own will beat stronger. Lose your life in the lives of the needy for Jesus' sake and you'll find it. Leave your self-interests and personal preoccupations behind and see what wonderful things God has in store for you.

For many years I had the privilege of working closely with Dr. Bob Pierce, founder of World Vision. Bob believed that God had called him to remote places in the world, and he literally gave away everything he had as he saw the need around him. I believe Bob would have done the same if God had called him to pastor a church in New York City or grow corn in Iowa. Somehow this man got right to the core of a person's need and then did something about it. The prayer of his life, written in the flyleaf of his dilapidated old Bible, is the prayer for all of us who want to unleash a little love in our own world: "Let my heart be broken with the things that break the heart of God." So be it! [24] ◀

Touching Both Body and Soul

Paul's letters to the first-century believers are full of exhortations to godly living and specific commands about particular problems. But at some point in most of his letters, Paul also writes passionately about something that was near and dear to his heart: the love of God in Christ. Here's what he told the Ephesians:

"Be imitators of God, therefore, as dearly loved children and live a life of love, just as Christ loved us and gave himself up for us as a fragrant offering and sacrifice to God" (Ephesians 5:1-2).

And he had a similar message for the Thessalonians:

"May the Lord make your love increase and overflow for each other and for everyone else, just as ours does for you" (1 Thessalonians 3:12).

Love Is All That Matters

If I speak in the tongues of men and of angels, but have not love, I am only a resounding gong or a clanging cymbal. If I have the gift of prophecy and can fathom all mysteries and all knowledge, and if I have a faith that can move mountains, but have not love, I am nothing. If I give all I possess to the poor and surrender my body to the flames, but have not love, I gain nothing.

Love is patient, love is kind. It does not envy, it does not boast, it is not proud. It is not rude, it is not self-seeking, it is not easily angered, it keeps no record of wrongs. Love does not delight in evil but rejoices with the truth. It always protects, always trusts, always hopes, always perseveres.

Love never fails. But where there are prophecies, they will cease; where there are tongues, they will be stilled; where there is knowledge, it will pass away. For we know in part and we prophesy in part, but when perfection comes, the imperfect disappears. When I was a child, I talked like a child, I thought like a

continued on the next page

It is not love in the abstract that counts.
Men have loved brotherhood, the workers, the poor—
but they have not loved "personally." It is the hardest
thing in the world to love. . . . It is never the brothers
next to us, but the brothers in the abstract
that are easy to love.

—DOROTHY DAY

Paul knew that loving as God loved required a combination of the spiritual and the physical, care for souls and care for bodies. But have some contemporary Christians neglected this important balance? Christian statesman Charles Colson believes many have. Here, Colson pleads the case for a balanced, holistic approach toward living out the message of Jesus:

▶ "Now that I've decided to follow Christ, how do I best serve Him?" This is the question I hear most frequently from serious new Christians.

Surely we are pressed by needs on every side. So many need to hear the Good News—more than one billion people globally have never even heard the name of Christ.

There are so many physical needs as well. Starvation, disease, and simple diarrhea kill off forty thousand children worldwide every day. Infant mortality rates in some rural Mississippi communities are as high as some Third World areas because of a lack of medical care and hygienic training.

In America's inner cities, drugs, crime, and poverty pass from generation to generation—a way of life and a way of making a living. Homeless people sleep on heating grates; the suffering of the mentally ill, the terminally ill, and the emotionally ruined is all around us.

So many needs, both spiritual and physical. And in its commendable fervor to respond, the Church has, uncommendably, split those needs into a false dichotomy.

If I had my time again, I would be stronger on social injustices and less involved in parties and politics.

—BILLY GRAHAM

Keeping Body and Soul Together. What exactly does the Lord require of us? He requires what Jesus Christ modeled during His public ministry—the Good News in word and in deed. At dinner with His disciples, as He walked through the marketplace, as children crowded around Him, Jesus continually pointed the way to the Father. At the same time, He fed the poor, He healed the blind, the sick, and the lame, and He affirmed the dignity of women, Samaritans, and other social outcasts of the day.

Before Christ ascended to heaven, He left clear commands to His followers: "As you go, preach, making disciples and baptizing them in the name of the Father and the Son and the Holy Ghost." God's Old Testament commands are equally compelling: "Impress [the words of God] on your children. Talk about them when you sit at home and when you walk along the road, when you lie down and when you get up." If we believe in the absolute authority of the inerrant Scriptures, we must take those commands to heart. For the believer, living the law of God, spreading His Word, and leading men and women to Christ should be as natural as breathing.

So, too, should be the acts of doing the gospel. In his epistle, James told the people of God that "pure religion and undefiled is this: 'to feed the orphans and comfort the widow in her distress.'" The Apostle Paul helped to raise funds for famine relief and commended the Macedonian Christians for their rich generosity in giving to their brothers and sisters in physical need.

In the Book of Micah, God called all of the mountains and hills to witness as He told the people of Israel what it is that He expected of them. "What does the Lord require of you?" He asks. "To act justly and to love mercy and to walk humbly with your God."

What Justice Demands, Mercy Pays. Of all of the demands upon the Christian, justice and mercy—not to mention humility—are perhaps the most often misunderstood.

child, I reasoned like a child. When I became a man, I put childish ways behind me. Now we see but a poor reflection as in a mirror; then we shall see face to face. Now I know in part; then I shall know fully, even as I am fully known.

And now these three remain: faith, hope and love. But the greatest of these is love (1 Corinthians 13:1-13).

119

Sorrow for Sinners

Look now at warring Christendom, what smallest drop of pity towards sinners is to be found in it? Or how could a spirit all hellish, more fully contrive and hasten their destruction? It stirs up and kindles every passion of fallen nature that is contrary to the all-humble, all-meek, all-loving, all-forgiving, all-saving Spirit of Christ. It unites, it drives, and compels nameless numbers of unconverted sinners to fall, murdering and murdered among flashes of fire, with the wrath and swiftness of lightning, into a fire infinitely worse than that in which they died.

O sad subject for thanksgiving days, whether in popish or Protestant churches! For if there is a joy of all the angels in heaven for one sinner that repents, what a joy must there be in hell over such multitudes of sinners, not suffered to repent? And if they who have "converted many to righteousness, shall shine as the stars in the firmament for ever," what Chorazin's woe may they not justly fear, whose proud wrath and

continued on the next page

Justice is a hard standard. Justice demands absolute conformity with God's holy character—righteousness in our hearts, righteousness in our conversations, righteousness in our jobs and lives, righteousness in our institutions. Because God is a holy God, He cannot be in fellowship with unjust people.

At the same time, God is a merciful God. He woos His people and calls them back to Himself. But His justice—consistency with His own decrees—means that sin has to be paid for with death.

And so He placed His only Son, Jesus Christ, on the altar as a sacrifice for the sins of mankind. Christ—in fact, God Himself—paid the price. Even Enoch, who walked with God, even Abraham, who pleased God, even Noah, who was chosen to father a new race of people after the Flood, could not have died for our sins. They had their own sins.

Why didn't God simply forgive and forget and let us begin again? Because His standard of justice, which demanded righteousness or death, could not be put aside.

So God shook heaven and earth, merging justice and mercy at the Cross by fulfilling the demands of justice through the one perfect sacrifice, His only Son, Jesus Christ.

When the Scriptures tell us to do justice and to love mercy, they require of us nothing less than the glorious, full-bodied justice and mercy that God Himself showed.

Half the world is starving; the other half is on a diet. We are not privileged because we deserve to be. Privilege accepted should mean responsibility accepted.

MADELEINE L'ENGLE

You Can't Have One Without the Other. But just as we so often separate evangelism and social activism, many in the Church today divide justice and mercy as well. Even worse, they secularize these holy terms. Conservatives seem to emphasize justice over mercy, then compound the problem by adopting the secular definition of justice, that is, punishing wrongdoers and seeing that everyone "gets his due." So every man, woman, and child must carry his or her own weight—no matter how heavy the odds against them—as if poverty could only be God's judgment and punishment for indolence.

Meanwhile, many a liberal latches onto mercy, believing it requires him to provide food, shelter, clothes, and entertainment for anyone who cannot provide it for themselves. So justice and mercy have been divorced from one another, and Christians take up sides, choosing their church—not to mention their political party—according to a destructive dichotomy.

This false dichotomy between justice and mercy creates unhealthy extremes in our political and social policies in the United States. I think it is because believers have not stood in the gap. The Church has too often bought into the secular definitions of these godly terms, thus ruining the possibility of a witness of what our Lord requires of us—to do justice and to love mercy. Nor have we been a particularly convincing witness of "walking humbly" with our God.

Too often Christian movements have trumpeted their presence and plans in victorious, triumphal language that has made their eventual demise all the more humiliating. The Religious Right that heralded its own high hopes for restoring morality to America through political means waned in a decade, its leaders burned out and its agenda unfulfilled.

Meanwhile, mainline churches sold their souls to social relevance and are now experiencing record declines in attendance. To many secular observers, the Church today is irrelevant.

But if the Church regained the wholeness of the biblical vision of justice and mercy, we could shake our society to its roots. Surely that is what happened to the world of an obscure sixteenth-century monk who cowered in terror of the judgment of God, writing in his journal that he saw himself before God "as a sinner troubled in conscience . . . without confidence that my merit would assuage Him." Therefore, "I did not love a just and angry God," he confessed, "but rather hated and murmured against Him."

Miserable, this monk studied the Epistle to the Romans and suddenly came to an unexpected moment of epiphany, seeing "the connection between the justice of God and the statement, 'the just shall live by faith.' Then I grasped that the justice of God is that righteousness by which, through grace and sheer mercy, God justified us through faith. Thereupon I felt myself to be reborn and to have gone

vain glory have robbed such numberless troops of poor wretches, of all time and place of knowing what righteousness they wanted, for the salvation of their immortal souls.

Here my pen trembles in my hand; but when, O when will one single Christian church, people, or language, tremble at the share they have in this death of sinners! [25]

—*William Law*

through open doors into paradise. The whole of Scripture took on new meaning, and whereas before the justice of God had filled me with hate, now it became to me inexpressibly sweet in greater love. This passage of Paul became to me a gate to heaven."

The justice this monk had so feared, a tumbrel to God's gallows, became the chariot that carried him to God's mercy seat of grace as well as a means by which the Church, and Western civilization at large, was forever changed. The Reformation that developed from Martin Luther's conversion brought millions of people to saving faith in Christ and went on to reform ecclesiastical, political, and social structures. This vision of the Church revealed the glorious truth that the justice of God is His righteousness flowing with "sheer mercy" to all who will believe.

The present division between the haves and have-nots in the body of Christ is a major hindrance to world evangelism.

Ronald J. Sider

The Gospel—Live! This, of course, is the call to all of us today. Compelled by thankfulness for God's personal mercy to each of us, we must go out and "ladle soup" as well as preach the Word with a free, fervent love for Christ and those He loves. We are to bear witness of God's righteousness. That is, lead men and women to be declared just by faith in Christ, and work to cause the structures of society to reflect God's standards of justice. We must exercise justice and mercy in the arenas of need all around us, wherever we find them.

Justice and mercy are always costly. It hurts to sacrifice resources, time, and comfort to help bear the burdens of the hurting. But this cost is nothing when compared to God's mercy that justified the sins of the world through the death of His only Son. Our devotion to Him compels us to obey Him, to do the gospel with all of our energies by whatever means we can. As we do so, we will open for those in physical and spiritual need Luther's gate of heaven. [26] ◄

*If you want my estate, you may have it; if you want
my body, I willingly give it up. If you want to put me
in irons or kill me, I am content. I will not flee to the
people for protection, or cling to the altar. Rather, I
choose to be sacrificed for the sake of the altar.*

—AMBROSE

Answering the Calls

As we have seen, Jesus issues two calls to men and women who hear
His voice and want to do what He asks: "Come, follow me" and "Go
and make disciples."

In the following sections, we will explore all that can be learned
by examining the ways Christians have answered these calls over the
past 20 centuries.

Section Three

I Am with You:
We All Do the Work of Discipleship

It had been an unbelievably unsettling time for the disciples. Jesus had prophesied His own violent death and then risen from the grave, making a number of appearances to some of His followers.

These appearances culminated with the resurrected Jesus and His eleven remaining disciples going to a mountain, where He gave them all a seemingly impossible task: "Go and make disciples of all nations."

Then Jesus concluded His command with a brief comment that has reassured millions of His disciples over the past 20 centuries: "I am with you always, to the very end of the age."

Even today, followers of Jesus live with the tension that exists between these two statements: the command to go and the assurance of continuing fellowship and assistance.

For throughout Christian history, the thing that has made discipleship possible hasn't been the wisdom and expertise of Jesus' disciples or the effectiveness of their programs and methods. Rather, ordinary men and women throughout the world have taken up Jesus' call because they have loved Him, they have obeyed Him, and they have welcomed His supernatural guidance and presence in their lives.

For we know, brothers loved by God, that he has chosen you, because our gospel came to you not simply with words, but also with power, with the Holy Spirit and with deep conviction.

1 THESSALONIANS 1:4-5A

All Are Called to Disciple

The ways people related to God in the centuries before Jesus were governed by a complex set of laws and rituals administered by an elite group of holy priests. But Jesus changed all that, opening wide the doors to God and anointing all His disciples to serve as priests of God:

"But you are a chosen people, a royal priesthood, a holy nation, a people belonging to God, that you may declare the praises of him who called you out of darkness into his wonderful light" (1 Peter 2:9).

God Chooses Us to Use Us

We have to do with a God about whom thick clouds and great darkness gather. We have to do with a God whose ways are not our ways and whose thoughts are not our thoughts. We have to do with a God whose understanding advances beyond man's as a mind of an Einstein surpasses that of an ant. We have to do with a deity whose designs include not just cultures and countries, but the cosmos; not just the hour, but the ages; not just individuals, but the family of man. Moreover, when we are caught in confining and oppressive circumstances we should console and counsel ourselves with the idea that God's relationship with us is one in which he not only does things for us, but he gets things done by us and through us. God chooses us in order to use us. We are not simply God's sheep, fed and tended by him. We are his servants, running errands and doing chores. We are not just his allies. We are his agents and ambassadors. We are not merely his dependents. We are also his disciples to whom he

continued on the next page

Instead of being called out and separated for life and trained by other priests, the earliest disciples of Jesus simply passed on the life-changing knowledge they themselves had received. And that's pretty much what followers of Jesus have been doing ever since, as Paul writes:

"For what I received I passed on to you as of first importance: that Christ died for our sins according to the Scriptures, that he was buried, that he was raised on the third day according to the Scriptures, and that he appeared to Peter, and then to the Twelve" (1 Corinthians 15:3-5).

The place God calls you to is where your deep gladness and the world's deep hunger meet.

〜FREDERICK BUECHNER

Paul himself is a prime example of the radical new ways followers of Jesus would spread God's truth. He had not been among Jesus' earliest followers, and in fact had persecuted the first believers. But after miraculously experiencing the presence and resurrection power of Christ, Paul devoted the rest of his life to proclaiming the dual call to love God and serve him through a life of disciple making:

"But we ought always to thank God for you, brothers loved by the Lord, because from the beginning God chose you to be saved through the sanctifying work of the Spirit and through belief in the truth. He called you to this through our gospel, that you might share in the glory of our Lord Jesus Christ" (2 Thessalonians 2:13-14).

I went to early service alone, and to the 11 o'clock with the children. The preacher was a stranger; he gave out his text, "Go work for me today in my vineyard." To me it was a trumpet call; I never heard any of the sermon. I could hardly keep from off my knees until it was finished; it was just as if God's voice had called me, and the intense rest and joy were beyond all words.

〜ISABELLA GILMORE

At great personal cost, Paul traveled throughout the world of his day inviting people to follow Jesus and then encouraging them to go out and invite others to do the same:

"So do not be ashamed to testify about our Lord, or ashamed of me his prisoner. But join with me in suffering for the gospel, by the power of God, who has saved us and called us to a holy life—not because of anything we have done but because of his own purpose and grace" (2 Timothy 1:8-9a).

Laborers in God's Vineyard

Over the last 20 centuries, Christian saints and scholars have written libraries full of books on discipleship techniques and methods, and we will be looking at many of these resources in the following section.

My great concern is not whether God is on our side; my great concern is to be on God's side, for God is always right.

ABRAHAM LINCOLN

But as we will see, Jesus never devised a detailed plan on how to do discipleship. Rather, He explained the process of bringing people into a relationship with God in the same way He described the amazing mysteries of the kingdom: through parables and other means.

"Again, the kingdom of heaven is like a merchant looking for fine pearls," He told His disciples one day. "When he found one of great value, he went away and sold everything he had and bought it."

The field of the Lord has been lying fallow, bristling with the thistles of unbelief. Now it has been ploughed by your teaching, and is bringing forth an abundant harvest of true faith.

GREGORY II

During that same discourse, He told another parable—one that His fishermen disciples would be sure to comprehend:

"Once again, the kingdom of heaven is like a net that was let down into the lake and caught all kinds of fish. When it was full, the fishermen pulled it up on the shore. Then they sat down and collected the good fish in baskets, but threw the bad away. This is how it will be at

gives tough assignments. We are not just God's guest. We are his host.

We are more than his creation; we are his channels. We are not merely members of Christ's body; we are means to his ends. We are holders of both a sonship and a servantship. We have a charge to keep, a race to run, and a course to finish. [1]

—Manuel Scott

Scott, pastor of Calvary Baptist Church in Los Angeles, made these comments in a paper he presented to the International Congress on World Evangelization in Lausanne, Switzerland, 1974.

129

Wanted: Soldiers for Jesus

What is the need of the hour?

For a beggar with a tin cup, it's a dime. For a woman being taken to the hospital, it's a doctor. But what is it in Christian work? I started to list the things we often feel are the need—those things which, if supplied, would end our troubles.

Some say, "If I just had a larger staff. …Many a minister would like to have an assistant, and many a mission would like to have more missionaries.

Others say, "We don't need more workers, but better facilities. If we just had more office space and more buildings and a bigger base of operation, then we could do the job."

In some parts of the world they say it's better communications we lack, or better transportation, or better health care, or literature.

Many feel the need is an open door into some closed country.

Some say, "If we just had more time," or "If I just weren't so old, if I were only young again." People have said to me, "Daws, if I had known when I

continued on the next page

the end of the age. The angels will come and separate the wicked from the righteous and throw them into the fiery furnace, where there will be weeping and gnashing of teeth" (Matthew 13:47-50).

Another parable of the kingdom used the metaphor of laborers in a vineyard. As we see, the landowner has more concern about employing new workers and gathering the harvest than observing every jot and tittle of Jewish labor laws:

"For the kingdom of heaven is like a landowner who went out early in the morning to hire men to work in his vineyard. He agreed to pay them a denarius for the day and sent them into his vineyard.

"About the third hour he went out and saw others standing in the marketplace doing nothing. He told them, 'You also go and work in my vineyard, and I will pay you whatever is right.' So they went.

"He went out again about the sixth hour and the ninth hour and did the same thing. About the eleventh hour he went out and found still others standing around. He asked them, 'Why have you been standing here all day long doing nothing?'

"'Because no one has hired us,' they answered.

"He said to them, 'You also go and work in my vineyard.'

"When evening came, the owner of the vineyard said to his foreman, 'Call the workers and pay them their wages, beginning with the last ones hired and going on to the first.'

"The workers who were hired about the eleventh hour came and each received a denarius. So when those came who were hired first, they expected to receive more. But each one of them also received a denarius. When they received it, they began to grumble against the landowner. 'These men who were hired last worked only one hour,' they said, 'and you have made them equal to us who have borne the burden of the work and the heat of the day.'

The whole of human life is but a single day, to those who labour with love.

GREGORY OF NAZIANZUS

"But he answered one of them, 'Friend, I am not being unfair to you. Didn't you agree to work for a denarius? Take your pay and go. I want to give the man who was hired last the same as I gave you.

Don't I have the right to do what I want with my own money? Or are you envious because I am generous?'

"So the last will be first, and the first will be last" (Matthew 20:1-16).

A Life of Discipleship

At the First International Consultation on Discipleship in Eastbourne, England, Jill Briscoe asked the question, "What is discipleship?" Her answer was simple and profound: "It is simply mature Christians being what mature Christians should be and doing what mature Christians can do."

Faithfulness in carrying out present duties is the best preparation for the future.

❧FRANÇOIS FÉNELON

In her talk, Briscoe discussed some of the major characteristics of disciples:

▶ Disciples need to be people who have a sense of calling, a specific task, and a commitment to truth-telling in a world that has believed the lie. They are people who know how to handle their differences and who do it well, dealing with the unexpected, coping with the unresolved. Mature disciples do this all with a broken heart. His tears are on their faces. His hurt is in their hearts. And because His love and mercy surround them, they have hope when sometimes things appear to be hopeless.

By perseverance the snail reached the ark.

❧CHARLES HADDON SPURGEON

I think of Jesus saying to Peter (John 21), "Peter, when you were little, and you grew up, you always dressed yourself. But there will come a day when you'll stretch out your hands and somebody else will dress you, take you where you don't want to go." This He said

was twenty years old what I know now, I could have done a hundred times more for the Lord. Why didn't I?"

Often the biggest need seems to be money. Money is the answer to a larger staff, more facilities, better communications and transportation and literature. "If we just had more money."

What is the need of the hour? I don't believe it is any of these. I am convinced that the God of the universe is in control, and he will supply all these needs in his own way and in his own time, all else being right.

The need of the hour is an army of soldiers dedicated to Jesus Christ, who believe that he is God, that he can fulfill every promise he ever made, and that nothing is too hard for him. This is the only way we can accomplish what is on God's heart—getting the gospel to every creature. [2]

—*Dawson Trotman*

These words are part of one of the last messages Navigators founder Dawson Trotman gave to his staff members and trainees before his death in 1956.

Paul put a high premium on faithfulness and stick-to-itiveness. People who turned back really bugged him. Witness his reaction when John Mark quit during his first missionary junket; or remember Demas: "For Demas hath forsaken me, having loved this present world" (2 Timothy 4:10). Speaking of his preliminary trial in Rome, Paul said, "No one came to my support, but everyone deserted me" (2 Timothy 4:16). Timothy was not a quitter. He had his faults and his frailties, but he was faithful. And as Paul advised Timothy to train leaders to take his place, he suggested first of all that they be faithful, trustworthy, reliable men.

We live in a day of the short attention span. Most people are either flitters or quitters. But Timothy and those who follow in his train are disciples who stick with it.

Paul had warned Timothy repeatedly that the way wouldn't be easy. Back in Lystra when they first met, Paul had warned Timothy that "much tribulation" lay ahead of them. Timothy couldn't say that

continued on the next page

signifying by what death Peter would glorify God.

And when God came to Jeremiah He said, "I have some clothes for you to wear, Jeremiah. Up to now you've dressed yourself. You've been My servant, you've been My disciple, but you've gone your own way. And now it's going to be a question of asking you if you are ready to let Me get you out your clothes, so that you can be dressed fitly for what I have in mind for you."

I went into a child's room once and saw a poster on the wall showing a little boy after a football match. At the top of it it said, "I quit." And his body language was saying it all. He sat alone on the bench. But on the bottom of the poster was a cross, and in little letters it said, "I didn't." I quit, and Jesus says, "Well, I didn't." And one of the themes coming through everything I say is the theme that disciples don't quit. They don't quit.

Great works are performed not by strength but by perseverance.

—SAMUEL JOHNSON

A Calling for Us All. This calling is for every child of God. It's not just for the Jeremiahs, the Moseses, the Abrahams, the Davids, the Matthews, Marks, Lukes and Johns, the Augustines, the Billy Sundays, the Dwight L. Moodys, the Billy Grahams, the Amy Carmichaels. It's not for pastors, missionaries, Christian stars, and personalities. There's only one bright morning star, and that's Jesus. It's not for singers or professional performers alone. It's for all those people. It's for little me and little you.

Little dust people, I love to call us. We're made of dust. Wearing dust clothes and sleeping in dust beds, and eating dust food. And all God has to do is say, "poof," and off we go. But we're dust dignified by divinity. Have you ever thought of that? Dust dignified by divinity. And that makes me feel really good. God chose me. God called me. And this is for every child of God. For every pastor's wife as much as it is for every pastor. God's calling is for every single born-again believer.

Those two words that Jesus Christ said, "Follow me," changed the world, as millions since have risen up to follow the call. What is this calling I'm talking about? It is this. It's Luke, chapter 5. It's Jesus saying to Peter, "Peter, will you follow Me?" And then in John 21, "Peter, will you love Me?" And again in John 21, "Peter, will you die for Me?"

Will you honor Me? Will you live for Me? Will you die for Me? That's the call. And every single believer is called to this: to this fellowship, to this maturity, to this discipleship. It's for every child of God, and that means me and that means you.

There are very few who in their hearts do not believe in God, but what they will not do is give Him exclusive right of way. . . . They are not ready to promise full allegiance to God alone. Many a professing Christian is a stumbling-block because his worship is divided. On Sunday he worships God; on weekdays God has little or no place in his thoughts.

—DWIGHT L. MOODY

The Calling Carries a Cost. It overrides all the major decisions of my life. Jesus said to Peter, "Leave it all and follow Me," and he did. He left everything including his wife, and followed Jesus. When Jeremiah asked God, "Can I get married?" God said, "Well, your calling overrides all the major decisions in your life. So, I am sorry Jeremiah, no." [See Jeremiah 16:1.] Then God tells him why, which is nice. He says, "The things that are going to happen to the women and children in the city—I want to spare you that. So you're not to get married, Jeremiah."

His calling, His plan in my life, overrides all the major decisions in my life. It overrides prosperity. Jeremiah again, Lamentations 3:17, "I've forgotten what prosperity is." And it might well be that God does not trust us with money so that we may fund His work and give us a good stewardship in that account. It might mean that we live poor and maybe die poor, as Jeremiah and Baruch certainly did.

And it's not an easy life. Bodily comforts might not be yours. As Lamentations 3:4 tells us, "He's made my skin and my flesh grow old, he's broken my bones." Yet as Jeremiah and Baruch abandoned themselves to God, as they submitted themselves to the Lord, who loved them and would give His Son to die for them, they found and fulfilled the central purpose for their lives. They found their reason for living.

he hadn't been warned.

All through Paul's last letter to Timothy are intimations of suffering: "Be thou partaker of the afflictions of the gospel" (2 Timothy 1:8); "Endure hardness, as a good soldier" (2:3); "All that will live godly in Christ Jesus shall suffer persecution" (3:12); "But watch thou in all things, endure afflictions" (4:5).

According to tradition, Brother Timothy was martyred in Ephesus about twenty years later, during the reign of the Emperor Domitian. [3]

—*William J. Petersen*

A Shining Light

I am the light of the world, the founder of the Christian religion said. What a stupendous phrase! And how particularly marvelous today, when one is conscious of so much darkness in the world! Let your light shine before men, he exhorted us. You know, sometimes ...someone asks me what I most want, what I should most like to do in the little that remains of my life, and I always nowadays truthfully answer—and it is truthful—"I should like my light to shine, even if only very fitfully, like a match struck in a dark, cavernous night and then flickering out."

—*Malcolm Muggeridge*

And that's what's wrong with the world that doesn't know Jesus: they have no purpose, they have no central calling in their life. They need to respond to THE call. The primary call.

Remember—Christianity proposes not to extinguish our natural desires. It promises to bring the desires under just control and direct them to their true object. In the case of both riches and of honor, it maintains the consistency of its character. But Christianity commands us not to set our hearts on earthly treasures. It reminds us that "we have in heaven a better and more enduring substance" than this world can bestow (Hebrews 10:34).

        —WILLIAM WILBERFORCE

Understanding the Work. Secondly the mark of maturity in a disciple is that he understands his work is in God's hands. Your plan in my life, Your work in my hand. What does He say? "I've called you. Before you were born I set you apart; I consecrated you for My secret use." The word means appointed, commissioned, ordained.

That's you, me, and all the other disciples in the world. He has appointed us to a task. That's the second recalling or calling. "I have set you apart to uproot, to tear down, to destroy, to build, and to plant."

It's a job description. A disciple is never going to be out of a job. He is guaranteed employment for the rest of his life. That's what our calling is all about: His plan in my life, His work in my hands. So a secondary call could be as a pastor, mother, machine operator, craftsman, missionary, shopkeeper, teacher, artist, women's ministry leader, secretary, helper, song leader. Those are our secondary callings. And this is very important, because when His work in our hands gets heavy, it's your primary calling that's going to keep you there so you don't quit.

And I think that we disciples sometimes get the callings mixed up. And if we are living for our secondary callings, then when things get difficult, we'll quit. What kept Jeremiah going in the pit, in the prison? It was his first calling, his primary calling. And so His work is in our hands. We are appointed to a task. We are anointed to perform.

There's something inside us that says, "I can do this." How did you find the task? You found it by finding your gift as you tried to meet a need. And as you met a need that you didn't know you had gifts to assist you with, you said, "Yeah, I can do this." I always feel as you discover the gift for the task that God has appointed before your embryonic existence, that there's a sort of stab of joy that comes.

The Spirit will teach us to love the Word, to meditate on it and to keep it. He will reveal the love of Christ to us, that we may love him fervently and with a pure heart. Then we shall begin to see that a life in the love of Christ in the midst of our daily life and distractions is a glorious possibility and a blessed reality.

—Andrew Murray

Having the Heart of God. A sign of maturity is when we care more about the things that break the heart of God than the things that break our heart. Now, I'm certainly not there yet, but I want to be. And I want to care about sin in my life and unholiness, and pride, and ambition because it causes tears on His face.

What I need is a humble, contrite heart that He will not despise. I believe that's what happened when God spoke to Baruch and he humbled himself and committed himself again to the task at hand. Then, he had a broken heart for the world and for the lost. And God's tears were on his face and on Jeremiah's face.

You read all Jeremiah's laments, "My eyes fail from weeping. I'm in torment within. My heart is poured out on the ground because my people are destroyed. Because children and infants faint. Women have cooked their own children. They became their food."

Jeremiah sits on the hillside watching the sack of Jerusalem, and he's weeping, not for himself, but for the things that break the heart of God. This beloved Israel had been uprooted by the hands of God in judgment. That's the mark, I believe, of a disciple.

Disciples don't quit, not even when the heart of your life's work goes up in flames. Because mature disciples have hope.

Listen to the words of Jeremiah. "I remember my affliction, my wondering, the bitterness and the gall. I well remember them. My soul is

135

**Paul: Disci-
pling as
Mother,
Father, and
Brother**

In the opening
two chapters of
his first letter to
the Thessalonians,
Paul identifies
three relational
models he em-
ployed in
ministering to
believers.

*The caring mother
(1 Thessalonians
2:7).* The chief
ingredient in
Paul's ministry at
this first level was
tender love. The
objective of the
caring mother
stage was to help
young believers
develop a desire
to grow, a heart
for the Lord, and
an eagerness for
ministry.

*The father
(1 Thessalonians
2:12).* The main
objective for the
father stage is to
equip them to
"live lives worthy
of God." This
means urging
them to do what
they know they
should. You rein-
force basic disci-
plines and help
them deepen
their commit-
ment. They are to
learn to live this
way because they
believe it is what
God wants them
to do.

The brother. In this
third stage,
though he was
physically absent
from them, we
can see his per-
sonal concern in
dealing with
them. First and

*continued on the
next page*

downcast within me yet this I call to mind and therefore, have I hope."

How do you hope when it's hopeless? Jeremiah tells us: "Because of the Lord's great love, we're not consumed." 4 ◄

Different Disciples, Different Ministries

What does it mean to be a disciple of Christ? Although there are certain basic requirements, the answers to this question are as numerous as there are disciples following the call.

Each one should use whatever gift he has received to serve others, faithfully administering God's grace in its various forms. If anyone speaks, he should do it as one speaking the very words of God. If anyone serves, he should do it with the strength God provides, so that in all things God may be praised through Jesus Christ. To him be the glory and the power for ever and ever. Amen.

∽1 PETER 4:10-11

Clyde S. Kilby was an American scholar specializing in C.S. Lewis and the Curator Emeritus of Wheaton College's Marion E. Wade Collection, which has many of Lewis' papers. He explored questions of discipleship and saintliness in an essay about the famed writer and thinker.

► Could a shabby creature with receding hairline, nicotine-stained teeth, and sloppy clothing—who lived in a house so desperately in need of repairs that one of its floors simply burst through—can such a man be a saint? A man who frequented a local pub and, in an anteroom where the smell of beer and smoke filled the air, talked and laughed so uproariously that other drinkers wondered if he and his friends were not drunk—can that sort of man be a saint? A big, hearty man capable of making a new suit look frowsy the second time worn and who enjoyed hiking twenty miles a day over hill and dale? A man who as scholar might ride roughshod over any opponent in intellectual debate?

If pressed, we should perhaps have difficulty in saying precisely what constitutes a holy person. Perhaps we would think of someone who possessed steadiness, quietness, contemplative habits, the regular reading of Scriptures and devotion to prayer. But less likely would we think of someone engaged in a busy, involved life.

Yet in C.S. Lewis both sets of characteristics met in a powerful witness to God's sanctifying grace.

We are so steeped in the antichrist philosopy—namely, that success consists in embracing not the values of the Sermon on the Mount but an infinity of material things, of sex and status—that we little sense how much of what passes for practical Christianity is really an apostate compromise with the spirit of the age.

~CARL F.H. HENRY

Writing and Practicing. Of course Lewis *wrote* of forgiveness, but did he *practice* it?

At twenty-six Lewis was elected to a Fellowship at Magdalen College, Oxford, one of the great universities of the world. He was expected to tutor pupils and deliver scholarly lectures. Oxford had been established by saintly men for the propagation of Christianity, but when Lewis went there it was far from its origin. Lewis found Magdalen "leftish, atheist, cynical, hard-boiled."

Yet in such an antagonistic atmosphere he became a Christian and in due course did not hesitate to write and publish books that would be sneered at by many of his colleagues. Not simply "religious" books—they might have been stomached—but works clearly intent on turning men to Jesus Christ.

One report went out that no one at Magdalen wanted to sit next to Lewis at table because he would immediately turn and ask, "Are you a Christian?" Both by nature and the dictates of good taste, Lewis was utterly opposed to putting anyone in a corner. Yet this was the sort of gossip that, along with his output of books on Christianity, finally prevented Lewis's being awarded a Professorship—though he

foremost he faithfully prayed for them and thanked God for them (1 Thessalonians 1:2). He also commended them for the success and fruit of their ministry, and rejoiced with them. We too should be faithful in praying for those we have helped spiritually, and in commending them for the good fruits of their ministry. [5]

—*Richard A. Cleveland*

Caring for Each Individual

To grow is to emerge gradually from a land where our vision is limited, where we are seeking and governed by egotistical pleasure, by our sympathies and antipathies, to a land of unlimited horizons and universal love, where we will be open to every person and desire their happiness.

—*Jean Vanier*

was regarded by many as the greatest scholar in the university.

For some twenty-five years Lewis knew what it was to be sneered at, to be called "saint" cynically, but still he was friendly with all his colleagues.

If Lewis had much to forgive at his college, he had more at home. At the time of World War I he had promised a buddy in the British army that, were the friend killed, he would attempt to care for his mother and her daughter. That led to long years of what Lewis' brother described as intolerable imposition, even domination, by a woman who possessed "an intense selfishness, an egotism, which excluded any presence of interest in any subject but herself, and an arrogant and ignorant dogmatism on every topic however abstruse."

We can choke God's word with a yawn; we can hinder the time that should be spent with God by remembering we have other things to do. "I haven't time!" Of course you have time! Take time, strangle some other interests and make time to realize that the center of power in your life is the Lord Jesus Christ and His Atonement.

≈OSWALD CHAMBERS

How quickly most of us would have conjured up plenty of excuses for escape from the promise made to a buddy leaving for the battlefront in France! But Lewis was steadfast to his promise during some thirty years of increasing vexation. When he spoke of the absolute necessity of forgiveness, he knew intimately what he was talking about.

What Makes a Saint? Was C.S. Lewis a saint, a holy man? The rather minimum evidence I have mentioned surely gives an affirmative answer, even such as to prod me into calling him a "real" saint and a person of particular and enticing holiness.

Who, according to Scripture, is a saint, a holy person? Simply one who believes God and, in the words of the first Psalm, "delights in the law of the Lord." We remember Paul's account of his happiness that the Macedonians had taken up a contribution for "the poor saints which are at Jerusalem." At the end of Hebrews, the writer sends salutations to "all the saints." Paul also tells of how, before his conversion on the Damascus Road, he vigorously shut up in prison many of the "saints" of that city.

A saint, then—a holy person—confesses the blessed name and attempts to live blamelessly before God.

As a child of God, you need to be prudent. You cannot simply walk around in this world as if nothing and no one can harm you. You remain extremely vulnerable. The same passions that make you love God may be used by the powers of evil.

—Henri Nouwen

In his lecture on Lewis Mr. Gresham declared that Lewis was "not a saint." Undoubtedly he did not wish to imply that Lewis was anything less than a devout Christian. Rather, perhaps he was thinking of the wide reading of Lewis' books (some forty million apparently now in print) as well as an outpouring of books and articles about him, and of the Lewis Societies and conferences and the danger of making him more than a man. Lewis himself would undoubtedly have responded to such things with warnings like Mr. Gresham's. Nevertheless Lewis was, by strictly biblical standards, a true saint, a genuinely holy man. [6] ◄

Members of the Body

People who heed the call to follow Christ aren't joining a club or a company, but rather, they are being grafted into the mystical, universal body of Christ. And as Paul repeatedly tells us, each one of us has a unique and important function, as do the various parts of the physical body:

"The body is a unit, though it is made up of many parts; and though all its parts are many, they form one body. So it is with Christ. For we were all baptized by one Spirit into one body—whether Jews or Greeks, slave or free—and we were all given the one Spirit to drink.

"Now the body is not made up of one part but of many. If the foot should say, 'Because I am not a hand, I do not belong to the body,' it would not for that reason cease to be part of the body. And if the ear should say, 'Because I am not an eye, I do not belong to the body,' it would not for that reason cease to be part of the body. If the whole body were an eye, where would the sense of hearing be? If the whole body were an ear, where would the sense of smell be? But in fact God has arranged the parts in the body, every one of them, just as he wanted them to be. If they were all one part, where would the body be? As it is, there are many parts, but one body.

———

God the Father, Son, and Holy Ghost isn't a consulting firm we bring in to give us expert advice on how to run our lives. The gospel life isn't something we learn about and then put together with instructions from the manufacturer; it's something we become as God does his work of creation and salvation in us and as we accustom ourselves to a life of belief and obedience and prayer.

—EUGENE H. PETERSON

———

"The eye cannot say to the hand, 'I don't need you!' And the head cannot say to the feet, 'I don't need you!' On the contrary, those parts of the body that seem to be weaker are indispensable, and the parts that we think are less honorable we treat with special honor. And the parts that are unpresentable are treated with special modesty, while our presentable parts need no special treatment. But God has combined the members of the body and has given greater honor to the parts that lacked it, so that there should be no division in the body, but that its parts should have equal concern for each other. If one part suffers, every part suffers with it; if one part is honored, every part rejoices with it.

"Now you are the body of Christ, and each one of you is a part of it. And in the church God has appointed first of all apostles, second prophets, third teachers, then workers of miracles, also those having gifts of healing, those able to help others, those with gifts of administration, and those speaking in different kinds of tongues" (1 Corinthians 12:12-28).

But rather than merely employing the body motif as a cute rhetorical device, Paul sees the idea of the body as a radical way of understanding our diverse callings. For Paul, Christian service is not a matter of leaders and followers. Instead, all disciples have vital ministries to perform, no matter their perceived rank:

"Just as each of us has one body with many members, and these members do not all have the same function, so in Christ we who are many form one body, and each member belongs to all the others. We have different gifts, according to the grace given us. If a man's gift is prophesying, let him use it in proportion to his faith. If it is serving, let him serve; if it is teaching, let him teach; if it is encouraging, let him encourage; if it is contributing to the needs of others, let him give generously; if it is leadership, let him govern diligently; if it is showing mercy, let him do it cheerfully" (Romans 12:4-8).

And for Paul, these were not merely theoretical ideas, but profoundly practical guidelines for ministry. The concept that different disciples should engage in varied forms of ministry helped the early church surmount one of its most challenging controversies—the issue of ministry to both Jews and Gentiles:

". . . I had been entrusted with the task of preaching the gospel to the Gentiles, just as Peter had been to the Jews. For God, who was at work in the ministry of Peter as an apostle to the Jews, was also at work in my ministry as an apostle to the Gentiles" (Galatians 2:7-8).

Work for the Loud and the Quiet

The New Testament prominently features some of the early church's best preachers and orators like Peter and Paul. And as we have seen, one of the most celebrated Christians of the 20th century was writer C.S. Lewis.

A word aptly spoken is like apples
of gold in settings of silver.
—PROVERBS 25:11

But it's not only polished speakers or published writers who are commissioned to disciple others. Gregory the Great believed that both the verbose and the quiet had important roles to play in God's work.

Gregory (c. 540–604) was a Roman statesman who became a

monk, an abbot, a deacon, and ultimately a pope. One of his most influential books was entitled *Pastoral Care* (c. 591), which included the following words of advice:

▶ The taciturn (those who are temperamentally disinclined to talk) are to be admonished in one way, those given to much talking in another.

It should be suggested to the taciturn that, while shunning some vices inadvertently, they are unconsciously involved in worse. For they often bridle the tongue beyond moderation . . . and so, their thoughts seethe the more in the mind. . . . Their mind is sometimes puffed up in pride, and it scorns as weaklings those whom it hears speaking. And when the mouth of its body is closed, it does not recognize how much it exposes itself by pride to vices. The man represses the tongue, but lifts up his mind, and without any regard to his bad qualities, he accuses others within his own heart, the more freely, as he does so the more secretly.

The taciturn are, therefore, to be admonished to aim carefully at knowing not only how they should appear outwardly, but also how to hold themselves inwardly, so as to fear the hidden judgment [of God] on their thoughts more than the [disapproval] of their speech by their neighbors. For it is written: "My son, attend to my wisdom, and incline thy ear to my prudence, that thou mayest guard thy thoughts" (Proverbs 5:1).

[Thus,] the various occasions are to be prudently judged: When the tongue ought to be restrained, it should not be unprofitably loosened in speech. When it could speak with profit, it should not indolently withhold speech. The prophet considers this matter well when he says: "Set a watch, O Lord, before my mouth, and a door round about my lips" (Psalm 141:3). He does not ask that a wall be set before his mouth, but a door, which, you see, can be opened and closed. We must take care to learn when speech should open the mouth . . . at the proper time, and when, on the contrary, silence should becomingly keep it closed.

But those who are addicted to much talking are to be admonished to observe vigilantly from how great a degree of [righteousness] they lapse, when they fall to using a multitude of words. . . . It is written: "As a city that lieth open and is not compassed with walls, so is a man that cannot refrain from his own spirit speaking" (Proverbs 25:28). For the citadel of the mind without a wall of silence is exposed to the darts of the enemy, and when it casts itself by words out of itself, it is patently exposed to the enemy.

By our neglect to guard against idle words, we come to utter harmful ones: At first we are satisfied to talk about the affairs of others, then the tongue gnaws with detraction the lives of those of whom we speak, and finally we break out into open slanders. Hence, provocations are sown, quarrels arise, the torches of hatred are lit, peace of heart is extinguished. Therefore it is well said by Solomon: "The beginning of quarrels is as when one letteth out water from a dam" (Proverbs 17:14).

Moreover, one addicted to much speaking fails entirely to keep on the straight path of righteousness: "In the multitude of words there shall not lack sin" (Proverbs 10:19). . . . Hence James says: "And if any man thinketh himself to be religious, not bridling his tongue, but deceiving his own heart, this man's religion is vain" (James 1:26). Hence, again, he says: "Let every man be swift to hear, but slow to speak" (James 1:19).

That is why the Truth in person admonishes us saying: "Every idle word that men shall speak, they shall render an account for it in the day of judgment" (Matthew 12:36). That is to say, a word is idle that has no justification of real necessity or no intention of pious usefulness. If, therefore, an account is exacted for idle words, let us consider what penalty is in store for much speaking. 7 ◀

Evolving Approaches

When Jesus taught His disciples about the kingdom of God, He alluded to nearby farmers and fields to illustrate His ideas. Today, many people experience inner transformation through the help of a Christian counselor.

No gift is more precious than good advice.

⌒DESIDERIUS ERASMUS

But even though the ways disciples help and instruct others are constantly changing (and are influenced by cultural trends), the basics of discipleship haven't changed over 20 centuries.

Theologian Bruce Demarest points this out by illustrating how spiritual direction, which is one of the oldest forms of discipleship, bears many similarities to more contemporary counseling approaches:

▶ There is a close relationship between three caring ministries practiced by Christians helpers: counseling psychology, pastoral counseling, and spiritual direction. They relate to each other as three overlapping circles:

Counseling psychology primarily deals with resolution of emotional conflicts, which affect every aspect of the person. Empathy, acceptance, and strength communicated by the Christian therapist plays a large role in the healing process. When the inner conflict that troubles the client is satisfactorily resolved, psychological counseling ends.

Pastoral counseling is usually performed in a local church or hospital ward. It focuses on a pressing problem in the life of the person seeking a helping pastor. The problem may be tension within the family unit, lack of vocational direction, or a serious health problem involving risky surgery. When by God's grace the problem is resolved, pastoral counseling usually ends.

Spiritual direction is the oldest of the three helping ministries. As we've seen, it's the form of soulcare in which a mature and gifted Christian assists another believer to grow in relationship with God, in Christ. As a catalyst for spiritual change, the spiritual director "gets out of the way" and points the disciple under the Spirit's leading to God, the source of all spiritual growth and satisfaction.

It should be clear that all three ministries seek the maturation of the Christian man or woman. Each ministry has its own special focus and task. But because we are integrated beings, the three ministries share some common ground. They are distinct but related ministries that God uses to bring healing and wholeness to His children. In the real world, psychological counseling often deals with the client's relationship with God. Pastoral counseling often addresses emotional obstacles to wholeness. And spiritual direction often confronts problems of daily living. Caregivers cannot be experts in every field. But the more competent they are in these three disciplines, the more effective under God they are likely to be.[8] ◀

Advice is like snow; the softer it falls, the longer it dwells upon, and the deeper it sinks into the mind.

≈Samuel Taylor Coleridge

Each disciple of Jesus disciples others in his or her unique way, and God doesn't condone one "authorized" approach or judge people for doing things their own way. And as with many aspects of the Christian life, the emphasis isn't so much on methodology or results as it is on the motivation with which the work is done.

We can see this in the following words of Jesus, which are often applied exclusively to tithing but can also help us understand the freedom we have to explore different ways of discipling others:

"As he looked up, Jesus saw the rich putting their gifts into the temple treasury. He also saw a poor widow put in two very small copper coins. 'I tell you the truth,' he said, 'this poor widow has put in more than all the others. All these people gave their gifts out of their wealth; but she out of her poverty put in all she had to live on'" (Luke 21:1-4).

Circles of Influence

In the opening chapter of the Book of Acts, Christ commissioned His followers to evangelize the world, telling them:

"But you will receive power when the Holy Spirit comes on you; and you will be my witnesses in Jerusalem, and in all Judea and Samaria, and to the ends of the earth" (Acts 1:8).

God comes to each soul as it is and we, as brothers and sisters of the same family, can love, respect, affirm, and encourage each other in our spiritual efforts, united in the same goal—if not in the same approach.

≈Peggy Wilkinson, O.C.D.S.

The way in which Jesus' instructions first cover Jerusalem, then the surrounding region, and finally the entire world have led some

Christian thinkers to believe that Jesus was suggesting a phased approach using the concept of concentric circles.

It's not clear whether Jesus meant to suggest a methodological approach that focused on nearby places first and on farther away places later, but throughout the centuries, many believers have repeatedly demonstrated that one of the best places to disciple others is in the home.

Offer hospitality to one another
without grumbling.
~1 PETER 4:9

We know that the earliest Christians met together in one another's homes, but even in later centuries, when churches constructed ecclesiastical facilities around the world, homes have remained a favored place for instructing others in the ways of God.

Family Ties

Jesus didn't exactly support the family values party line that day when He was speaking to a crowd:

"Someone told him, 'Your mother and brothers are standing outside, wanting to speak to you.'

"He replied to him, 'Who is my mother, and who are my brothers?' Pointing to his disciples, he said, 'Here are my mother and my brothers. For whoever does the will of my Father in heaven is my brother and sister and mother'" (Matthew 12:47-50).

The family should be a place where each new human
being can have an early atmosphere conducive to the
development of constructive creativity.
~EDITH SCHAEFFER

Still it's clear that the Christian faith places a premium on the values of hearth and home, for the home is where parents can train children and where family members can encourage one another.

This kind of close-range discipleship is at once the most effective and also the most challenging. Family members can more easily see both one another's virtues and failings than can others who don't share the same house.

Unfortunately, things don't always work out as planned. Pastor and author Joseph Stowell wrote about the parents of writer Ernest Hemingway, who failed to pass on their faith to their son in a deep and lasting way:

▶ Ernest Hemingway grew up in a solid evangelical Christian home in Oak Park, Illinois. His grandparents were missionaries, and his father was a devoted churchman and best of friends with evangelist Dwight Lyman Moody. Hemingway's family conformed to the strictest codes of Christianity, and as a boy and young man Hemingway was active in the life of his church, serving as a choirboy.

Then came the First World War, and Hemingway went away as a war correspondent and saw the death and despair that only a war like that can bring. His youthful enthusiasm for Christianity was soured to the point where he progressively, through the next several years, rejected his upbringing and denied the validity and credibility of the Christ that he once had embraced.

Or had he?

While we certainly don't know all that transpired, it would seem fair to say that Ernest Hemingway never developed a truly personal relationship with Christ. Living in an environment, going through catechism, conforming to the codes, and expressing a general affirmation of the truths of Scripture are not really what genuine Christianity consists of.

Every effort to make society sensitive to the importance
of the family is a great service to humanity.
　　　　　　　☙Pope John Paul II

Authentic Christianity is composed of non-negotiated followers who are progressively moving toward Christ and who understand all of life and all of this world in the context of His teaching and His truth. If we aren't cultivating a living, vital relationship with Jesus Christ, then we, too, can respond as Hemingway did when either life's questions are agonizingly unanswerable or when our inner

Available to Touch Others

We offer hospitality when we create a loving climate in which others can bloom. The Bible records many examples of this kind of ministry:

Mary, Martha, and Lazarus opened their home to Jesus to feed Him and give Him a comfortable place as a base from which to conduct His teaching ministry.

When Jesus healed Peter's mother-in-law, her first act was to get up and serve her guests (Mark 1:29-31).

Simon the leper, Zacchaeus, Levi, and many others opened their homes to Jesus.

The early Church believers met together in each other's homes to pray, praise, worship, fellowship, and eat together. Perhaps the comfortable environment of a home or the relaxed atmosphere around a meal helped make people receptive to the teaching.

In addition to providing examples of hospitality, Scripture gives us specific instructions to practice this kind of loving care for others. Paul listed it as a necessary qualification of an elder in the church (1 Timothy 3:2; Titus 1:8.)

continued on the next page

impulses are too seductive for us to resist. Relating to systems, rituals, and rules as a point of allegiance is never enough to keep us unflinchingly loyal.

The point really is not Hemingway's life. It's my life and your life. The point is whether we are simply fellow travelers along for the ride for reasons other than Christ, or are genuinely pursuing a relationship with Him. [9] ◄

Hospitality is about relationship—one cannot be hospitable without guests. God not only plays the host for us and becomes the banquet for us; God also has become guest for us. This is one of the deep meanings of the incarnation, that God let go of hosting long enough to become guest as well.

≈MATTHEW FOX

Simple Hospitality, Not a Picture-perfect Hotel

A quick survey of New Testament teaching on the requirements for church leaders turns up numerous references to the importance of practicing hospitality, including this one from one of Paul's letters to Timothy:

"Here is a trustworthy saying: If anyone sets his heart on being an overseer, he desires a noble task. Now the overseer must be above reproach, the husband of but one wife, temperate, self-controlled, respectable, hospitable, able to teach, not given to drunkenness, not violent but gentle, not quarrelsome, not a lover of money" (1 Timothy 3:1-3);

. . . another from Titus:

"Rather he must be hospitable, one who loves what is good, who is self-controlled, upright, holy and disciplined" (Titus 1:8);

Christians should offer their brethren simple and unpretentious hospitality.

≈ST. BASIL

. . . this one from Romans:

"Share with God's people who are in need. Practice hospitality" (Romans 12:13);

. . . and this passage from Hebrews:

"Do not forget to entertain strangers, for by so doing some people have entertained angels without knowing it" (Hebrews 13:2).

But even though it is commanded and is one of the easiest forms of discipleship for virtually anyone to practice, today hospitality is seldom seen, falling victim to a rapidly increasing pace of life. The following article by Judith Couchman explains why hospitality is important and gives practical suggestions for making it work in your life.

Practicing Hospitality in a Hectic World

▶ My sister Barbara and her family visited me in Colorado recently. They arrived during lunch time and could stay only briefly, since they were driving from Arizona to Nebraska. So I assembled sandwiches, and we plopped in the dining room to munch and talk. About two hours later I handed Barb a bag of snacks for the road, and the threesome climbed into their truck, bade a wistful good-bye, and traveled toward home, refreshed.

> To give our Lord a good hospitality,
> Mary and Martha must combine.
>
> ⮞TERESA OF AVILA

For me, creating a quick lunch for out-of-towners marked a major mind-set change about hospitality. In the past I'd have spent hours preparing for their visit—cleaning the house, shopping for groceries, cooking a sumptuous meal, arranging a memorable table setting— even though our time together was short. This time the place mats didn't even match!

God weaves miracles into our hearts. In my case, it's the miracle of offering a simple, flawed hospitality instead of striving for the proverbial "hostess with the mostest" award. A hospitality that—in a hectic and complicated world—nurtures guests without overwhelming and depleting the host.

Paul's instructions in Romans 12:9-13 emphasize that this ministry of love in action belongs not just to elders, but should be a trademark of all believers:" Share with God's people who are in need. Practice hospitality."

The emphasis in our practice of hospitality should be on how we give of ourselves to minister to others—not on how we perform to entertain others. The Bible commands us to carry out this ministry; it does not set up requirements for housing or meals. We do not need a large, beautifully decorated, immaculately tidy house in order to invite others into our home. "Breaking bread" with others does not require serving filet mignon or lobster tails. The issue is not spending money, but spending our time—not giving things, but giving ourselves. [10]

—*Rachel Crabb*

Rachael Crabb has worked with Stonecroft Ministries and is the coauthor of The Personal Touch: Encouraging Others Through Hospitality.

Called to Hospitality. In this age of the ubiquitous Martha Stewart, it's easy to feel unsettled about hospitality. After watching Martha mastermind a summer feast for 50, we can decide we're too busy, uncreative, or financially limited to invite company into our homes. Or we may aspire toward her perfection but wind up too depleted to enjoy the guests when they arrive.

If time, money, and energy were the true measuring sticks for hospitality, then most of us should lock the front door and watch television. But thankfully, our guideline for hosting guests derives from the Bible. In Romans 12 Paul presented a litany for growing strong in the faith. Interestingly, he instructed Christ's followers to "practice hospitality" along with the reminders to "keep your spiritual fervor" and be "faithful in prayer" (Romans 12:11-13). The apostle considered hospitality an everyday practice and priority, integrating it with the keys to spiritual growth and vitality.

It is equally offensive to speed a guest who would like
to stay and to detain one
who is anxious to leave.

꧁Homer

Yet Paul wasn't referring to "entertaining" as we think of it today. Entertaining emphasizes planning, acquiring resources, and managing an event. Hospitality centers on inviting people into our lives and sharing from what we have, on helping guests feel relaxed and part of the household. Instead of dazzling people with our social skills, we pour God's warmth into their souls. This approach patterns after the early church when believers shared everything in common and eschewed the need to "perform" and impress one another (Acts 2:44).

It is nothing won to admit men with an open door,
and to receive them with a shut and reserved
countenance.

꧁Francis Bacon

The New Testament provides glimpses into the open lives of 1st-century Christians. "They broke bread in their homes and ate together with *glad and sincere hearts*" (Acts 2:46, emphasis mine), and "day after day, in the temple courts and from house to house, they never stopped teaching and proclaiming the good news that Jesus is the Christ" (Acts 5:42).

But how do we apply this ancient directive, these generous role models, to our hectic times? Here are several tips:

1. *Make the time.* If we're convinced of hospitality's necessity for the soul, we'll find the time to be hospitable. I've learned that when it seems I can't afford the time to invite people in—and I welcome them anyway—these gatherings have ranked among my most satisfying.

Uncovering the time for guests can be as simple as adding a plate to the dinner table when a friend unexpectedly stops by, or as organized as reserving alternating Saturday nights for visitors. It may mean giving up some minor involvements or breaking a couch-potato habit, but the benefits of hospitality outweigh the adjustments.

2. *Give up perfection.* If we want to relax about hospitality, we must forsake the quest for perfection. I'm not advocating that we never fix a gourmet meal, decorate for a party, or straighten up the house. But when perfection grows more important than people, we're missing the point. Hospitality is about being together, and when we refuse to fret, choose to laugh away the mishaps, and delight in our guests, it proves we truly care about them.

3. *Stay flexible.* Peter wrote, "Offer hospitality to one another without grumbling" (1 Peter 4:9). When people arrive without notice or when our least-favorite relatives vacation at our house, a flexible attitude can guide us through. These episodes also give us the opportunity to express Christ's love in gritty situations. Jesus said that with God, all things are possible (Matthew 19:26), and that includes serving with a smile and an open heart when we'd rather be eating snacks and channel surfing in bed.

4. *Be yourself.* Successful hospitality pivots on doing what makes us comfortable so we can comfort our guests. When we're being our real selves instead of who we think we should be, and doing what's natural for us instead of meeting somebody else's expectations, we're most apt to provide a haven of hospitality in a hectic world.

Outreach to Friends and Neighbors

Herb and Janice were anything but experts when they started an evangelistic Bible study in their home, but that didn't stop them. Two other Christian couples agreed to help—Keith and Cheryl as co-hosts, Dave and Denise by leading discussions.

The couples spent three months planning, listing friends and neighbors who might come, and praying. They sent out more than fifty invitations, knowing that many people might agree to come but would cancel at the last minute.

When the day of the first meeting arrived, nine people showed up—nervous, hesitant, not sure what to expect. The group was off and running! The leaders planned that first meeting to be as nonthreatening as possible. They spent the first hour making everyone comfortable with social talk and finger foods, and then a guest speaker gave a short talk on "The Relevance of Christianity in Society Today." Afterward, Herb explained that in subsequent meetings they would be studying the Bible, and all materials would be provided. Even verbal participation was voluntary.

continued on the next page

5. *Focus on souls.* We touch our visitors' souls by creating a comfortable atmosphere, listening carefully to their words and hearts, offering kindness and encouragement, sharing at a spiritual level, honoring them with touches of grace or beauty, fostering fun times or providing a hideaway to rest—anything that fills inner needs and renews spirits. In turn, we can humbly allow guests to nurture and spiritually refuel us. Caring for the soul constitutes a give-and-take relationship.

This approach elevates hospitality to a spiritual level, for such "soulfulness" models God's personal relationship and accommodation toward us. He who invited us into a love-filled family circle where we'd find acceptance, encouragement, and inspiration for living in the day to day, urges us to do the same for one another through the avenue of hospitality. When we look at it that way, the question becomes, "How can I not invite people into my home?" [11] ◄

Sharing Your Home and Your Life

When you meet someone in an office or a restaurant, you can share conversation. But when you invite someone to share your home with you, you share more of yourself.

Happiness is to be found only in the home where God is loved and honored, where each one loves, and helps, and cares for the others.

◄—THEOPHANES VENARD

Pamela Toussaint lives and works in Brooklyn, New York, where her ministry focuses on providing a positive role model to inner-city youth. A few years ago, she and her girlfriend opened their apartment to a young woman who was transitioning out of the state foster care system. Pamela and her friend hosted Felicia for a year, and the time made a powerful difference in the young lady's life. As she thought about the experience, Pamela also concluded that sharing one's home or apartment with someone who needs a place to stay seemed like something Jesus would have done:

► Having a young believer live with you may sound radical, but it's actually the kind of discipleship Jesus modeled. Many Christians meet periodically over coffee with a younger believer. Yet Jesus lived with His disciples. He ate, slept, prayed, and even cried with them. The disciples grew just from hanging out with Jesus.

Jesus' life provides the ultimate blueprint for whole-life discipleship. His disciples shared His everyday life—His highest and lowest moments. They saw Him from all sides, not just as a performer of miracles but also as a man who bore the Father's burdens, got angry, and even wept. His investment in their lives would reap tremendous returns after His departure.

We, too, have deposits to make in the lives of our brothers and sisters in the faith. If you have ever tried to teach a new believer about the Christian life, you know that it takes more than a book lesson. Many things need to be taught, prayed about, explained further, and, most of all, demonstrated, again and again, before they "click" in the mind of a young believer. 12 ◄

There is no such thing as "my" bread. All bread is ours and is given to me, to others through me and to me through others.

~MEISTER ECKHART

Although she thinks it's a good thing to do, Pamela admits that practicing this kind of hospitality isn't for everybody. Here are some of the practical lessons she learned along the way:

► *Pray.* Ask God to show you opportunities for discipleship and to give you a servant's heart.

• *Don't do it alone.* We discovered that two mature believers in the home is the best situation. A co-laborer will often bring qualities you lack. The church is another important source of support. Develop a support system among Christians friends who will encourage, pray, find resources, and possibly help financially.

• *Determine in advance the length of your commitment.* If possible, clearly determine how long you are committed to housing a young disciple in your home. This period of time may correspond to a natural

The next meeting began with a discussion of who Jesus was. Answers ranged from "Jesus is alive and walking around today" to "He's just another guru." So the group began studying a chapter of the Gospel of John at each monthly meeting to find out who Jesus is.

Since those first meetings, the group has settled into a comfortable format—reading a selected Scripture passage and an hour of Bible-related discussion, followed by refreshments and talk.

The leaders are committed to building friendships, spending time together, and really listening and caring during the social times. But overcoming skepticism about biblical concepts hasn't been easy. "The prevalence of cults and negative press about television evangelists have made many people wary of any spiritual involvement," says Denise. "We've had to think about the whole picture, not just the study itself. We realize we're in this for the long haul, but as long as our small-group members are asking questions, we'll be there for them." 13

—*Stephen Sorenson and Yvonne Baker*

153

season in life, such as a school year. If you are helping someone in a crisis situation, you may not have this luxury. However, establishing the time period before the disciple moves in keeps him or her from moving into undefined, semipermanent residence with you.

• *Be clear about house rules and expectations.* Clearly communicate your expectations regarding household responsibilities. We posted our rules on the refrigerator door. If your disciple begins to slack off a bit, address the issue at once so that resentment doesn't build.

• *Understand their world.* If you choose to disciple a young person, familiarize yourself with teen culture—the music, television shows, and magazines they enjoy. Understanding his or her world and interests creates common ground that will be invaluable as you develop a deeper relationship.

• *Be teachable.* God will reveal ugly realities about you and your attitude through this process. It will be a humbling, character-building experience through which you will grow deeper in your relationship with the Lord. [14] ◄

The core of the Christian gospel is a promise and an invitation to belong in, to be at home in, the abolition of all exclusiveness, in sharing the outgoing life of a non-excluding God with the whole of creation.

—ELIZABETH TEMPLETON

Reaching the World at Work

How many times has someone made a clear-cut distinction between having a regular job and being involved in so-called "full-time Christian service"? And how many times have people cringed when hearing the distinction drawn so clearly?

Interestingly, the idea that "spiritual" work like being a pastor or a missionary means more to God than "secular" work like being a carpenter or a secretary isn't a biblical concept at all, but simply reflects the ways in which people place clergy on spiritual pedestals.

Doug Sherman and William Hendricks set out to correct this error by defending the dignity of all work and boldly proclaiming that the workplace remains one of the best places to disciple others:

154

▶ I [Doug] have a friend who operates a company that makes pallets, the platforms used to make it easier for forklifts to load and unload stacks of goods.

I've spent hours encouraging my friend to live a life that pleases God. We've studied the Scriptures together, prayed together, and talked about his spiritual life at length. But I've discovered that nothing motivates my friend to practice his Christianity more than relating what he does all day on the job to what he believes God wants done in the world.

Act as though you could hear the Divine call to participate through free and creative activity in the Divine work.

☜NICOLAS BERDYAEV

But does God want pallets made? Does it matter to Him, or not? If it does, then my friend should do it with his whole heart, knowing that he is "working for the Lord, not for men" (Colossians 3:23). If not, he is wasting his life.

I must believe no work beneath me, since Jesus was a carpenter for thirty years, and Joseph all his life.

☜CHARLES DE FOUCAULD

The same holds true for you, too, no matter what your work—especially if you have a "secular" career. Unless you can connect what you do all day with what you think God wants you doing, you will never find ultimate meaning in your work—or in your relationship with God. How can you make that connection?

The question, of course, assumes that there is a connection. Many Christians think God cares mainly about the work of "ministry"—preaching and teaching, evangelism and missions, and so forth. Jobs like manufacturing pallets, they think, are second class in the divine economy. They hold what I call the Two-Story view of work. They carve life into "secular" and "sacred" categories and assign work to the "secular" category, or "first story," assuming that God cares only about "sacred" areas of life, the "upper story." Work has no inherent

God of the Mundane

I should like to bring the routine of my daily life before You, O Lord, to discuss the long days and tedious hours that are filled with everything else but You.

Look at this routine, O God of Mildness. Look upon us men, who are practically nothing else but routine. In Your loving mercy, look at my soul, a road crowded by a dense and endless column of bedraggled refugees, a bomb-pocked highway on which countless trivialities, much empty talk and pointless activity, idle curiosity and ludicrous pretensions of importance all roll forward in a never-ending stream.

When it stands before You and Your infallible Truthfulness, doesn't my soul look just like a market place where the second-hand dealers from all corners of the globe have assembled to sell the shabby riches of this world? Isn't it just like a noisy bazaar, where I and the rest of mankind display our cheap trinkets to the restless, milling crowds? [15]

—*Karl Rahner*

**Five Good
Things about
Your Job**
1. Through work
we love people
by serving them.
2. Through work
we meet our own
needs.
3. Through work
we meet our fam-
ily's needs.
4. Through work
we earn money
to give to
others.
5. Through work
we love God.
—Doug Sherman
and William
Hendricks

value in their view. Nothing about it recommends it as a worthwhile or noble human activity.

Do your work in peace.

        ≈JOHN THE DWARF

You can see where this thinking leads. If my friend wants to please God, he must feel guilty for working in a "secular" career. He should concentrate less and less on work, and more and more on "the things of God." In fact, he might even decide to sell his business and go into the ministry. After all, that's what really counts to God.

Many people have entered the ministry through just this sort of reasoning process. I don't fault them for their zeal. But I'm astonished at their sub-biblical view of work.

Our Saviour says that a good tree, that is, a good heart as well as a soul on fire with charity, can do nothing but good and holy works. This is why St. Augustine could say "Love, and do what you will"— that is, possess love and charity, and then do what you will. It is as though he said "Charity cannot sin."

        ≈ANGELA MERICI

Work's Intrinsic Value. The Bible's view of work stands in bold contrast to the Two-Story view. Work is not something outside of God's concern. Instead, it is a major part of human life that God takes very seriously.

Work has intrinsic value—it is inherently worth doing. Why? There are two reasons:

God is a Worker. You may never have thought of God as a worker, but that is how He first reveals Himself in Scripture. In Genesis 1, God says He created the heavens and the earth; Genesis 2:2 calls this activity "work." It uses the same Hebrew word that refers to man's work in the Ten Commandments.

God didn't stop working after Creation. He continues to work, upholding the creation (Colossians 1:16-17; Hebrews 1:3). He also meets His creatures' many needs (Psalm 104). He is working out His purposes in history (e.g., Deuteronomy 11:1-7). And of course He accomplished the great work of Atonement at the Cross. No wonder Psalm 111 says "Great are the works of the Lord."

The greatness of work is inside man.
—POPE JOHN PAUL II

God is a worker. This alone tells us that work must be significant, that it must have intrinsic value. For by definition, God can do nothing that is not inherently good, or else He would violate His own nature and character. The fact that God calls what He does work and calls it good means that work has intrinsic worth.

God Created People to Be His Coworkers. Most of us know that man was created in God's image. But since God is a worker, man—created in God's image—must be a worker, too. And that is precisely what Genesis says he is: "Then God said, 'Let us make man in our image, in our likeness, and let them rule over the fish of the sea and the birds of the air, over the livestock, over all the earth, and over all the creatures that move along the ground'" (Genesis 1:26).

Not only is God a worker, but man is a worker, too. Mankind's ruling over other creatures, subduing the creation, and eating the produce of the earth all point to man as a worker. In fact, Ecclesiastes 3:13 calls man's work a gift of God.

But here's a twist on what we have said so far: Man was created not to work for himself, but to work as a coworker with God. God placed man in the garden "to work it and take care of it" (Genesis 2:8, 15). God planted the garden; man cultivated it. The first partnership! What an incredible privilege!

All legitimate work is an extension of God's work. By legitimate work I mean work that somehow contributes to what God wants done in the world, not to what He does not want done. Of course, because of sin, none of our work completely fulfills God's intentions. But this does not take away from the inherent dignity that God has assigned to work.

Good for the body is the work of the body,
good for the soul is the work of the soul, and
good for either the work of the other.

❧HENRY DAVID THOREAU

"Whatever you do," Paul wrote, "work at it with all your heart, as working for the Lord, not for men, since you know that you will receive an inheritance from the Lord as a reward" (Colossians 3:23-24). When we work with this attitude, we fulfill the highest and noblest destiny to which anyone can aspire—we are partners with God in accomplishing His work in the world. 16 ◀

Called to Lead

All people are called to disciple others, including both laypeople and church leaders. And even though laypeople and leaders are equal in God's sight, leaders face additional challenges and, if they are to be successful, must meet other tests.

He who has never learned to obey
cannot be a good commander.

❧ARISTOTLE

J. Oswald Sanders (1902–1992) taught pastors and missionaries at the Christian Leaders Training College in New Guinea and worked with Overseas Missionary Fellowship. In his book *Spiritual Leadership*, Sanders tried to help others find and develop their gifts:

▶ Spiritual leadership is a blending of natural and spiritual qualities. Even the natural qualities are not self-produced but God-given, and therefore reach their highest effectiveness when employed in the service of God and for His glory.

Personality is a prime factor in natural leadership. The spiritual leader, however, influences others not by the power of his own personality alone but by that personality irradiated, interpenetrated, and empowered by the Holy Spirit. Because he permits the Holy Spirit undisputed control of his life, the Spirit's power can flow unhindered through him to others.

Spiritual leadership is a matter of superior power, and that can never be self-generated. There is no such thing as a self-made spiritual leader. Nevertheless, because qualities of natural leadership are by no means unimportant in spiritual leadership, there is value in seeking to discover leadership potential both in oneself and in others.

Tools for Assessment. Most people have latent and undeveloped traits that, through lack of self-analysis and consequent lack of self-knowledge, may long remain undiscovered. An objective study of the following suggested standards of self-measurement could result in the discovery of such qualities where they exist, as well as the detection of incipient weaknesses that would make one unfit for leadership.

1. Have you ever broken yourself of a bad habit? To lead others, one must be master of oneself.

2. Do you retain control of yourself when things go wrong? The leader who loses self-control in testing circumstances forfeits respect and loses influence. He must be calm in crisis and resilient in adversity and disappointment.

3. Do you think independently? While using to the full the thoughts of others, the leader cannot afford to let others do his thinking or make his decisions for him.

4. Can you handle criticism objectively and remain unmoved by it? Do you turn it to good account? The humble man can derive benefit from petty and even malicious criticism.

5. Can you use disappointments creatively?

6. Do you readily secure the cooperation and win the respect and confidence of others?

7. Do you possess the ability to secure discipline without having to resort to a show of authority? True leadership is an internal quality of the spirit and requires no external show of force.

8. Have you qualified for the beatitude pronounced on the peacemaker? It is much easier to keep the peace than to make peace where it has been shattered. An important function in leadership is conciliation—the ability to discover common ground between

---

The Wise Manager

Who then is the faithful and wise manager, whom the master puts in charge of his servants to give them their food allowance at the proper time? It will be good for that servant whom the master finds doing so when he returns. I tell you the truth, he will put him in charge of all his possessions. But suppose the servant says to himself, "My master is taking a long time in coming," and he then begins to beat the menservants and maidservants and to eat and drink and get drunk. The master of that servant will come on a day when he does not expect him and at an hour he is not aware of. He will cut him to pieces and assign him a place with the unbelievers (Luke 12:42-46).

159

opposing viewpoints and then induce both parties to accept it.

9. Are you entrusted with the handling of difficult and delicate situations?

10. Can you induce people to do happily some legitimate thing that they would not normally wish to do?

11. Can you accept opposition to your viewpoint or decision without considering it a personal affront and reacting accordingly? Leaders must expect opposition and not be offended by it.

12. Do you find it easy to make and keep friends? Your circle of loyal friends is an index of the quality and extent of your leadership.

13. Are you unduly dependent on the praise or approval of others? Can you hold a steady course in the face of disapproval and even temporary loss of confidence?

14. Are you at ease in the presence of your superiors or strangers?

15. Do your subordinates appear at ease in your presence? A leader should give an impression of sympathetic understanding and friendliness that will put others at ease.

16. Are you really interested in people? In people of all types and all races? Or do you entertain respect of persons? Is there hidden racial prejudice? An anti-social person is unlikely to make a good leader.

17. Do you possess tact? Can you anticipate the likely effect of a statement before you make it?

18. Do you possess a strong and steady will? A leader will not long retain his position if he is vacillating.

19. Do you nurse resentments, or do you readily forgive injuries done to you?

20. Are you reasonably optimistic? Pessimism is no asset to a leader.

21. Are you in the grip of a master passion such as that of Paul, who said, "This one thing I do"? Such a singleness of motive will focus all one's energies and powers on the desired objective.

22. Do you welcome responsibility?

It will not be sufficient merely to engage in this exercise in self-analysis superficially and pay no further heed to the discoveries made. Something must be done about it. Why not take some of the points of conscious weakness and failure and, in cooperation with the Holy Spirit who is the Spirit of discipline, concentrate on strengthening or correcting them?

---

*The final test of a leader is that he leaves behind him
in other men the conviction and the will to carry on.*
~WALTER LIPPMANN

Those desirable qualities were all present in their fullness in the symmetrical character of our Lord, and each Christian should make it his constant prayer that they might more rapidly be incorporated into his own personality. [19] ◄

Wisdom on Leadership: Old and New

More than three centuries ago, English Puritan writer Richard Baxter encouraged pastors and spiritual leaders to zealous lives and ministries in his book, *The Reformed Pastor.* Much of his advice is as timely today as it was then.

► Content not yourselves with being in a state of grace, but be also careful that your graces are kept in vigorous and lively exercise, and that you preach to yourselves the sermons which you study, before you preach them to others. If you did this for your own sakes, it would not be lost labor; but I am speaking to you upon the public account, that you would do it for the sake of the Church, When your minds are in a holy, heavenly frame, your people are likely to partake of the fruits of it. Your prayers, and praises, and doctrine will be sweet and heavenly to them. They will likely feel when you have been much with God: that which is most on your hearts, is like to be most in their ears.

We are the nurses of Christ's little ones. If we forbear taking food ourselves, we shall famish them; it will soon be visible in their leanness, and dull discharge of their several duties. If we let our love decline, we are not like to raise up theirs. If we abate our holy care and fear, it will appear in our preaching: if the matter show it not, the manner will. If we feed on unwholesome food, either errors or fruitless controversies, our hearers are like to fare the worse for it. O brethren, watch therefore over your own hearts: keep out lusts and passions, and worldly inclinations; keep up the life of faith, and love,

Not Too Fast!

Three pitfalls await young believers who are thrust into premature leadership:

1. Pride. Paul exhorted Timothy not to put a new convert into the position of spiritual leadership (an overseer in this case) "or he may [become] puffed up with conceit" (1 Timothy 3:6, NSRV). Romans 12:3 instructs us not to think more highly of ourselves than we ought, but to exercise sober judgment about our own importance. People who are new to their relationship with Jesus do not usually have such judgment.

2. Judgment. The Bible emphasizes that spiritual responsibility will result in greater accountability, and we ought not to give a novice such responsibility and accountability too soon. James exhorted his readers: "Not many of you should presume to be teachers . . . because you know that we who teach will be judged more strictly" (James 3:1). This stricter judgment must come eventually, but it should be reserved for those who have had opportunity to mature.

and zeal: be much at home, and be much with God. If it be not your daily business to study your own hearts, and to subdue corruption, and to walk with God—if you make not this a work to which you constantly attend, all will go wrong, and you will starve your hearers; or, if you have an affected fervency, you cannot expect a blessing to attend it from on high.

A stander-by may sometimes, perhaps, see more of the game than he that plays it.

✎ JONATHAN SWIFT

When you are studying what to say to your people, if you have any concern for their souls, you will oft be thinking with yourself, "How shall I get within them? and what shall I say, that is most likely to convince them, and convert them, and promote their salvation!" And should you not as diligently think with yourself, "How shall I live, and what shall I do, and how shall I dispose of all that I have, as may most tend to the saving of men's souls?" Brethren, if the saving of souls be your end, you will certainly intend it out of the pulpit as well as in it! If it be your end, you will live for it, and contribute all your endeavors to attain it. Let me then entreat you, brethren, to do well, as well as say well. Be "zealous of good works." Spare not for any cost, if it may promote your Master's work. Maintain your innocence, and walk without offense. Let your lives condemn sin, and persuade men to duty. Would you have your people more careful of their souls, than you are of yours?

Sin travels faster than they that ride in chariots.

✎ CHARLES DUDLEY WARNER

Your sins have more hypocrisy in them than other men's, by how much the more you have spoken against them. O what a heinous thing is it in us, to study how to disgrace sin to the utmost, and make it as odious in the eyes of our people as we can, and when we have done, to live in it, and secretly cherish that which we publicly disgrace! What vile hypocrisy is it, to make it our daily work to cry it down, and yet to keep to it; to call it publicly all naught, and pri-

continued on the next page

vately to make it our bed-fellow and companion; to bind heavy burdens on others, and not to touch them ourselves with a finger! What can you say to this in judgment? Did you think as ill of sin as you spoke, or did you not? If you did not, why would you dissemblingly speak against it? If you did, why would you keep it and commit it? O bear not that badge of a hypocritical Pharisee, "They say, but do not." Many a minister of the gospel will be confounded, and not be able to look up, by reason of this heavy charge of hypocrisy. 20 ◀

Servant Leadership

Centuries after Richard Baxter wrote his advice to leaders, some of the most prominent contemporary Christian leaders were asked for their thoughts on the current state of leadership. Two of them faulted today's leaders for failing to exhibit the same kind of servant leadership demonstrated by Jesus.

> *Every day bring God sacrifices and be the priest in this reasonable service, offering thy body and the virtue of thy soul.*
>
> ☜St. John Chrysostom

As Chaplain of the United States Senate, Richard Halverson spent most of his days with the high and mighty, but his heart tended toward the lowly and downcast:

▶ There is no shortage of entrepreneur-leaders. But there is a shortage of servant-leaders. When I hear leader, I think servant. As a pastor, I define myself as, "a servant to the servants of the Servant."

Unfortunately we in the evangelical church are so celebrity-conscious that we have a distorted perception of what a leader is. In truth, the people we perceive to be the leaders may not be the real leaders in the Church of Jesus Christ. As the vice president of IBM once said, authority and leadership are not determined by our outer position, but by our inner purpose and direction.

When I think about how the church can raise up leaders, I think of 2 Timothy 3:16-17: "All Scripture is God-breathed and is useful for teaching, rebuking, correcting," and then it says, "and training in

3. Shallowness. If we believe the instruction of Jesus that followers will grow to be like their teachers (Luke 6:40), then immature leaders will promote immaturity in a ministry or fellowship. If we desire to be people who are firmly planted with deep roots (Psalm 1), then we must work hard to build depth into ourselves and into our ministries. 21

—*Paul Borthwick*

163

A Radical Approach

Although Jesus was not a revolutionary in the political sense, many of His teachings were startling and revolutionary, and none more so than those on leadership. In the contemporary world, the term *servant* has a very lowly connotation, but that was not so as Jesus used it. Indeed, He elevated it, equating it with greatness, and that was certainly a revolutionary concept. Most of us would have no objection to being masters, but servanthood holds little attraction.

Christ's view of His kingdom was that of a community of members serving one another—mutual service. Paul advocates the same idea: "Through love serve one another" (Galatians 5:13). And of course our loving service is to spread to the needy world around us. But in the life of the church today, it is usually the few who serve the many.

Jesus well knew that such an other-worldly concept would not be welcomed by a self-pleasing world of men. But nothing less than

continued on the next page

righteousness." Why? "So that the man of God may be thoroughly equipped for every good work."

The Bible says our goal should be righteousness. But when we think of leadership training, we generally think in terms of skills. Our Christian bookstores are full of "how-to" books. In my opinion, these books speak primarily to the flesh, offering only simple, superficial ways for us to live our lives. The damage this has done to the influence of the Body of Christ in the world today is immeasurable. We've got an explosion of evangelical ministries, yet we have growing social decay. Apparently, all the "skills" and "how-to's" taught in the evangelical community have not had much moral impact on our society. The church does not need more "leadership training." What we need is "righteousness training." [22] ◀

Author and speaker Elisabeth Elliot agreed:

▶ I believe the church will be more effective in raising up leaders when we begin to teach and exemplify servanthood. We too often imply that leadership is something visible: teaching, preaching, singing. But the power of servanthood is what ultimately leads to true leadership. We have this idea in the church that leadership is a recognizable, admirable position that is accompanied by a certain amount of prestige. I think the reason that it's often hard to find Sunday school teachers and other leaders is because there's no prestige connected to the position.

People want leadership, but only on their terms. We are consumed by our greed for distinction. To raise up the kind of leadership we need in the church today, we must make very plain what leadership means in the gospels: "He that would be greatest among you must be the servant of all." Stephen was willing to serve tables. Moses and David started by being willing to take care of sheep. People are often doing ordinary things when God calls them to do what turn out to be great things.

Great works do not always lie in our way, but every moment we may do little ones excellently, that is, with great love.

—St. Francis de Sales

164

Jesus said: "If you're willing to be last, then you will be first. If you're willing to do the small things, then I will make you ruler over many things." It's one of those biblical paradoxes where the principle of the Cross goes into operation—you gain by losing; become great by becoming small. When we as the Church evade the Cross we are cutting ourselves off from the possibility of true spiritual leadership. And that is the kind of leadership that we need today more than ever. 23 ◄

Caring Enough to Love

P rior to the 19th century and the invention of the telegraph, the fastest way to get information from one place to another was by a galloping horse. By the end of the 20th century, information could be transmitted from one computer to another on the opposite of the world almost instantaneously.

Comfort in tribulation can be secured only on the sure ground of faith holding as true the words of Scripture and the teaching of the Church.

Thomas More

Inventions like the telegraph, the computer, and the television have transformed our world (and made it a good bit more noisy and hectic). But such technological marvels have also tempted some people to believe that it is possible to disciple people without intense interpersonal contact.

One young American who was preparing for missionary service in Africa finally saw how relationship-starved people in the West were when he learned more about the more laid-back, relational cultures that prevail in other parts of the world:

"I discovered that I had much to learn from my African brothers. We in the West are so time-oriented and activity-oriented that it often takes away from relationships with people. How often do we say, 'I haven't gotten a thing done all afternoon,' even though we spent the entire afternoon talking with a friend? But when I talked with men

that was what He required of those who desired to rise to leadership in His kingdom. The contrast between the world's idea of leadership and that of Christ is brought into sharp focus in Mark 10:42-43: "You know that those who are recognized as rulers of the Gentiles lord it over them; and their great men exercise authority over them. But it is not [to be] so among you. But whoever wishes to become great among you shall be your servant; and whoever wishes to be first among you shall be slave of all." 24

—J. Oswald Sanders

Comfort from Sufferings

Praise be to the God and Father of our Lord Jesus Christ, the Father of compassion and the God of all comfort, who comforts us in all our troubles, so that we can comfort those in any trouble with the comfort we ourselves have received from God. For just as the sufferings of Christ flow over into our lives, so also through Christ our comfort overflows. If we are distressed, it is for your comfort and salvation; if we are comforted, it is for your comfort, which produces in you patient endurance of the same sufferings we suffer. And our hope for you is firm, because we know that just as you share in our sufferings, so also you share in our comfort (2 Corinthians 1:3-7).

from Africa, I would not have thought time existed. They would spend hours with me . . . and would not feel it was anything unusual. 'It is nothing,' was their typical reply when I thanked them for their generous giving of time.

"Now, in considering how Jesus related to people, doesn't the Africans' 'people orientation' seem more Christlike than the busy, activity-filled orientation of our Western culture?"

The New Testament features plenty of occasions when Jesus spoke to crowds or Peter and Paul preached to the masses, but the bulk of the Gospels and Epistles consist of small-scale and often messy interactions between people who know each other.

Paul's letters, in particular, overflow with human emotion for beloved brethren:

"I hope in the Lord Jesus to send Timothy to you soon, that I also may be cheered when I receive news about you. I have no one else like him, who takes a genuine interest in your welfare. For everyone looks out for his own interests, not those of Jesus Christ" (Philippians 2:19-21).

Or as Paul wrote the believers Colosse:

"Therefore, as God's chosen people, holy and dearly loved, clothe yourselves with compassion, kindness, humility, gentleness and patience. Bear with each other and forgive whatever grievances you may have against one another. Forgive as the Lord forgave you. And over all these virtues put on love, which binds them all together in perfect unity" (Colossians 3:12-14).

No matter how much we say we love someone, that love will never manifest itself unless we practice what one writer called "the ministry of hanging around."

I have always loved to think of devoted suffering as the highest, purest, perhaps the only quite pure form of action.
—FRIEDRICH VON HUGEL

For missionary author Amy Carmichael, this meant caring more for others than we care for ourselves. She had a term for this attitude. She called it Calvary love:

▶ If I can easily discuss the shortcomings and the sins of any; if I can speak in a casual way even of a child's misdoings, then I know nothing of Calvary love.

If I am perturbed by the reproach and misunderstanding that may follow action taken for the good of souls for whom I must give account; if I cannot commit the matter and go on in peace and in silence, remembering Gethsemane and the Cross, then I know nothing of Calvary love.

If my attitude be one of fear, not faith, about one who has disappointed me; if I say, "Just what I expected," if a fall occurs, then I know nothing of Calvary love.

If I say, "Yes, I forgive, but I cannot forget," as though the God who twice a day washes all the sands on all the shores of the world could not wash such memories from my mind, then I know nothing of Calvary love.

If by doing some work which the undiscerning consider "not spiritual work" I can best help others, and I inwardly rebel, thinking it is the spiritual for which I crave, when in truth it is the interesting and exciting, then I know nothing of Calvary love.

If I cast up a confessed, repented, and forsaken sin against another, and allow that sin to color my thinking and feed my suspicions, then I know nothing of Calvary love.

If I am afraid to speak the truth, lest I lose affection, or lest the one concerned should say, "You do not understand," or because I fear to lose my reputation for kindness; if I put my own good name before the other's highest good, then I know nothing of Calvary love.

If I fear to hold another to the highest because it is so much easier to avoid doing so, then I know nothing of Calvary love.

If I myself dominate myself, if my thoughts revolve round myself, if I am so occupied with myself I rarely have "a heart at leisure from itself," then I know nothing of Calvary love.

If I cannot in honest happiness take the second place (or the twentieth); if I cannot take the first without making a fuss about my unworthiness, then I know nothing of Calvary love.

If monotony tries me, and I cannot stand drudgery; if stupid people fret me and little ruffles set me on edge; if I make much of the trifles of life, then I know nothing of Calvary love.

Small Is Beautiful

In a small group, person meets person; communication takes place at the personal level. This is why, contradictory as it may seem, a small group may really reach more people than the mass communication media. The mass media may reach millions superficially but few profoundly.

—*Howard Snyder*

If I want to be known as the doer of something that has proved the right thing, or as the one who suggested that it should be done, then I know nothing of Calvary love.

If in the fellowship of service I seek to attach a friend to myself, so that others are caused to feel unwanted; if my friendships do not draw others deeper in, but are ungenerous (to myself, for myself), then I know nothing of Calvary love.

If I slip into the place that can be filled by Christ alone, making myself the first necessity of a soul instead of leading it to fasten upon Him, then I know nothing of Calvary love.

If I refuse to allow one who is dear to me to suffer for the sake of Christ; if I do not see such suffering as the greatest honor that can be offered to any follower of the Crucified, then I know nothing of Calvary love.

If, when an answer I did not expect comes to a prayer which I believed I truly meant, I shrink back from it; if the burden my Lord asks me to bear be not the burden of my heart's choice, and I fret inwardly and do not welcome His will, then I know nothing of Calvary love. [25] ◄

Maxims for Servants of God

In addition to writing his classic work, *The Dark Night of the Soul* (1582–84), John of the Cross (1542–1591), who was a Spanish friar, theologian, poet, and religious reformer, composed maxims over a period of many years. These are some of his finest on the topic of servanthood:

► God desires [even] the least degree of obedience and submissiveness more than all those services you think of rendering Him.
• God is more pleased by one work, however small, done secretly, without desire that it be known, than a thousand done with desire that men know of them. The person who works for God with purest love not only cares nothing about whether men see him, but doesn't even seek that God Himself know of them. Such a person would not cease to render God the same services, with the same joy and purity of love, even if God were never to know of them.
• He who does not allow his appetites to carry him away will soar

in his spirit as swiftly as a bird that lacks no feathers.

• Well and good if all things change, Lord God, provided we are rooted in You.

• My spirit has become dry because it forgets to feed on You.

• Lord, my God, You are not a stranger to him who does not estrange himself from You. How do they say that it is You who absent Yourself?

• The soul that journeys to God, but does not shake off its cares and quiet its appetites, is like one who drags a cart uphill.

• Think not that pleasing God lies so much in doing a great deal as in doing it with good will, without possessiveness and [regard to] human respect.

• Do not think that, because the virtues you have in mind do not shine in your neighbor, he will not be precious in God's sight for something of which you are not thinking.

• See that you are not suddenly saddened by the adversities of this world, for you do not know the good they bring, being ordained in the judgments of God for the everlasting joy of the elect.

• What does it profit you to give God one thing if He asks of you another? Consider what it is God wants, and then do it. You will as a result better satisfy your heart than with that toward which you yourself are inclined.

• Since, when the hour of reckoning comes, you will be sorry for not having used this time in the service of God, why not arrange and use it now as you would wish to have done were you dying?

• Preserve a habitual remembrance of eternal life, recalling that those who hold themselves the lowest and the poorest and least of all will enjoy the highest dominion and glory in God.

• Rejoice habitually in God, who is your salvation, and reflect that it is good to suffer in any way for Him who is good.

• He who seeks not the cross of Christ seeks not the glory of Christ.

• All the goodness we possess is lent to us, and God considers it His own work.

• Any thought not centered on God is stolen from Him.

• The devil fears a soul united to God as he does God Himself.

• More is gained in one hour from God's good things than in a whole lifetime from our own.

• Do not excuse yourself or refuse to be corrected by all; listen to every reproof with a serene countenance; think that God utters it.

• It is a serious evil to have more regard for God's blessings than for God Himself.

• Never give up prayer; and should you find dryness and difficulty, persevere in it for this very reason. God often desires to see what love your soul has, and love is not tried by ease and satisfaction.

• Remember always that everything that happens to you, whether prosperous or adverse, comes from God, so that you neither become puffed up in prosperity nor discouraged in adversity.

• Remember always that you came here for no other reason than to be a saint; thus let nothing reign in your soul which does not lead you to sanctity.

• He is meek who knows how to suffer his neighbor and himself.

• Whoever flees prayer flees all that is good.

• Conquering the tongue is better than fasting on bread and water.

• Suffering for God is better than working miracles.

• In all things, both high and low, let God be your goal.[26] ◀

Section *Four*

TEACHING THEM TO OBEY:
Disciple-making Methods and Models

Jesus commanded His disciples to "go and make disciples of all nations, baptizing them in the name of the Father and of the Son and of the Holy Spirit, and teaching them to obey everything I have commanded you" (Matthew 28:19-20).

Ever since, followers of Jesus have wondered how they should best complete such a gargantuan task. But Jesus never gave His disciples a detailed step-by-step plan for how they should disciple others.

When asked about how the kingdom of God would grow, He responded with parables:

"Listen! A farmer went out to sow his seed. As he was scattering the seed, some fell along the path, and the birds came and ate it up. Some fell on rocky places, where it did not have much soil. It sprang up quickly, because the soil was shallow. But when the sun came up, the plants were scorched, and they withered because they had no root. Other seed fell among thorns, which grew up and choked the plants, so that they did not bear grain. Still other seed fell on good soil. It came up, grew and produced a crop, multiplying thirty, sixty, or even a hundred times" (Mark 4:3-8).

Jesus concluded His remarks on this subject with the words, "He who has ears to hear, let him hear" (v. 9). But apparently some of His disciples heard but didn't understand, so Jesus spelled things out in greater detail:

"Don't you understand this parable? How then will you understand any parable? The farmer sows the word. Some people are like seed along the path, where the word is sown. As soon as they hear it, Satan comes and takes away the word that was sown in them. Others, like seed sown on rocky places, hear the word and at once receive it with joy. But since they have no root, they last only a short time. When trouble or persecution comes because of the word, they quickly fall away. Still others, like seed sown among thorns, hear the word; but the worries of this life, the deceitfulness of wealth and the desires for other things come in and choke the word, making it unfruitful. Others, like seed sown on good soil, hear the word, accept it, and produce a crop—thirty, sixty or even a hundred times what was sown" (vv. 13-20).

Some have understood Jesus to be recommending that, in the interests of economy and efficiency, we should not waste seed by

173

scattering it on the rocks or other places we judge to be infertile or unresponsive. But in another parable, Jesus emphasizes the importance of continuing to seek out anyone anywhere who will welcome God's offer of eternal life:

"A certain man was preparing a great banquet and invited many guests. At the time of the banquet he sent his servant to tell those who had been invited, 'Come, for everything is now ready.'

"But they all alike began to make excuses. The first said, 'I have just bought a field, and I must go and see it. Please excuse me.'

"Another said, 'I have just bought five yoke of oxen, and I'm on my way to try them out. Please excuse me.'

"Still another said, 'I just got married, so I can't come.'

"The servant came back and reported this to his master. Then the owner of the house became angry and ordered his servant, 'Go out quickly into the streets and alleys of the town and bring in the poor, the crippled, the blind and the lame.'

"'Sir,' the servant said, 'what you ordered has been done, but there is still room.'

"Then the master told his servant, 'Go out to the roads and country lanes and make them come in, so that my house will be full. I tell you, not one of those men who were invited will get a taste of my banquet'" (Luke 14:16-24).

Even the Apostle Paul, the early church's great systematic theologian, gave sparse instructions about discipleship, writing at one point:

"Therefore encourage one another and build each other up, just as in fact you are doing" (1 Thessalonians 5:11).

And he told Timothy, his closest disciple:

"You then, my son, be strong in the grace that is in Christ Jesus. And the things you have heard me say in the presence of many witnesses entrust to reliable men who will also be qualified to teach others" (2 Timothy 2:1-2).

Through the centuries, Christians have attempted to define the minimum requirements God expects of believers. The Heidelberg Catechism of 1563 asked, "How many things are necessary for thee to know, that thou, enjoying this comfort, mayest live and die happily?" The answer was short and simple: "Three; the first, how great my sins and miseries are; the second, how I may be delivered from all my sins and miseries; the third, how I shall express my gratitude to God for such deliverance." [1]

Making Disciples: The Perennial Problem

T hroughout the ages, followers of Jesus have created elaborate systems for discipling believers. And there was a flourishing of such systems during the second half of the 20th century, as many ministries and leaders increasingly focused on the task of discipleship. But according to many observers, the task is far from complete.

"Nondiscipleship is the elephant in the church," wrote Dallas Willard in his acclaimed 1998 book, *The Divine Conspiracy:*

▶ It is not the much discussed moral failures, financial abuses, or the amazing general similarity between Christians and non-Christians. These are only effects of the underlying problem. The fundamental negative reality among Christian believers now is their failure to be constantly learning how to live their lives in The Kingdom Among Us. And it is an *accepted* reality. The division of professing Christians into those for whom it is a matter of whole-life devotion to God and those who maintain a consumer, or client, relationship to the church has now been an accepted reality for over fifteen hundred years. [2] ◀

And even Jim Petersen, a Navigators executive and longtime advocate for discipleship, bemoaned the current state of affairs in the opening sentences of his 1993 book, *Lifestyle Discipleship,* writing, "Thirty years of discipleship programs, and we are not discipled." As he wrote:

▶ If you have been around the Christian community at all, you know about discipleship. It is there on the right-hand side of the page of the church bulletin. The discipleship group meets on Tuesdays for breakfast at Underwood's Restaurant. In our bigger churches, we have pastors of discipleship. Our Christian bookstores always have a section reserved for discipleship materials. There you will find everything from a study booklet for new believers to complete courses in discipleship. Many of us have taken the course.

Occasional high days, answers to prayer now and then, temporary blessings, make an uneven and spasmodic Christian life. But to live day in and out, all kinds of days, in simple dependence on Christ as the branch on the vine, constantly abiding, that is the supreme experience.

~VANCE HAVNER

It was in the late 1950s that I first heard about discipleship. I was just getting started in my Christian life and was casting about trying to figure out how to make it work for me.Then I met some people who talked about Scripture memory, quiet times, and personal Bible study. One of them was Ed Reis. Their goals were to live as disciples of Jesus Christ and to multiply their numbers until they filled the world.

I can't decide whether I was naive or arrogant in those days, but I was certainly mistaken. I believed the world would never be quite the same once this movement of discipleship had swept through it. Three decades have now passed. The gospel has done well in many parts of the world in these years. But in our Western society there has been a change in spiritual climate that is not at all what I envisioned. 3 ◄

No Blueprint Available
According to Dallas Willard, the search for a divine blueprint for discipleship is futile, because Jesus gave us no such directive:

▶ Not only is the outcome of our progression in the kingdom not under our control, but we are not told in any systematic way how to do our part in the process. Well, at least we are not told in precise terms—certainly not in formulas. This is because the process is to be a walk with a person. But it is also because what is needed is very much an individual matter, a response to the particular needs of individual disciples. Perfectly general instructions simply cannot be given.

The assumption of the way of Jesus is that we will, once we have

176

decided to "hear and do," do whatever is required to carry out the decision. The precise details of this process will be modeled and picked up by the devoted individual from the group, from redemptive history, and from the good sense of humankind. And that is exactly what we see when we look at the history of Jesus' people. 4 ◄

*Let us so live that when we come to die
even the undertaker will be sorry.*

≈MARK TWAIN

Willard does deduce two "primary objectives" of discipleship, and he finds much wisdom on these points from Paul's letter to the Colossians:

► The first objective is to bring apprentices to the point where they dearly love and constantly delight in that "heavenly Father" real to earth in Jesus and are quite certain that there is no "catch limit," to the goodness of his intentions or to his power to carry them out.

The second primary objective of a curriculum for Christlikeness is to remove our automatic responses against the kingdom of God, to free the apprentices of domination, of "enslavement" (John 8:34; Romans 6:6), to their old habitual patterns of thought, feeling, and action. These are the "automatic" patterns of response that were ground into the embodied social self during its long life outside The Kingdom Among Us. They make up "the sin that is in my members" which, as Paul so brilliantly understood, brings it about that "wishing to do the good is mine, but the doing of it is not" (Romans 7:18). 5 ◄

Still, Willard concludes that details about precise steps in the discipleship process are, of necessity, relatively few:

► And of course it is Jesus above all who shows us how to live in the kingdom. Genuine apostolic succession is a matter of being with him, learning to be like him, along with all those faithful ones who have gone before us. Jesus is the ultimate object of imitation. . . . But then come those directly after Jesus who imitate him. And so it goes on down through the ages. The history of the people

No More Fear of God

Our evangelical culture tends to take the awesome reality of a transcendent God who is worthy to be feared and downsize Him so He could fit into our "buddy system." The way we talk about Him, the way we pray, and, more strikingly, the way we live shows that we have somehow lost our sense of being appropriately awestruck in the presence of a holy and all-powerful God. It's been a long time since we've heard a good sermon on the "fear of God." If God were to show up visibly, many of us think we'd run up to Him and high-five Him for the good things He has done. [7]

—Joseph M. Stowell

of God is an exhaustible treasure that draws its substance from the person of Jesus alive then, alive now, alive always, in himself and in others.

We do not just hear what Jesus said to do and try to do that. Rather, we also notice what he did, and we do that too. We notice, for example, that he spent extended times in solitude and silence, and we enter solitude and silence with him. We note what a thorough student of the Scriptures he was, and we follow him, the Living Word, into the depths of the written word. We notice how he used worship and prayer, how he served those around him, and so forth. We have Bibles with red letters to indicate what he said. Might we not make a good use of a Bible that has green letters for what he did? Green for "go," or "do it"?[6] ◄

Spiritual Problems or Cultural Problems?

Bob Briner, who was both a mainstream media executive and an author of books on Christian living, suggested that some of the church's deepest problems were really cultural problems concerning how Christians relate to the larger world. As he wrote in his best-known book, *Roaring Lambs:*

► Let's face it. Despite the fact that roughly 80 percent of Americans claim to believe in Jesus as the Son of God, we're not doing so hot. Collectively, as the church of Jesus Christ—the church against which the gates of hell shall not prevail—we're struggling.

I can almost hear the chorus of defense. What do you mean we're struggling! Church attendance is at its highest in decades. Look at all the big, active churches we've built. Consider the tremendous contributions of Christian television-networks that span the globe with the message of the Gospel. And what about the church-based antiabortion victories? Why, we've gotten so strong that the President listens to us on this and other issues.

But despite all the fancy buildings, sophisticated programs, and highly visible presence, it is my contention that the church is almost a nonentity when it comes to shaping culture. In the arts, entertainment, media, education, and other culture-shaping venues of our country, the church has abdicated its role as salt and light.

Culturally, we are lambs. Meek, lowly, easily dismissed cuddly creatures that are fun to watch but never a threat to the status quo. It's time for those lambs to roar.

The church doesn't need renewal. It needs revolution. Until we start thinking in terms of revolution instead of compromise, until we are willing to give up all the cultural presuppositions we have allowed to become the criteria for our thinking and doing, the church will continue to pat itself on the back with token steps of renewal.

⟞MIKE YACONELLI

Less Than Success. Do you honestly believe that our big churches and highly visible Christian leaders have brought about a movement that is taken seriously in this country?

We feel we are making a difference because we are so important to ourselves. We have created a phenomenal subculture with our own media, entertainment, educational system, and political hierarchy so that we have the sense that we're doing a lot. But what we've really done is create a ghetto that is easily dismissed by the rest of society.

I'm afraid many in the world view us as a flock of lambs grazing in the safe pastures surrounding our churches that have been designed to blend right in with the neighborhood landscape. We're good neighbors. We look like everyone else. And except for Sunday morning, we follow the same patterns of behavior as those who have little or no interest in religion. Our lives are divided into sections labeled religious and secular, and neither category seems to affect the other. Consequently, our religious views are not taken very seriously.

It's time for the lambs to roar.

What I'm calling for is a radically different way of thinking about our world. Instead of running from it, we need to rush into it. And instead of just hanging around the fringes of our culture, we need to be right smack dab in the middle of it.

Why not believe that one day the most critically acclaimed director in Hollywood could be an active Christian layman in his church? Why not hope that the Pulitzer Prize for investigative reporting could go to a Christian journalist on staff at a major daily newspaper? Is it really too much of a stretch to think that a major exhibit at the Museum of Modern Art could feature the works of an artist on staff at one of our fine Christian colleges? Am I out of my mind to suggest that your son or daughter could be the principal dancer for the Joffrey Ballet Company, leading a weekly Bible study for other dancers in what was once considered a profession that was morally bankrupt?[8] ◄

One or Many?

Jesus instructed His disciples both in group settings and one-on-one. Likewise, the early church used both approaches. In some circles, debate rages as to which approach works best, but as Waylon B. Moore argued in his book *Multiplying Disciples: The New Testament Method for Church Growth,* both approaches have their advantages.

Moore provided 12 solid reasons in favor of each approach:

► *In defense of individual discipleship:*

1. Anyone in the local church can do individual discipling. He simply shares with another what the Lord is doing in his life, and leads the other in the steps he has already taken.

2. Individual ministry already is modeled in the church by personal counseling to the lost, the sick, the bereaved, and others with expressed needs. It is equally logical to give personal time to people who desire spiritual growth.

3. Christ's ministry was to love his disciples and to lay down his life for them. Working with an individual reflects the kind of commitment Christ had for each of his men.

4. Few people have the time or capacity to be intimately involved in the lives of a large number of individuals. Anyone can make time for working with one person.

5. Individual discipling has the closeness of friendship and the precision of a teacher-apprentice relationship.

6. The method of individual discipling is flexible in schedule and intensity. Training and Bible study assignments can be paced according to individual needs. Spiritual growth is thus more rapid and effective.

7. This method of individual discipling is readily copied. We do

unto others what has been done unto us.

8. Exhortation, correction, and admonition can be quickly and easily given in individual relationships.

9. The life of the discipler reinforces the truth of the message, and can be closely observed by the disciple.

10. The needs of the disciple come to the surface in the privacy of individual ministry.

11. Both the relationship and the results seem more lasting in individual discipling.

12. Discipling on a one-to-one level is the most rapid way I know to develop spiritual leaders who can multiply disciples.

And in defense of corporate discipleship:

1. Group ministry is the method most often used in the local church, so people feel at ease with it and expect its methodology.

2. It is a fluid method. An individual can move in and out of the group without destroying either the group or his relationship with those attending.

3. The group method allows people to participate without feeling put on the spot. Some people are not ready for one-to-one discipling.

4. A variety of teaching methods can be used in the group setting.

5. General doctrine can be easily taught to several people at once.

6. Bible study is highly stimulating as different members discuss together their research and application.

7. Momentum can grow in groups. A spirit of adventure and unity can eventually motivate those who are less eager at first.

8. Giving general correction and exhortation in a group is more subtle than directly confronting individuals.

9. A group counseling effect can result from people becoming interested in and praying for the needs of others.

10. Groups are effective channels for funneling people into a more intensive one-to-one relationship and training time.

11. The Holy Spirit can use the background and experiences of a number of people to teach each member of the group.

12. The spiritual gifts of all the members can collectively provide strength and ministry to the group. 9 ◄

Finding Your Vision for Ministry

Since there is no divinely ordained blueprint for discipleship, and since various approaches seem to have their pluses and minuses, it's important for disciples to develop a vision for their own approach to discipleship. George Barna suggested ways to do just that:

▶ I define vision as a comprehensive sense of personal ministry. It means knowing where you are with the Lord, where your ministry is going, and how you're going to get there. Vision is the "big picture" of the opportunities open to you, a divinely inspired insight into how you can minister effectively in your world.

Where there is no revelation,
the people cast off restraint.
⊸PROVERBS 29:18A

But vision is even more than just a mental landscape of the past, present, and future. It is also the driving force behind the activity of a true servant of God. It is the energy and assurance that guides us through unforeseen difficulties, or stimulates us to act when fatigue, discouragement, or ambivalence threaten to defeat us.

Developing Your Vision. Vision is the key to ministry. But how do you get it? Here are eight factors that I believe are critical to developing vision. I've uncovered them by studying the Bible and the lives of people of vision.

1. *Commitment.* To arrive at a vision for service, make God your first priority (Matthew 6:33). Above all else, desire to know God's will for your life and to achieve it. Apply the principle of planned neglect: Plan to neglect everything that sidetracks you from accomplishing your vision for ministry.

The word of God is plain in itself; and if there appear
any obscurity in one place, the Holy Ghost, which is
never contrarious to himself, explains
the same more clearly in other places.
⊸JOHN KNOX

2. *Praise.* God created us so that we can praise Him. Praise establishes and strengthens your bond with God, and results in the humility necessary for true service. Make it one of the foundations of your vision.

3. *Study.* Peter taught that those who serve most effectively have matured in their faith. Maturity requires the intimate knowledge and application of God's holy Word. Just as knowledge without response is poor stewardship, so action without knowledge is impetuous foolishness. Through His Word, God reveals the means of ministry open to us. We can receive that revelation only when we are richly dwelling in His Word (Colossians 3:16).

4. *Prayer.* Jesus and Paul modeled prayer as a source of guidance. If you truly seek God's vision for your life, then turn to Him in prayer. Through praising, requesting, and listening, you will gain God's direction (Matthew 7:7-8).

5. *Self-evaluation.* We all have special gifts for ministry (1 Peter 4:10). By relying upon these God-given talents and energies, you will be able to accomplish the tasks set before you. Use any of the many tools available to discover your unique capacities and interests. Then be sensitive to opportunities to utilize those skills and talents at the right time, and in appropriate ways.

God is endlessly imaginative, and the function of discernment is to enter creatively into God's vision for the world and to collaborate with the Spirit in making that vision a reality.

─DAVID LONSDALE

---

6. *Research.* Before deciding how to carry out the ministry you feel God is leading you into, take time to gather information about your world. Carefully analyze the conditions around you. The more you understand your context for ministry, the better prepared you will be to take advantage of the opportunities that lie within it.

At this stage you may find that the vision looms larger than you anticipated, or is different from what you expected. Mother Teresa planned on teaching middle-class girls before adopting God's vision for her life. Not until she had spent time examining the conditions in the cities did she understand her calling.

It's Out of Your Hands

In training we want to help people maximize their potential for Jesus Christ. In the training process, it must be remembered that the trainer cannot take upon himself the work of the Holy Spirit. He cannot reach down inside a person and change his sense of values—though often he wishes he could when he meets people who appear to be giving their lives to the wrong things, and whose sense of values seems to be warped.

All the trainer can do is help a disciple become what he wants to be. If a person does not see things from God's point of view, if he does not surrender his life to Jesus as Lord, if he is unwilling to pay the price of being Christ's servant, there is very little that can be done to disciple him. [But] if a person is committed to Jesus Christ and highly motivated to do His will, the training process becomes simple, even enjoyable.

In the final analysis, the trainer can contribute to a person's development in only two areas: (1) the giving of time, and (2) the opportunity to learn. All

continued on the next page

7. *Counsel.* Especially before making major decisions, the wise person seeks advice from others who are mature in the Lord (Proverbs 11:14; 12:15). Try out your ideas on a few people you trust and respect. Ask them not only for their reaction, but also to pray that you will have wisdom and discernment in your decision. Each of us has experiences that God can use in guiding others' decision-making. Fellow believers who know you can offer a more objective assessment of how well your vision fits your gifts and abilities.

---

*What a great gift it would be if we could see
a little of the great vision of Jesus—if we
could see beyond our small lives.*

᠊᠊᠊J. HEINRICH ARNOLD

---

8. *Action.* Once you define your vision for ministry, go after it. Vision without action is defiance of God (James 4:17). Be prepared for difficulties, even persecution, remembering that it is one mark of an individual who is making a difference (2 Timothy 3:12; 1 Peter 4:12-15).

You are God's instrument for ministry. You can discover His vision for how He will use you. Now I'd like to challenge you to pursue it. 10 ◀

---

*Timothy, my son, I give you this instruction in keeping
with the prophecies once made about you, so that by
following them you may fight the good fight, holding
on to faith and a good conscience. Some have rejected
these and so have shipwrecked their faith.*

᠊᠊᠊1 TIMOTHY 1:18-19.

Discipleship at Close Range

Jesus frequently spoke to the masses, teaching them about the things of God by referring to earthly things they could easily understand.

But Jesus also stole away from the crowds, both for times of intimate communion with His father and for times of intense teaching with His closest disciples. As Mark tells us:

"Jesus did not want anyone to know where they were, because he was teaching his disciples" (Mark 9:30b-31).

And Matthew shows us how Christ desired to be alone with His disciples in the days before His crucifixion:

"The Teacher says: My appointed time is near. I am going to celebrate the Passover with my disciples at your house" (Matthew 26:18b).

To teach is to learn twice.

≈JOSEPH JOUBERT

Jesus selected an even smaller group of companions to be with him in the Garden of Gethsemane during His final evening (Matthew 26:36-38).

In doing this, Jesus was modeling an approach that was later called "spiritual direction" and has been one of the more common methods of one-on-one discipleship throughout the first 20 centuries of Christian history.

Theologian Howard Baker discussed spiritual direction in his 1998 book, *Soul Keeping:*

▶ In our Christian past, spiritual men and women understood the ways of the soul and how to guide others into a deeper, closer experience with God. Like Jeremiah before them, they directed Christians to "ask for the ancient paths, where the good way is, and walk in it; and you shall find rest for your souls" (Jeremiah 6:16). The paths of the soul are "ancient" because they seem to be the oldest paths on which men and women have found God, pressing through their personal turmoil to seek direct knowledge of Him.

Abraham, pondering the glory of the stars, encountered the One who spoke with creating power from beyond the cold indifference of the visible universe. Job pressed his soul along the path of frustration at the injustice of life and was given a new vision of the vastness of God's ways.

A teacher is better than two books.

≈GERMAN PROVERB

---

other factors conducive to change and growth—a feeling of personal responsibility, willingness to work sacrificially, attitudes of teachability and flexibility, native intelligence—are either inherited or controlled by the person himself.

The trainer, therefore, must yield the total responsibility for change to the person he is training. [11]

—Walter A. Henrichsen

The Apostle Paul pursued God through the experiences that nearly brought him to despair at the impossible task of founding the young church, and after that he was given profound understanding of God's glory and plan in forming a "body of Christ" to share in God's suffering for His lost children.

Throughout the centuries, great saints and spiritual directors—like Francis of Assisi and Teresa of Avila in the Middle Ages, and contemporaries like Henri Nouwen—also learned the secret of focusing the passion of their whole being by walking the narrow way of Jesus that leads to life (Matthew 7:14).

The trouble with trying to seek God completely on our own is that we can so easily sink back into complacency and self-deception. Learning to live "in Christ" is incredibly challenging work. We would rather turn to easy distractions. We would rather blame God when life does not go our way, or piously tell ourselves we'll let Him explain Himself when we get to heaven, but we are called to seek Him and find Him now.

My joy in learning is partly that it enables me to teach.

SENECA

Today, we are beginning to rediscover the value of accepting guidance from a spiritual director. Christians of the past recognized the need to have someone "coach" them along in spiritual growth. The one offering direction was not a "guru" who had supposedly achieved perfection and therefore stood above them. Nor were they privy to "mystical secrets" or given ability to hear special voices and see secret visions on another's behalf. Instead, the spiritual director was a companion who could walk right beside someone, able to give direction because he or she understood the way to go through the dilemma and have a closer relationship with God on the other side of it. The spiritual director kept God in sight when the person had lost sight of Him. Who else could give us spiritual direction out of where we are struggling, stuck, or lost but one who has been there before—one who has learned how to fix his or her heart on things above? [12] ◄

Available for Questions

One of the reasons one-on-one discipleship works so well is because students can ask their teacher questions and explore the deeper meaning of the wisdom being shared.

Of course, students often have a way of asking questions that are difficult or troubling, or that test the teacher's knowledge. But according to Henri Nouwen, there's nothing wrong with that.

▶ Teachers can only be teachers when there are students who want to be students. Without a question, an answer is experienced as manipulation; without a struggle, help is considered interference; and without the desire to learn, the offer to teach is easily felt as oppression. Therefore, our first task is not to offer information, advice, or even guidance, but to allow others to come into touch with their own struggles, pains, doubts, and insecurities—in short, to affirm their life as quest.

If wisdom were offered me with the proviso that I should keep it shut up and refrain from declaring it, I should refuse. There's no delight in owning anything unshared.

⊸SENECA

That is quite a difficult task since it runs counter to the mainstream of education that wants to give knowledge to understand, skills to control, and power to conquer. In religious education, we encounter a God who cannot be understood, we discover realities that cannot be controlled, and we realize that our hope is hidden not in the possession of power but in the confession of weakness. As long as a religion is perceived by the student and treated by the teacher as another field to be mastered—with competition, grades, and rewards—only hostility and resentment can be expected. The main questions of religion—Who am I? Where have I come from? Where am I going?—are not questions with an answer but questions that open us to new questions which lead us deeper into the unspeakable mystery of existence.

What needs affirmation is the validity of these questions. What needs to be said is: "Yes, yes indeed, these are the questions. Don't hesitate to raise them. Don't be afraid to enter them." Teaching religion,

---

Jesus Trains His Disciples

When Jesus was preparing His disciples for their future role, He displayed a superb training method. He taught them by example as well as by precept, and His teaching was incidental rather than formal. He arranged retreats for special instruction, but in the main their characters were developed in the highways of life rather than in isolation. Their experiences in daily life afforded the opportunity of inculcating spiritual principles and values. He employed the internship method (e.g., Luke 10:17-24), and that enabled them to learn by their failures as well as their successes (Mark 9:14-29). They learned to exercise faith for their daily needs. [13]

—*J. Oswald Sanders*

Guidelines for One-on-One Discipleship

1. Make sure you are well prepared. Pray before spending one-to-one time with someone, and organize yourself.
2. Remember that you can't lead anyone further than you have gone. You cannot lay solid foundations in someone else's life with what are only sketchy outlines in your own.
3. You teach by the example of your life. The person who is ministering one to one must be what he is trying to teach.
4. Tailor your help to meet the need of the individual. Every person is different.
5. Repeat everything. "He tells us everything over and over again, a line at a time and in such simple words!" (Isaiah 28:10, The Living Bible).
6. In everything, show him how. We are generally too long in telling people what to do, and too short in showing them how.
7. Give achievable assignments. If you happen to be shoveling everything you have at the person you are individually following up—throw away your shovel. Get out an eye-dropper or a thimble.
8. Take nothing

continued on the next page

therefore, is first of all the affirmation of the basic human quest for meaning. Teaching means the creation of the space in which the validity of the questions does not depend on the availability of answers but on their capacity to open us to new perspectives and horizons. Teaching means to allow all the daily experiences of life such as loneliness, fear, anxiety, insecurity, doubt, ignorance, need for affection, support, and understanding, and the long cry for love to be recognized as an essential part of the quest for meaning.

This quest, precisely because it does not lead to ready answers but to new questions, is extremely painful and at times even excruciating. But when we ignore, and thus deny, this pain in our students, we deprive them of their humanity. The pain of the human search is a growing pain. When we prevent that pain from entering into consciousness, we suffocate the forces of human development. [14] ◀

Shaping the Heart Requires Relationship

We live in a mass-media, instant-communications age. When a top government official makes a speech in Washington or a terrorist wreaks havoc in the Middle East, we can watch the episode on our TVs in a matter of minutes.

Persons are fine things, but they cost so much!
— EMERSON

Still, discipleship is something that takes time and requires close contact, as Roger Fleming demonstrates:

▶ Jesus made disciples by His life. One does not teach faith and love with words alone. Disciples' hearts cannot be set on fire by theories. Fire kindles fire; iron sharpens iron; faith calls forth faith; life begets life.

Multitudes heard His words but only this circle saw Him walk on water and command a legion of demons, beheld Him transformed in supernatural radiance on a mountain top; witnessed Him sweat blood in a garden. Multitudes heard testimonies of those He healed, but only a small circle saw His love in the way He touched a leper or drew a blind man away from the crowd. Thousands enjoyed a feast on the mountain ignorant of all that passed between the Teacher and His pupils who served them.

His words often confused this hardy band of followers, but His Life discomfited and even offended them. Not only would He go through Samaria, but also He would talk privately with a "wicked" woman of that race. He joined tax collectors and other low life at their tables and seemed intent on offending all religious officials. He put off dignitaries and received children.

And it was His Life that convinced them of the truth of His words. Even when they did not understand what He said, they continued to follow Him, convicted by all they had heard and seen, that Jesus Christ had the words of eternal life (John 6:69).

On the eve of His crucifixion, He could say to the Father, "I have made Your name known to them . . . they have received Your words . . . they have obeyed Your word . . . now they know. . . ." Three years of life-on-life involvement turned His words into deep personal conviction born out of their experiences with Him (cf. John 17:6-8).

God with us. The Life of Jesus Christ, Immanuel, served as a living pattern to shape His disciples so that His astonished enemies observed that these unlettered, ordinary men who stood so boldly before them had been with Jesus (Acts 4:13). No textbook gave these men such courage. They had carefully observed their Master's Life (1 John 1:1) and now by the power of His indwelling spirit they imitated Him.

A man, to be greatly good, must imagine intensely and comprehensively; he must put himself in the place of another and of many others; the pains and pleasures of his species must become his own.

—SHELLEY

The Bible studiously avoids our Western concept of education in matters of true discipleship. God schools His people in the context of ordinary, and sometimes extraordinary, circumstances of life.

Jesus radically transformed concepts held by the Twelve about God, about Himself, about His kingdom, about His message. He

for granted. Check and double-check his progress on past commitments.

9. Keep emphasizing the lordship of Christ. Jesus said, "Anyone who does not carry his cross and follow me cannot be my disciple" (Luke 14:27)

10. Help him establish his goals in life—the goals of knowing Christ and making Him known.

11. Meet his needs through the Scriptures.

12. Keep sharing with him the importance of the "basics"—God's Word, prayer, fellowship, witnessing, and keeping Christ at the center of everything.

13. Explain the 2 Timothy 2:2 principle—concentrating on faithful men who will be able to teach others also. Teach him to give his life to a few, who in turn will multiply into many.

14. Thank him for his fellowship. Thank God for this time as well.

15. Remember Psalm 127:1—"Unless the Lord builds the house, its builders labor in vain." It is God who builds disciples.[15]

—Jack Griffin

drew them after Him in a fast-paced, demanding work where they could watch Him deal with nature and demons, and with people from every station in life. He gave them jobs to do and problems to solve. He pushed them to the limits of their endurance (Mark 6:30-56) and drew them aside for periods of reflection and rest (Mark 7:24). He led them into deepest sorrow (John 16:20-22) and then, at last, they shared an incomparable joy together in an upper room.

They learned their lessons in open-air classrooms surrounded by filthy beggars, mutilated lepers, thronging multitudes, and malicious officials. Always they fastened their attention on Jesus to see what He would do. Later their own lives reflected His. [16] ◀

Discipleship Through Mentoring

Mentoring, which is an intimate, one-on-one form of relating and discipling, has been around for centuries, but it is experiencing renewed popularity in our own day.

He teaches me to be good that does me good.

~THOMAS FULLER

James Houston explained why during a lecture he gave at the International Consultation on Discipleship:

▶ The human heart cries out against reductionism. And that is what we are facing in our culture. A mentor, you see, is different. He or she is not someone who can give you all the answers. He or she is someone who can cry with you when there is no answer, someone who can weep with you when you are wounded and there is no healing.

A mentor is simply a companion in your situation. Now, it may be that hopefully that mentor has already gone through experiences that are new to us, and therefore we seek that help from that wise man or woman. Clearly what we are looking for in a mentor is someone that has more depth than whatever the fixer can ever give to us. And so, the call for mentors in our culture today may be a social awakening to recognize that our lives are too shallow, that we have become too cheated by the morals with which we live. And so it may be like the return of the prodigal son, an awareness of the unreality of the far country compared with the need for coming home to a relational life.

The crab instructs its young, "Walk
straight ahead—like me."
　　　　　　&—HINDUSTANI PROVERB

Perhaps the desire for mentors may indicate the isolation of the self within our contemporary society and that this alienation that we are suffering from is increasingly more intensified. How few of us have ever had a soul friend. How few of us have someone that we can confide in with all the secrets of our life? So, who will be that role model with whom I can live life more fully and more intimately, more confidently?

I think too we live in a day of tarnished leaders and fallen idols. So we become disillusioned about our heroes. We are looking for those who appear, having more integrity because they are not concerned with success. They are concerned only with righteousness. Many of us as Christians come to a real crisis in our lives when we recognize that to pursue success is to pursue the mirage of reductionism. To pursue righteousness is far more comprehensive. But, of course it is much more costly. To be faithful is far more imperative than to be successful in the Christian life. How absurd that Christians should pursue success when it is a symbol of the cross that is the symbol of discipleship.

The mentoring relationship of one Christian to another should be one that accepts the role and the importance of mystery in the Christian life. It is a great mystery that we are made in the image and likeness of God, created for a covenant relationship with Him, redeemed by His Son through grace. So, a mentor is someone who walks with me through the mystery of our relationship as well as the mystery of our being. And indeed the mystery of our destiny. [17] ◄

We need someone, I say, on whom our character may
mold itself: you'll never make the
crooked straight without a ruler.
　　　　　　&—SENECA

Houston also discussed how the mentoring process works:

▶ Just as the master craftsman in the middle ages trained the apprentice, or the tutor taught the student, it has been a long tradition that to learn implies far more than what we mean by it today. It implies instruction, guidance, counsel, imitation, affirmation, encouragement, growth in relationship; even an abiding friendship is all involved in what we mean by this word. And thus the interface between disciple and mentor raises the question today: is one discipled appropriately without all these deep relational connotations? Is what we do in the Sunday School class enough? Can we carry out the Great Commission to make disciples of all nations only as scholars or as technicians, or indeed as organizing pragmatists?

So let's turn them to New Testament discipleship. The Christian patterns of discipleship in the New Testament are richly varied. They interact continually with the particularities of each community which each of the gospels and each of the epistles addresses distinctively. So we immediately are impressed to see that there's no stereotype version of discipleship in the New Testament, unlike so many of our prior church traditions that we represent here. Yet there's a basic core and dominant tradition that runs throughout the whole of Scripture and that is a symbol of the way of life. Obedience then to the Word of God is the essential core meaning that Judaism later adopted, though however binding it might be was of course what divided the jury into different groups, and schools.

But the theme of walking runs throughout the Bible. From when Yahweh walked with Adam in the cool of the evening, or indeed as both Enoch and Noah walked with God, until in the Book of Revelation itself the faithful remnant "follow the Lamb wherever he goes." They did this regardless of the cost of martyrdom. There's a way to walk, and there's a mission to be fulfilled.

Now as we study the world that the New Testament writers encountered the spiritual guide was at the very heart of classical education. Such a spiritual guide encouraged his pupil to participate actively by entering into dialogue at every stage of instruction. We do a lot of preaching, a lot of teaching, but we have very little dialogue. So we can learn from the classical mentors.

---

*The whole secret of a teacher's force lies in the
conviction that men are convertible.*

≈ EMERSON

The relation between master and pupil should be one of transparency. And so the polemics of Christian discipleship take up what was a great theme of classical education. The whole purpose of classical mentoring was to be god-like. And the whole of the New Testament is how we should be truly God-like. Not in the classical way, but in the spirit of Jesus Christ. [18] ◄

Making Contact

We are surrounded by people who would like to know about the love of Jesus and who would like to see it demonstrated in a way they can understand and appreciate.

---

*Man becomes a holy thing, a neighbor, only if we
realize that he is the property of God and that Jesus
Christ died for him.*

≈ HELMUT THIELICKE

For writer Stephen Sorenson, life offers plenty of opportunities for us to do just that, and many of them are as simple as applying Jesus' words to "love our neighbors as ourselves" (Matthew 19:19). Here, Sorenson offers thirteen practical ways to love our neighbors:

► 1. *Exchange simple greetings.* If you are consistently friendly when you meet people on the stairs, in the elevator, or during a neighborhood walk, eventually you'll have the opportunity to get to know them.

2. *Pass along a compliment.* Solomon wrote, "How good is a timely word!" (Proverbs 15:23) A cheerful word can still open doors to relationships, even in our impersonal society. For example, nearly every time I drove past a certain house down the road from us, I noticed that something had been improved. The trash had disappeared. A new picnic area had sprouted. The house was repainted. And so on. One day I

**Long-
Distance
Discipling**
Even from a dis-
tance, you can
help someone
grow. Here are
some sugges-
tions:
1. Write a letter.
"More than
kisses, letters
mingle souls,"
wrote John
Donne. The Bible
is a collection of
messages and
letters from God.
The New Testa-
ment contains 23
letters from Paul
and others to
churches and
individuals
throughout the
Mediterranean
world who
needed help and
encouragement.
2. Send a fax or
e-mail. You can
send letters, Bible
studies, or a list
of recommended
books to anyone
in the world who
has the same
equipment—and
receive a reply
the same day or
hour! And
because many
people have free
or low-cost e-
mail access, it can
be a much
cheaper alterna-
tive than talking
on the tele-
phone.
3. Make a phone
call. The tele-
phone is another
natural and
effective way to
communicate
with along-dis-
tance disciple.
Just as you meet
regularly when
you're discipling
someone face to

told the owners, "I just wanted to tell you that I think you're doing a great job with this house," I said. "It's really looking good." Immediately, their faces beamed. We talked for nearly twenty minutes.

3. *When somebody new moves in, demonstrate some Christian hospitality.* Stop by with cookies. Pass along information on where to buy certain items. Answer questions about local activities. Offer to help in any way possible. What a difference a smile can make!

4. *Share a meal.* Jesus knew how significant sharing a meal could be. He often met with "sinners" in their homes and spoke to thousands of people at mealtimes.

5. *Share a book.* Sharing food for the stomach is one thing. Have you considered sharing food for the mind? Do you have a book that one of your neighbors might enjoy reading? It's easy to loan out books, particularly as you learn your neighbors' interests.

6. *Share a skill.* If you are particularly good at interior decorating, fixing a car, greasing bicycle wheel bearings, landscaping, and so on, set aside a few hours on a weekend. Let other neighbors know when you will be using your particular skill and that you are willing to pass on a few tips or do some hands-on work. Then see what happens. Perhaps no one will drop by, in which case you can simply catch up on your own work. On the other hand, neighbors may stop by.

For this I think charity, to love God for himself and our neighbor for God.

~Thomas Browne

---

7. *Share your recreation.* You may be surprised at how pleased a neighbor will be to join you in a favorite activity. If you are a mountain-bike aficionado and you notice that a neighbor also has a bike, why not suggest a time to ride a trail together? If you enjoy taking your family to a local pool, invite a neighbor or neighbor's child to tag along. Perhaps the local library is starting a new film series. Or your church has put together a special drama presentation. Or you have been given free tickets to a downtown event. Quite often people will be honored that you invite them. Even if they can't come, the invitation will mean a great deal.

8. *Volunteer advice.* Perhaps you've learned about something the

*continued on the
next page*

hard way, and your neighbor hasn't. If he or she is open-minded, doesn't have an attack dog who hates you, and is home when you are awake, try sharing an idea that has worked for you.

9. *Meet obvious needs.* The opportunity to meet others' needs is not always obvious. Occasionally we have to initiate the action, not merely respond to the situation.

10. *Ask for help.* We all have strengths and weaknesses. One way of compensating for our weaknesses, and getting to know our neighbors better in the process, is to ask for help. (Sometimes it's better to receive than to give!)

I say that Christ, the sinless Son of God, might be living now in the world as our next-door neighbor and perhaps we not find it out.

&—JOHN HENRY NEWMAN

---

11. *Organize neighborhood activities.* Everybody has to eat, and few people will turn down the chance to grill a few burgers and sample other people's tasty dishes. In one neighborhood, a random gathering of people on the Fourth of July became a tradition. The residents closed off the street for a block party and brought their favorite foods. From about noon until dark, neighbors talked, threw Frisbees, and played with everybody's children. If you live in an apartment, see if you can reserve the clubhouse or block off part of the parking lot. Or arrange for everyone to meet at a nearby park.

12. *Form a neighborhood play group.* If you have small children at home, talk with your neighbors about forming a play group. You, the neighbors, and the children could get together at designated times at one another's homes or in a local park. If all goes well, the children will have fun with their peers, and you'll have a great time visiting and relaxing with new friends. If you like kids and want to meet their parents, a play area may be just the ticket.

13. *Get active in a community group or cause.* Almost every neighborhood has groups active in community affairs. Perhaps you could help start a crime-prevention group. Or maybe an issue is coming up at a public hearing. The keys here are participation and common interests.

face, you can set up a regular time to talk on the phone. A number of resources can help you become a more effective long-distance discipler. If you're not a letter writer or are uncertain what spiritually focused correspondence should look like, two books in particular are valuable. In *Letters of Francis A. Schaeffer* (Crossway) you'll find examples of letters that speak from a loving heart as they deal with the concerns of living daily with Christ. *Letters to an American Lady* (Eerdmans) is a collection of letters written over a period of 13 years by C.S. Lewis to encourage a woman he never met face to face to grow in her faith. [19]

—Joyce W. Sackett

*The love of our neighbor is the only door out of the
dungeon of the self.*
—GEORGE MACDONALD

Everybody likes to be appreciated and cared for. As Christians, we have a wonderful opportunity to express Christ's love to those around us. We don't have to go far to see great needs or hurting, harried people. We don't have to go far to meet people who may become supportive friends. But we have to be willing to take the first steps and trust God to do the rest. [20] ◄

The Community of the Committed

At the International Consultation on Discipleship, Stuart Briscoe gave a talk entitled "The Church Where Disciples Are Made." Here, Briscoe demonstrates that discipleship can happen in group settings too.

► Two things we know that come from the lips of the Lord Jesus. The first one is that He is absolutely committed to building His church. The gates of hell will not prevail against it. The second thing we know is, He has every intention of thrusting out His church into all regions of the world to make disciples. It seems, therefore, pretty obvious to me that there is an indissoluble link between the church and the making of disciples.

*Help us to help each other, Lord
Each other's cross to bear,
Let each his friendly aid afford,
And feel his brother's care.*
—CHARLES WESLEY

Here are some of the things that were apparently going on in the church in Antioch that contributed to the making of disciples. In Acts 11:19 we read, "Those who had been scattered by the persecution in connection with Stephen traveled as far as Phoenicia, Cyprus and Antioch telling," there's the word, "telling," the message only to Jews. Some of them were men who held Hellenistic views, and they decided that they weren't going to tell the message just to Jews. They decided that they would tell the message to Greeks also. And this is what we are told they told. It said that they were telling the good news about the Lord Jesus.

What you can reasonably expect in the community of believers is that you are producing people who know how to tell the good news about the Lord Jesus. Now obviously people differ. There's a difference between the way a Jew thinks and the way a Greek thinks. So, if you're going to tell the message to the Jew, you will use one format. If you're going to tell the message to the Greek, you'll use another format. But the important thing is that the content of the message is more significant than the style of communication. Don't get so wrapped up in style that you lose focus on the content. And the content is very simple. It is the Lord Jesus.

On the day of Pentecost after Peter had come to the conclusion of his sermon he said, "This Jesus whom you crucified, God has made both Lord and Christ." Make no mistake about it. We preach a Savior. Make no mistake about it, we tell people about the Lord. In fact we're told in the Acts of the Apostles, that at one stage after Saul of Tarsus got converted and the archenemy was now the wonderful missionary, that the churches had some rest and peace and living in the fear of the Lord they were multiplied. We rejoice in the fact that Jesus is our Savior and we celebrate His saving grace, but we come before Him with a sense of reverence and awe, for He is the Lord.

So in the church that we're are part of, we ask ourselves a question. If we're in the business of making disciples, are we training people, are we developing people, who know how to tell people in different ways the simple basic message of the Lord Jesus? That's a big question.

If I long to improve my brother, the first step
toward doing so is to improve myself.

 CHRISTINA ROSSETTI

Dream and Reality

Innumerable times a whole Christian community has broken down because it had sprung from a wish dream. The serious Christian, set down for the first time in a Christian community, is likely to bring with him a very definite idea of what Christian life together should be and to try to realize it. But God's grace speedily shatters such dreams. Just as surely as God desires to lead us to a knowledge of genuine Christian fellowship, so surely must we be overwhelmed by a great disillusionment with others, with Christians in general, and, if we are fortunate, with ourselves. [21]

—*Dietrich Bonhoeffer*

**Advantages
of the Cell
Church
Approach**
The cell church is
a perfect setting
for making disci-
ples. The cell
church system
within the cell
church is an ideal
program for the
monitoring, the
mentoring, and
the maturing of
new believers.
From the outset
we must clearly
understand the
term cell church.
And there you
see a cell church
versus a church
with cells. There is
a major differ-
ence between
the two.

There are many
churches with all
sorts of small
groups that
would call them-
selves a cell
church. But in
reality they are
churches with
cells of some sort.
In a church with
cells, each cell is
only one of the
many optional
programs in
which the mem-
bers can partici-
pate. Does that
make sense? The
church with cells
has got other
things as well.
They've got this
group going,
they've got that
activity. And now
I'm not saying
that a cell church
hasn't got activi-
ties or programs,
but none of the
programs will
compete with the
cell. In a cell
church the cell
forms the center
and the life of the
church and every
program is
designed to assist
and support the
cell and never to
compete with the
cell.

*continued on the
next page*

From Decisions to Discipleship. It is not difficult to get decisions. It is not difficult to get people to respond to an invitation, particularly if you word the invitation carefully. But it is a matter of the
hand of the Lord, gripping speaker and hearer alike, that will bring
a person to the point of turning to God from idols, from darkness to
light, from the power of Satan to the power of God, and change him
or her from worshiping idols to serving the living and true God and
living in the constant expectation of the glorious return of the Lord
Jesus and the ultimate establishment of His kingdom. And that's what
we can realistically expect to see in churches that are making disciples. Telling and turning.

---

*The fullness of the Christian life cannot be known
except in fellowship—fellowship with
God and fellowship with one another.*
—W.E. SANGSTER

What kind of a teaching example did they get? Well, they got it
from Barnabas, this most delightful Christian gentleman. His name was
Jose, or Joseph. But he had some land, you remember, in Cyprus and
he sold it and brought the proceeds and gave it to the church. They
were very grateful for this. And they gave him another name, Barnabas, son of encouragement. He was one of those positive, encouraging people. What a delight it is to have them in the church.

Three words are used to describe Barnabas. He was a *good* man.
He was a *glad* man. And he was a *great* man. If you want to have a
mentoring relationship, what could be better than to have an older
person who is known for being good, for being glad, and for being
great. There was sheer goodness in this man. If it hadn't been for this
good man, Barnabas, we might have lost the Apostle Paul.

It takes a great man not to protect his turf. It takes a great man
to be able to say, "I'm just absolutely thrilled to see what is happening here even if it's being done the way I wouldn't do it." It takes a
great man to say, "I'm expendable. And if you're going to be able to
do it better, let me step back and let you do it."

Properly speaking, the Church is just the people of God, just humanly remade in Christ. It should therefore have as much variety as the human race itself.

⮜LESSLIE NEWBIGIN

And that's how you teach people in the church—by example. By the good man, the great man, and the glad man. But we know also they taught them by exposition. We know that this was the style. The early church was coming out of the synagogue. We know that in the synagogue it was customary to read from the Scriptures. We know that it was customary to give an exposition of the Scriptures. And may I just say that all the modern methods to the contrary, there is still nothing that will take the place of the reading and the exposition of the Word of God. 22 ◀

Mastering Methods

Carl Wilson, who worked in churches and with Campus Crusade for Christ, carefully studied the Gospels to arrive at the following seven steps Jesus used in discipling His followers:

▶ During the first step, John the Baptist and Jesus sought to lead people to Repentance and Faith. They called them to change their minds about their past life of sin and accept a new life with God. They warned of the coming judgment and talked about the meaning of sin. But they also taught their listeners about God's love and His forgiveness of the sinner. Many were converted, being persuaded to turn from their selfish, sinful lives and to trust God.

Spiritual growth most likely takes place in a context of routine and discipline.

⮜GORDON T. SMITH

During the second step, Enlightenment and Guidance, Jesus helped His followers understand who He was so that they would trust

In the cell church everyone is a member of a cell. New people coming to the church first become members of a cell and then members of the church. So everyone in the church can be properly discipled for their ministry to each other and their missions in the community. Everyone can be properly discipled. Why? Because everyone is in a cell. It's not a new program. It's a new lifestyle.

The cell church has as its goal the development of a new lifestyle of caring and sharing relationships for everyone in the church. We didn't set out in the cell church to make it a place for discipleship. But what we discovered was that we started reproducing after our own kind in a way we never did before. We discovered that discipleship became automatic. We've found that as the new believers are coming into the church and getting involved in the cells, they are being taken care of. They are being discipled. So, we jumped in and formed a discipleship program, highlighted it, and discovered we're onto something here. 23

—*Pastor Deryck Stone of South Africa*

199

Him as their leader. He taught them that He was the Messiah and He showed them His power—that of the glorious Son of God. They were led to understand that there was continued acceptance and forgiveness through Him. They learned to follow Him obediently.

In the third step, Ministry Training and Appreciation of Benefits, Jesus called men to commit themselves publicly to minister with Him, trusting God to draw men to Himself and help them grow. Jesus called these men, saying, "Come, follow me . . . and I will make you fishers of men" (Mark 1:17). He taught them the principles of evangelism. He showed them His love for the sinner and His power to forgive sin and give new life. He demonstrated His power over physical evil. He taught them that He was the Lawgiver who brought freedom from the curse of the Law to all who followed Him and that He had the authority to judge all men at the resurrection and to justify the believer.

Every art and every discipline has a particular objective, that is to say, a target and an end peculiarly its own. Someone keenly engaged in any one art calmly and freely endures every toil, danger, and loss.

JOHN CASSIAN

The fourth step is Leadership Development and Government Under God. In this step Jesus organized His kingdom and gave men responsible leadership roles, instructing them and giving them authority. One theme of His teaching was the kingdom. He proclaimed its blessings and talked about the new law of inner righteousness. He contrasted the kingdom of heaven with Satan's, and He used parables to teach them how God's kingdom would grow.

The purpose of the fifth step, Reevaluation and Separation, is to bring a person to trust God for the eternal things of life above the temporal. At this time, Jesus challenged the status quo. He offered His followers heavenly bread instead of earthly bread, divine authority over human authority, and assurance of eternal life and future glory rather than eternal damnation. This led to a hostile separation by the world.

During the sixth step, Participation and Delegation, Jesus brought His disciples to the point of trusting Him both to work in other members of the body and to cope with those outside of and suspicious of the body of Christ. Jesus reviewed with the seventy new apostles what He had already taught the Twelve, who now observed how Jesus delegated to the Seventy. In addition, He taught them how to relate to others and what the priorities of the Christian life are. He also warned them about evils that would harm the Christian life. During this time of "Body Life," Jesus taught them how to relate to those who demanded legal obedience, those who wanted to work independently rather than as a unit, those who rejected them, false teachers, a brother who sinned, and others.

This must be our ground and our anchor-hold, that
Christ is our only perfect righteousness.

⟪MARTIN LUTHER

In the seventh step, Exchanged Life and Worldwide Challenge, a person learns how to rest in the sufficiency of the risen Christ through the Holy Spirit. The disciples, who had become professionals in the Christian ministry and who were confident in themselves, discovered through the crucifixion and the resurrection that the flesh is inadequate. They learned of God's sovereignty, the crucifixion of the flesh, and sufficiency of Christ in and through His Holy Spirit who is in the world. They learned that His kingdom is not to be confined to Israel, but to be worldwide. 25 ◀

A Recipe for Holy Living

LeRoy Eims, an executive with The Navigators, developed a lengthier list of "essentials of a healthy Christian" in his 1992 book, *The Basic Ingredients of Spiritual Growth*. That list included these elements:

1. *Quiet time.* Many thousands of Christians have discovered the blessings that God showers down upon His people as we meet with Him day by day, reflect on His Word, claim the promises He makes, face the rigors of discipleship, unburden our hearts in prayer, offer the sacrifice of praise, and in everything give thanks.

2. *Bible reading.* Bible reading can easily get lost in the shuffle. But

Following Up

For new Christians all the world is new. They have before them a grand new life with all its potentialities for blessing and profit and use. They can either fall into a nominal Christian existence and be of little help—or an actual hindrance—to the cause of Christ, or they can move victoriously into a life of fruitfulness and glory to the Lord.

The patient, tender care of those able to instruct and equip men and women for the Christian walk—this is the embodiment of what we commonly term follow-up.

Perhaps yours is a church where a few do the work that many should be doing. But the majority of Christians should have a part, and perhaps would be willing to do so if they but knew what to do and felt qualified to do it. Follow-up is something in which the whole church may participate. 26

—Dawson Trotman

that need not happen. And one of the greatest preventatives against defeat in regular Bible reading is to realize the importance that God places on it. God is very clear in His desire that His people read the Bible every day. Just look at the instructions He gave to the ruler of Israel: "He shall read it all the days of his life, that he may learn to fear the Lord his God and be careful to observe all the words of this law and these statutes, that his heart may not be lifted above his brethren, that he may not turn aside from the commandment to the right hand or to the left and that he may prolong his days in his kingdom, he and his children in the midst of Israel" (Deuteronomy 17:18-20).

Make your friends your teachers and mingle
the pleasures of conversation with the
advantages of instruction.
—BALTASAR GRACIAN

---

3. *Study.* I believe our greatest motivation for Bible study is found in the words of Jesus Himself. Referring to the Scriptures, our Lord said, "These are they which testify of Me" (John 5:39). The great desire of all Christians should be to have a growing knowledge of the Lord Jesus Christ. "For my determined purpose is that I may know Him, that I may progressively become more deeply and intimately acquainted with Him, perceiving and recognizing . . . the wonders of His person more strongly and more clearly" (Philippians 3:10, AMP). And how do we grow in our knowledge of Christ? Through the study of the Scriptures, because the Scriptures reveal Him to our hearts.

4. *Meditation.* One of the outstanding benefits of careful Bible study is that it can lead to the blessed practice of meditation. Today meditation is a lost art. We are people on the go, active, busy, and in a hurry. So the idea of taking out a portion of a day to sit and do nothing but reflect is considered by many a waste of time.

However, God commands us to slow down, sit down, and think upon His Word. "Meditate on these things; give yourself entirely to them, that your progress may be evident to all" (1 Timothy 4:15).

5. *Scripture memory.* Scripture memory seems to be the least popular form of Scripture intake. Just why do you think this is so? What is it about Scripture memory that turns people off? Could it be

that we have been led to believe that Scripture memory is not for people like you and me? Could it be that somewhere we have gotten the idea that Scripture memory is just for children?

In my own church we have made Scripture memory a vital part of the life of our Sunday School. A little child showing up for class on Sunday morning meets the Scripture Memory Lady sitting just outside the classroom door. She welcomes the child with a friendly smile and asks, "Did you memorize your verse for Sunday School this morning?" When the child says, "Yes," and recites the verse, the Scripture Memory Lady puts a gold star on the chart beside the child's name. There is no lady outside the door of my class.

When you meditate, imagine that Jesus Christ in person is about to talk about the most important thing in the world. Give him your complete attention.

FRANÇOIS FÉNELON

Are we quietly convincing ourselves that Scripture memory is for kids? But think with me for a moment. Who was it who wrote, "How can a young man cleanse his way? By taking heed according to Your Word. . . . Your Word I have hidden in my heart, that I might not sin against You" (Psalm 119:9, 11). Was it a child who wrote those words? Or were they written exclusively for children? No. These are words of David, the King of Israel, and one of the greatest military leaders the world has ever known. These are the words of a man who discovered the power of the Word of God lodged in his heart.

6. *Fellowship.* We need each other. We need each other's love and concern and prayers. And if a person has no good solid biblical fellowship with his brothers and sisters in Christ, but tries to go it alone, at some point he will run into trouble. God never intended for us to hold ourselves aloof from the care and concern of our fellow Christians. In fact, the Lord likens us to a body where "the eye cannot say to the hand, 'I have no need of you'" (1 Corinthians 12:21).

7. *Church.* I would rather worship God on Sunday morning in my home church than anything else I can think of. I suppose there are many who don't believe me, but it's true. If you offer me the opportunity to go snorkeling in the South China Sea, or gaze at Paris on a

bright spring morning from atop the Eiffel Tower, or go shopping in Hong Kong, or ski in the Swiss Alps, or attend a concert in the Sydney Opera House, or take the grandkids to Disneyland, or go to my home church and worship the Lord—I'll go to church.

If you are helping young Christians learn to walk with the Lord and serve Him, be patient with them in their attitude toward the church. Pray for them, keep them involved, and let the Holy Spirit woo them to a wholehearted involvement in and love for His church.

8. *Witnessing*. The reason people come down with spiritual lockjaw and find it difficult to give a word of witness is all too often due to a simple misunderstanding. To help us clear up this tragic misunderstanding, let's look at the people involved in the ministry of witnessing. The first is a gracious and loving God who wants all men to be saved and come to the knowledge of the truth (1 Timothy 2:4). The Apostle Peter describes this gracious loving God as the one who is "not willing that any should perish but that all should come to repentance" (2 Peter 3:9).

Wonder is the basis of worship.

—THOMAS CARLYLE

The second is a person seeking the truth. These people are everywhere—in the neighborhood where you live, down at the office or plant where you work, over at the club where you exercise—everywhere. And here is the exciting thing.

Right now the Holy Spirit, the third person in this saga of salvation, is working night and day to create a hunger for God in the hearts of these seeking souls and is devising means to bring these people across your path.

Therefore, the fourth person involved is a willing witness. Jesus said, "As the Father has sent Me, I also send you" (John 20:21). That is where you come in. That is your cue to get involved in this process. And remember this: God does not need your ability, but He does need your availability. He hunts for people who are willing to get involved.

9. *Follow-up*. Paul speaks of a mighty conflict that rages around him and the spiritual warfare into which these new babes have been

thrust. He fears that enticing words will inflict damage on their order and steadfastness. These two words he uses, "order" and "steadfastness," are military terms that carry the picture of an enemy breakthrough of what was once a solid formation of soldiers, something like the U.S. Army experienced at the Battle of the Bulge in Europe, during World War II. So Paul's desire for these new babes is that they might have strong, solid roots from which they can grow and become firmly established in the faith. [27] ◀

Showing and Telling

It is a truism that people learn the most when they use both their ears and their eyes for hearing and seeing the truths being put forth. Robert E. Coleman emphasized this point in his influential book *The Master Plan of Evangelism,* which illustrated the importance of doing with five major examples.

▶ The men and women we help spiritually will inevitably learn standards for living through what they see in us.

Of course, in a technical sense, life precedes action; but in a thoroughly practical point of view, we live by what we do. One must breathe, eat, exercise, and carry on work normally if he is to grow. Where these functions of the body are neglected, life will cease to be. That is why the effort of Jesus to get across to his followers the secrets of his spiritual influence needs to be considered as a deliberate course of his master strategy. He knew what was important.

God's mercy was not increased when Jesus came to earth, it was illustrated! Illustrated in a way we can understand. Jesus knows.

— EUGENIA PRICE

Showing the Way. Take, for example, his prayer life. Surely it was no accident that Jesus often let his disciples see him conversing with the Father. They could see the strength which it gave to his life, and though they could not understand fully what it was all about,

Get Real
Our non-Christian contemporaries are looking for something real. What we offer them must be genuine enough to withstand a careful and thorough probing. Sick of phony solutions, they're even more fed up with phony people. They aren't fooled by the pious person whose religion goes only skin-deep. Nor are they attracted by naive wishful thinkers who aren't ready to face up to life's harsh realities. In presenting the Christian answer, we must demonstrate its relevance as a realistic solution in specific situations. There's only one way to do this: by being realistic about Christianity and about ourselves. [28]

— *Paul E. Little*

they must have realized that this was part of his secret of life. Note that Jesus did not force the lesson upon them, but rather he just kept praying until at last the disciples got so hungry that they asked him to teach them what he was doing.

Seizing his opportunity when it did come, Jesus proceeded to give them a lesson which their hearts were prepared to receive. He explained to them some of the more basic principles of prayer, and then before he finished, he illustrated what he meant by repeating before them a model prayer (Luke 11:1-11; Matthew 6:9-13). Whatever it took, Jesus was determined to get this lesson across.

Another aspect of Jesus' life which was vividly portrayed to the disciples was the importance and use of the Holy Scriptures. This was evident both in maintaining his own personal devotion and in winning others to the Way. Often he would take special pains to impress upon his followers the meaning of some passage in the Bible, and he never ceased to use the Scriptures in his conversation with them. Altogether there are at least sixty-six references to the Old Testament in his dialogues with the disciples in the four Gospels, to say nothing of the more than ninety allusions to it in his speaking with others.

All this served to show the disciples how they too should know and use the Scriptures in their own life. The principles of Bible exhortation were practiced before them so repeatedly that they could not help but catch on to at least some of the rules for basic scriptural interpretation and application. Moreover, the ability of Jesus to recall so freely Old Testament passages must have impressed the disciples with the necessity of learning the Scriptures by heart, and letting them become the authority for their pronouncements.

Showing How God's Work Is Done. Through this manner of personal demonstration, every aspect of Jesus' personal discipline of life was bequeathed to his disciples, but what perhaps was most important in view of his ultimate purpose was that all the while he was teaching them how to win souls.

Practically everything Jesus said and did had some relevance to their work of evangelism, either by explaining a spiritual truth or revealing to them how they should deal with men. He did not have to work up teaching situations, but merely took advantage of those about him, and thus his teaching seemed perfectly realistic. In fact, for the most part, the disciples were absorbing it without even knowing that they were being trained to win people under like conditions for God.

This point, already alluded to several times, cannot be emphasized too much. Jesus was so much the Master in his teaching that he did not let his method obscure his lesson. He let his truth call attention to itself, and not the presentation. His method in this respect was to conceal the fact that he even had a method. He was his method.

This may be hard to imagine in this day of professional techniques and sure-fire gimmicks. In some quarters, it would almost appear we would be unable to proceed without a well-illustrated handbook or multi-colored chart showing us what to do. The least we might expect is a class in soul-winning. Yet, strange as it may seem, the disciples never had any of these things now considered so essential for the work.

What in me is dark illumine,
What is low raise and support;
That, to the height of this great argument,
I may assert Eternal Providence,
And justify the ways of
God to men.

⊸JOHN MILTON

All the disciples had to teach them was a Teacher who practiced with them what he expected them to learn. Evangelism was lived before them in spirit and in technique. Watching him they learned what it was all about. He led them to recognize the need inherent in all classes of people, and the best methods of approaching them. It wasn't outlined on the blackboard of a stuffy classroom nor written up in a "Do It Yourself" manual. His method was so real and practical that it just came naturally.

Classes Always in Session. This was as true in his approach to the masses as in his way of dealing with individuals. The disciples were always there to observe his word and deed. If the particular approach was not clear, all they had to do was to ask the Master to explain it to them.

For example, after Jesus told the story of the sower to "a very great multitude" (Mark 4:1-9; Matthew 13:1-9; Luke 8:4-8), his disciples

---

Being the Same Inside and Out

The life of a good religious ought to abound in every virtue so that he is interiorly what to others he appears to be. With good reason there ought to be much more within than appears on the outside, for He who sees within is God, whom we ought to reverence most highly wherever we are and in whose sight we ought to walk pure as the angels. Each day we ought to renew our resolutions and arouse ourselves to fervor as though it were the first day of our religious life. We ought to say: "Help me, O Lord God, in my good resolution and in Your holy service. Grant me now, this very day, to begin perfectly, for thus far I have done nothing."

If you cannot recollect yourself continuously, do so once a day at least, in the morning or in the evening. In the morning make a resolution and in the evening examine yourself on what you have said this day, what you have done and thought, for in these things perhaps you have often offended God and those about you. [30]

—*Thomas à Kempis*

Taking Christ Seriously

The reason of my humbly and affectionately addressing this discourse to the clergy, is not because it treats of things not of common concern to all Christians, but chiefly to invite and induce them, as far as I can, to the serious perusal of it; and because whatever is essential to Christian salvation, if either neglected, overlooked, or mistaken by them, is of the saddest consequence both to themselves and the churches in which they minister. [31]

—*William Law*

"asked him what this parable might be" (Luke 8:9; Mark 4:10; Matthew 13:10). Whereupon Jesus proceeded to explain to them in detail the meaning of the analogies used in the illustration. In fact, judging from the printed text, he spent three times the amount of time explaining this story to the disciples than he did in giving the initial lesson to the crowd (Matthew 13:10-23; Mark 4:10-25; Luke 8:9-18).

When the disciples seemed reluctant to confess their bewilderment, then Jesus often would have to take the initiative in clearing up the problem. The story of the rich young ruler is a typical incident. After Jesus dealt with him rather sternly, and the young ruler went away sorrowful because he loved his riches more than the kingdom of God, Jesus turned to his disciples and said: "It is hard for a rich man to enter into the kingdom of heaven" (Matthew 19:23; Mark 10:23; Luke 18:24). "The disciples were amazed at his words" (Mark 10:24). This led to an extended conversation in which Jesus explained the reason for his approach to this good moral man, while also using the opportunity to apply the principle to their own profession of faith (Mark 10:24-31; Matthew 19:24; Matthew 20:16; Luke 18:25-30).

The method of Jesus here was more than a continuous sermon; it was an object lesson as well. This was the secret of his influence in teaching. He did not ask anyone to do or be anything which first he had not demonstrated in his own life, thereby not only proving its workability, but also its relevance to his mission in life. And this he was able to do because he was constantly with his disciples. His training classes were never dismissed. Everything he said and did was a personal lesson in reality, and since the disciples were there to notice it, they were learning practically every moment of their waking day.

We have a real problem in this country when it comes to values. We have become the kind of societies that civilized countries used to send missionaries to.

⮜WILLIAM BENNETT

How else will his way ever be learned? It is well enough to tell people what we mean, but it is infinitely better to show them how to do it. People are looking for a demonstration, not an explanation.

We must take this truth to our lives. There can be no shirking or evading of our personal responsibility to show the way to those we are training, and this revelation must include the practical outworking in life of the deeper realities of the Spirit. This is the Master's method, and nothing else will ever suffice to train others to do his work. 32 ◄

Teaching As Jesus Did

Even if your life is a continuing demonstration of the truths of the Gospel, there will still come a time when you will need to teach some of these concepts to others. Teacher and writer Monte Unger discusses how we can become a "master teacher" by learning from the Master.

► What made Jesus a master teacher was the combination of His multitude of teaching techniques and the underlying principles that pervaded that teaching. Much has been written about His teaching techniques, but here are four of the principles that undergirded his three years of ministry.

1. *The principle of preparation.* A master teacher spends much time learning his or her subject. Jesus studied and prepared all His life for His final three years of intensive teaching ministry. It started when he was twelve and was found "sitting among the teachers, listening to them and asking them questions" (Luke 2:46). Even at that young age, "Everyone who heard him was amazed at his understanding and his answers" (Luke 2:47). Between the ages of twelve and thirty, Luke 2:52 says that He "grew in wisdom."

Much unhappiness has come into the world because of bewilderment and things left unsaid.

⌐DOSTOYEVSKY

Jesus knew the Scriptures better than the learned men of His day who were the teachers of the Law. Time and time again He pointed out something they'd overlooked, such as in Matthew 19:4 when He said, "'Haven't you read . . . ?'" and then spelled out God's deeper truths. This is as it should be: Master teachers know more about the subject than their students—that is why they're teaching them.

And master teachers continue to prepare themselves, an impor-

Expressing God's Word in Their Words

Paraphrasing is a way of making sure we understand something that is communicated to us. For instance, when I go to my doctor and she tells me what I must do to get well, sometimes she uses words I'm not sure I understand. I say to her, "Doctor, I want to make sure I get this right; let me say back to you what I think you said."

Paraphrasing can also be used to understand God's Word, putting the words of Scripture into the language of our neighborhoods and families, using current jargon and slang. Language changes rapidly. Words that mean one thing this year mean something quite different the next. You, and only you, are the expert on the language of today, the language your children speak, the language spoken by your associates at work.

That's not to say we do not need scholars who know the original Greek of the New Testament, but the scholars don't know nearly as well as you do the language spoken in the shopping malls of Wichita and Miami.

When you paraphrase the Bible, you are doing gospel work as valuable as that of any Bible

continued on the next page

translator. Not as many people, of course, are going to benefit. You may be writing for a few friends in a Bible study or for members of your own family. Yet, J. B. Phillips, whose paraphrase has sold in the millions, started by paraphrasing the Book of Colossians for his youth group in England. Kenneth Taylor, whose *Living Bible* has brought the Scriptures alive for millions of Bible readers, got started by paraphrasing the parables for his children.

To paraphrase the Bible, you need to understand the text as well as you are able. Read the text carefully. Look up words that stump you. Get out the Bible dictionary and make sure you know what Sadducee means and where the "Kidron" is.

Then, get out pencil and paper and write what you know you understand into the language you ordinarily use. If John were living today, how would he say it? If Paul were writing to your congregation, how would he put it? If Jesus were a guest in your home, with your children crawling all over Him, what

continued on the next page

tant part of which is following Jesus' example of taking time in solitude for prayer and rest (Matthew 14:13, 23).

2. *The principle of humble authority.* A master teacher serves his or her students by exhibiting nonauthoritarian authority.

Early on in the gospels we learn this about Jesus: "The crowds were amazed at his teaching, because he taught as one who had authority, and not as their teachers of the law" (Matthew 7:28-29). Their teachers were strict authoritarians more concerned with traditions than with the essence of the Law.

Jesus exhibited authority but was not authoritarian. There is a difference. Jesus spent much of His time combating the authoritarian "teachers of the law." In Mark 7:8 He says, "You have let go of the commands of God and are holding on to the traditions of men."

There is a difference between authoritarianism and one who teaches with authority.

3. *The principle of compassion.* A master teacher shows compassion for his or her students.

---

*Use what language you will, you can never
say anything but what you are.*

⮑EMERSON

Jesus modeled compassion. When Peter tried to emulate Jesus by walking on water, and began sinking, it would have been a great opportunity for Jesus to "clobber" Peter, to let him sink and swallow a few mouthfuls of water. Then He could have given him a good tongue-lashing and taught him a lesson he'd never forget.

Instead, "Immediately Jesus reached out his hand and caught him. 'You of little faith,' he said, 'why did you doubt?'" (Matthew 14:31) He cared for His disciple and helped him. He had compassion on the crowds (Matthew 9:36; 14:14; 15:32), on the blind men (Matthew 20:34), on the man with leprosy (Mark 1:41), and for all of Jerusalem (Luke 13:34). In all of these interactions and others, He taught His disciples about compassion.

While talking to the rich young man who had obeyed all the commandments but could not give up his riches, "Jesus looked at him and loved him" (Mark 10:21). Yes, Jesus spoke to the young man with authority, but also with love, not rigid authoritarianism. How did Mark know that Jesus loved the young man? Mark knew Jesus. He'd seen that look of compassion many times.

4. *The principle of awareness.* A master teacher is acutely aware of his or her students, the environment, and the teaching process.

A good teacher has "antennae" that absorb everything about the subtle and dynamic interplay in the teacher-subject-student process, the three elements present in every teaching episode. This is one reason a good teacher maintains eye contact with the audience. The teacher not only wants to keep the teaching personal, but he or she watches for nuances, indicators, flickers of disinterest, shadows of doubt, subtle noddings of agreement, or the pulling back in resistance.

Good communication is stimulating as black coffee,
and just as hard to sleep after.

~ANNE MORROW LINDBERGH

Jesus had absorptive antennae that kept Him in tune with everything going on around Him. He knew of that special touch of the bleeding woman who touched his cloak in Luke 8:44-46. "Someone touched me," he said. "I know that power has gone out from me." He was aware of the situation, even in the midst of a jostling crowd.

He was aware that day in the temple when the widow put only a small amount of money into the treasury. It became a teaching point, and to this day, like "the good Samaritan," the "widow's mite" is widely quoted, even in secular circles.

And Jesus was aware of what people were thinking. Many times He played mental chess with the scribes. He was already far in advance of their own thoughts, waiting for them to catch up, and when they did He tripped them. Matthew 9:4 says Jesus knew their thoughts. He knew their thoughts because He had prepared; He was aware in each situation of the direction the conversation would go. Because He knew their philosophy, He knew what they would say next.

Teachers are change agents. To learn is to change. Jesus wanted to pass on truths that would become a major world religion through only twelve key men. He would also have to teach them how to teach. But He only had time to teach the truths, not to give seminars

---

language would He use?

The ever-present danger in paraphrasing the Holy Scriptures is reduction. That is, in making a sentence clear we will have reduced it; in eliminating a difficulty or obscurity we will have inadvertently erased a mystery. There is so much in Scripture that our hearts and faith are not yet large enough to comprehend. The danger is that in our attempt to make the sentences plain we will have cut them down to the size of our individual understanding. That is one reason paraphrasing is best done in a group. Most paraphrases, and maybe the best ones, will never be published. Yours may never be known beyond the four walls of your Bible study. But if it witnesses of the living God, it will do honor to the Word of God. [33]

—*Eugene H. Peterson*

Peterson is the author of The Message, *a contemporary paraphrase of the Bible.*

on teaching. He solved His dilemma by being a living model of master teaching. He was a walking educational seminar. 34 ◀

---

*Precision of communication is important, more
important than ever, in our era of hair-trigger
balances, when a false, or misunderstood word
may create as much disaster
as a sudden thoughtless act.*

∞JAMES THURBER

Going Beyond Programs

P rograms and methodologies have helped many people boil discipleship down to a few teachable concepts, thus enabling more
believers to take up the task of discipling others.

---

*Have nothing to do with godless myths and old wives'
tales; rather, train yourself to be godly. For physical
training is of some value, but godliness has value for
all things, holding promise for both the present life
and the life to come.*

∞1 TIMOTHY 4:7-8

But at the same time, some Christian thinkers believe that some
of the programs have boiled discipleship down too far, allowing its
essence and true flavor to be dissipated in the process.

Jeff Jernigan, a Navigators vice president, has argued that "relying
too much on discipleship programs can actually hinder the work of
the Holy Spirit." He writes:

▶ Imagine you are walking through a garden and you notice a
butterfly struggling to emerge from its cocoon. What would happen
if, in an effort to help it, you took some scissors and snipped the
cocoon away?

In a few hours you would witness a tragedy. The wings, shrunken and shriveled, would not fill out with all their potential beauty. Instead of developing into a creature free to fly, the butterfly would drag a broken body through its short life. The constricting cocoon and the struggle necessary to be free from it are God's way of forcing fluid into the butterfly's wings. The "merciful" snip would have been in reality quite cruel.

Similarly, in well-intentioned efforts to help others grow spiritually, we may interfere with what God is doing in their lives. Trying to force people to follow rigid discipleship programs can actually stunt spiritual growth. Experience convinces me that an approach to discipling others based on methods alone is bound to fail.

The way to maturity is often difficult and ugly, forcing us to embrace our poverty before God. In helping others grow we must teach them to struggle well, not avoid the fight while building a shining exterior. Sometimes the struggle is exactly what they need. By trying to make things easy for people, we may actually cripple them. [36] ◄

All the disciples and followers of Jesus Christ must deny themselves. It is the fundamental law of admission into Christ's school, and the first and great lesson to be learned in this school, to deny ourselves; it is both the strait gate, and the narrow way; it is necessary in order to our learning all the other good lessons that are there taught.

꘍MATTHEW HENRY

Likewise, Navigators executive Randy Raysbrook has criticized something he calls "cookie-cutter discipleship," which is inspired more by modern management theory than biblical approaches to discipleship.

► Blame it on Frederick W. Taylor. Though he lived a century ago, he may still be affecting your understanding of disciplemaking. Taylor's influence was primarily in the industrial sector of America in the late 1890s. It was he who refined post-Industrial Revolution thought by advocating the standardization of tools and equipment in

213

the factory. His ideas helped Henry Ford increase efficiency by focusing on method and speed. His formula: The greatest production results when each worker is given a definite task to be performed in a definite time and in a definite manner.

God works immediately by his Spirit in and on the
will of his saints.
—JOHN OWEN

For many years my concept of discipling others was a product of Taylor's thinking. Unwittingly I had developed an industrialized perspective. I looked at statistics at the end of each year to determine if I was being fruitful in my ministry. That was the "greatest production" part of the formula. I was very aware of how long it took me to train someone to the point where he could reproduce himself. That was the "definite time" component of the formula. And I had sophisticated and well-refined plans by which I trained. That was the "definite manner."

I had to face the gruesome reality that I had become more a disciple of Taylor than Christ.

There seem to be two extremes when it comes to helping another grow in his walk with God. One extreme says the Christian life is primarily relationship, and therefore if you just love someone he will grow and mature. The other extreme says you can't build without plans, and you must have a set of well-defined training plans for a new Christian. Plans assure direction and continuity.

Those who have the gale of the Holy Spirit
go forward even in sleep.
—BROTHER LAWRENCE

Somewhere in between these two extremes we must find a divine balance that proclaims the primacy of relationship but also embraces the necessity of some order and structure. Without this delicate balance a discipling relationship could either become strictly social without healthy spiritual stimulation, or it could become a form of mechanical Christianity with its attendant hoop-jumping. [37] ◄

An Ancient Debate

Though such thoughts may seem new, they are merely the latest example of a heated debate that has engaged Christians for 20 centuries.

In the first century, the Apostle Paul struggled with the seemingly contradictory concepts of grace and law. As he saw it, few things were inherently sinful in themselves. Rather, obedience to Christ had to be understood in a much broader context:

"Therefore let us stop passing judgment on one another. Instead, make up your mind not to put any stumbling block or obstacle in your brother's way. As one who is in the Lord Jesus, I am fully convinced that no food is unclean in itself. But if anyone regards something as unclean, then for him it is unclean. If your brother is distressed because of what you eat, you are no longer acting in love. Do not by your eating destroy your brother for whom Christ died. Do not allow what you consider good to be spoken of as evil. For the kingdom of God is not a matter of eating and drinking, but of righteousness, peace and joy in the Holy Spirit, because anyone who serves Christ in this way is pleasing to God and approved by men.

"Let us therefore make every effort to do what leads to peace and to mutual edification. Do not destroy the work of God for the sake of food. All food is clean, but it is wrong for a man to eat anything that causes someone else to stumble. It is better not to eat meat or drink wine or to do anything else that will cause your brother to fall" (Romans 14:13-21).

When it is a question of our justification, we have to put away all thinking about the Law and our works, to embrace the mercy of God alone, and to turn our eyes away from ourselves and upon Jesus Christ alone.

~JOHN CALVIN

Centuries later, C.S. Lewis explored the same subject in his own inimitable style:

▶ Christians have often disputed as to whether what leads the Christian home is good actions, or Faith in Christ. I have no right

215

really to speak on such a difficult question, but it does seem to me like asking which blade in a pair of scissors is [more] necessary.

A serious moral effort is the only thing that will bring you to the point where you throw up the sponge. Faith in Christ is the only thing to save you from despair at that point: and out of that Faith in Him good actions must inevitably come.

Beauty and grace are performed whether or not we will sense them. The least we can do is try to be there.

—ANNIE DILLARD

There are two parodies of the truth which different sets of Christians have, in the past, been accused by other Christians of believing: perhaps they may make the truth clearer. One set [was] accused of saying, "Good actions are all that matters. The best good action is charity. The best kind of charity is giving money. The best thing to give money to is the Church. So hand us over 10,000 pounds and we will see you through." The answer to that nonsense, of course, would be that good actions done for that motive, done with the idea that heaven can be bought, would not be good actions at all, but only commercial speculations.

The other set [was] accused of saying, "Faith is all that matters. Consequently, if you have faith, it doesn't matter what you do. Sin away, my lad, and have a good time and Christ will see that it makes no difference in the end." The answer to that nonsense is that, if what you call your "faith" in Christ does not involve taking the slightest notice of what He says, then it is not Faith at all—not faith or trust in Him, but only intellectual acceptance of some theory about Him.

The Bible seems to clinch the matter when it puts the two things together into one amazing sentence. The first half is, "Work out your own salvation with fear and trembling" which looks as if everything depended on us and our good actions: but the second half goes on. "For it is God who worketh in you"—which looks as if God did everything and we nothing. I am afraid this is the sort of thing we come up against in Christianity. I am puzzled, but I am not surprised. You see, we are now trying to understand, and to separate into watertight compartments, what exactly God does and what man does when God and man are working together. And, of course, we begin by thinking it is like two men working together, so that you could say, "He did this bit and I did that."

Grace is love that cares and stoops and rescues.

—John Stott

But this way of thinking breaks down. God is not like that. He is inside you as well as outside: even if we could understand who did what, I do not think human language could properly express it. In the attempt to express it, different Churches say different things. But you will find that even those who insist most strongly on the importance of good actions tell you you need Faith; and even those who insist most strongly on Faith tell you to do good actions. At any rate that is as far as I go. [38] ◄

Holiness for Human Beings

Theologian Michael Wilkins defines discipleship like this: "Discipleship means living a fully human life in this world in union with Jesus Christ and His people, growing in conformity to His image, and helping others to know and become like Jesus."

The gospel is not simply a noble humanism; it is also a message of divine redemption.

—Christopher Butler

Occasionally, Wilkins has had to defend his view that being "fully human" is as an important aspect of discipleship and not a diversion away from godly living:

► The first time I gave that definition in public, while teaching a doctoral seminar in the Philippines for international students, one student—an exuberant teacher from a Bible college in Irian Jaya—had difficulty with one part of the definition.

"Professor Wilkins," he said, "I am troubled by the phrase, 'living a fully human life.' My students are converts from paganism. I don't want them to live more humanly. I want them to live more spiritually."

Continuing Repentance

The fact is, the ego doesn't die when Christ is invited in to set up His kingdom. The old self-reliant, self-centered sin nature attempts to regain the territory it lost to the Spirit of Christ. This sets up the need for a lifelong process of ongoing repentance. Each believer must learn how to cooperate with the indwelling Holy Spirit. His main concern is our growth in availability and obedience to our King. He never lets up on that objective. [39]

—Jan David Hettinga

217

Over the years, the one part of this definition that consistently is questioned is the expression, "living a fully human life." I can easily understand the concerns that Christians have about the expression. Since many of us are so aware of our sinfulness in this life, we tend to equate the sinful nature with our humanness. But this is a misguided understanding of our humanness. A better understanding comes from the intriguing statement of the early church father Irenaeus in the second century: "The glory of God is a human being fully alive."

When I first heard that statement quoted in a sermon, I puzzled over it for some time. But then I read Irenaeus' statement in the light of a profound declaration from the Apostle Paul, that man is "the image and glory of God" (1 Corinthians 11:7).

Paul looks back on the creation accounts and concludes that humans, created in the image of God, are the glory of God in this world. The very purpose of our existence is to manifest the glory of God in this world. We are His workmanship, God's creation, and so we bring praise and honor to God by living life fully as our Creator intended us to live it. New Testament scholar Gordon Fee insists, "By creating man in his own image God set his own glory in man. Man, therefore, exists to God's praise and honor, and is to live in relationship to God so as to be his glory."

This is similar to the way in which a work of art is an artist's glory, since it both gives expression to a part of the artist, and at the same time brings praise and honor to the artist's skills simply by being what it was intended to be.

Read this statement carefully, thoughtfully: Our humanness should not be considered inherently sinful. We have a sinful nature as a result of the Fall. However, the original creation of man and woman in the image of God did not include sin as a part of their nature. At their creation God declared them to be "very good" (Genesis 1:31).

God's purpose in redemption is glory, glory, glory.
WATCHMAN NEE

Sadly, many of our Christian teachings and activities actually encourage the opposite. They are so removed from regular activities of life that they create a false dichotomy between human life and

Christian life. Remember the stale old cliché, "He's so heavenly minded he's no earthly good"? Biblical discipleship has as its goal to make us heavenly minded and earthly good. [40] ◄

Achieving Discipline Without Legalism

Jerry Bridges, who has written books on both holiness and grace, discussed the tension between these two concepts in an article entitled "How to Develop Learners, Not Legalists." His insights are helpful:

► When I was first introduced to the idea of discipleship, I was given a list of seven spiritual disciplines I should practice every day—things such as a daily quiet time, Scripture memorization, Bible study, and prayer. As overwhelming as that list was, I did manage to survive and am extremely grateful for the spiritual disciplines I learned in the process. But I soon came to believe that my day-to-day relationship with God depended on how faithfully I performed those disciplines.

The greatest of faults, I should say,
is to be conscious of none.

☙THOMAS CARLYLE

No one actually told me God's blessing on my life was based on my performance. Still, I had developed a vague but very real impression that God's smile or frown depended on what I did. The frequent challenge to "be faithful" in my quiet time, while intrinsically good, probably helped create this impression. Soon, I was passing on this legalistic attitude to those I was seeking to disciple.

In recent years I've noticed an even stronger emphasis on discipleship by legalism. Not only do some people convey that God's smile or frown is dependent on a person's performance, they communicate by attitude and action that their own approval is based on a person's faithful performance of certain disciplines or attendance at certain Christian activities. The message is: People who don't do these things faithfully are not as "spiritual" or "committed" as those who do.

However, it is not rules that effectively disciple a person, it is God's grace. As the Apostle Paul said, "For the grace of God that brings salvation has appeared to all men. It teaches us to say 'No' to ungodli-

God's Strengthening Power
For this reason I kneel before the Father, from whom his whole family in heaven and on earth derives its name. I pray that out of his glorious riches he may strengthen you with power through his Spirit in your inner being, so that Christ may dwell in your hearts through faith. And I pray that you, being rooted and established in love, may have power, together with all the saints, to grasp how wide and long and high and deep is the love of Christ, and to know this love that surpasses knowledge—that you may be filled to the measure of all the fullness of God (Ephesians 3:14-19).

ness and worldly passions, and to live self-controlled, upright and godly lives in this present age" (Titus 2:11-12). Note that Paul says it is the grace of God—not a regimen of rules and activities—that teaches or disciples us. If we want to disciple others in a biblical manner, we must disciple by the grace of God, not by legalism. But this poses a problem.

Proclaim the Good News. Too many people set grace and discipline (or discipleship) in opposition to one other. Just as there is a strong element of legalistic discipleship within evangelicalism, there is an equally strong element of teaching that any emphasis on spiritual disciplines is a negation of God's grace.

How then can we apply Titus 2:11-12 in our discipling ministries? How can we disciple by grace? First, we must continue to teach the gospel to the people we are discipling. Our tendency is to proclaim this "good news" to people until they trust Christ; then we begin to teach them the demands of discipleship. But the gospel is the good news that God sent His Son into the world to die for all our sins— not just the sins we committed before we trusted Christ, but all our sins past, present, and future.

You don't always have to chop with the sword of truth. You can point with it, too.

*≈*ANNE LAMOTT

What do I mean when I say we must continue to preach the gospel to Christians? A believer recently said to a friend of mine, "I'm a failure." In an effort to encourage, my friend told this person, "No, you're not a failure." While I appreciate my friend's compassion, I would suggest a different response to such a statement and the attitude of despair lying behind it. I would suggest that we say something like this: "That's right. You are a failure, and so am I. But that's why Jesus came. He came to die for people who are failures." You see, this dear person needed to hear the gospel just as much that day as she did the day she trusted Christ as her Savior.

Jesus came for spiritual failures, not for the spiritually successful. He said, "It is not the healthy who need a doctor, but the sick. I have not come to call the righteous [the spiritually successful], but sinners [the spiritual failures] to repentance'" (Luke 5:31-32). We don't like to admit we're failures, but we really are! Jesus said we are to love the Lord our God with all our heart, soul, and mind, and to love our neighbor as ourselves (Matthew 22:37-38). By that standard, all of us are failures. None of us has even come close to loving God with all our hearts and our neighbors as ourselves.

Merit Is Spelled G-R-A-C-E. I believe the two greatest hindrances to discipleship are self-righteousness and guilt. Some people are not interested in pursuing true biblical discipleship because they are satisfied with their own performance. They have reduced the Christian life to measurable activities. Supposedly, they are the spiritually healthy Jesus spoke of who do not need the doctor (Luke 5:31-32).

Other believers are weighed down with guilt—often about the wrong things. They worry that they haven't succeeded in the spiritual disciplines as others seem to have done, or they've truly failed in a significant area of their lives and feel guilty about it. They haven't yet learned that Jesus died for those who have failed.

The gospel strips us of self-righteousness and frees us from guilt. The gospel, reiterated every day, reminds the seemingly "successful" disciple that he really is a sinner because "no sinner, no Savior." It reminds the seemingly "unsuccessful" disciple that Jesus died for all his failures to practice the disciplines of discipleship.

Once a person is able to put his failures into perspective, what next? We must help those we disciple realize that even their most diligent pursuit of spiritual disciplines never earns them one iota of favor from God. God's blessings come to us by His grace—through the merit of Jesus Christ. God's grace has been defined through the acrostic G-R-A-C-E, "God's Riches At Christ's Expense." This means that Jesus Christ has already merited for us every blessing and every answer to prayer we will ever receive. The practical outworking of this truth means that when I am "faithful" in my quiet time I do not earn God's blessing. Conversely, when I haven't been faithful I haven't forfeited God's blessing.

These things, good Lord, that we pray for,
give us Thy grace to labor for.
　　　　　—THOMAS MORE

This truth needs to be emphasized over and over, because we are all legalistic by nature. We don't have to be taught to relate to God on a performance basis; we do that naturally. Rather, we have to be taught over and over again that the only way we can truly relate to God is by His grace, through the merit of Jesus Christ. Why, then, should we be concerned with the practice of spiritual disciplines?

The Way to Spiritual Health. Although the spiritual disciplines do not earn God's favor, they are absolutely necessary for spiritual growth.

An analogy I sometimes use is that of a child eating the nutritious food his mother has prepared. Eating the food doesn't earn his mother's approval (though she is undoubtedly pleased that he is eating it), but it is vitally necessary for his physical growth and health. In the same way, practicing spiritual disciplines does not earn God's approval (though He is pleased), but they are vitally necessary for our spiritual growth.

All men who live with any degree of serenity live by
some assurance of grace.

REINHOLD NIEBUHR

Exposure to the truths of God's Word through the teaching of others and our own personal study, consistent prayer, and the fellowship of other believers are some of the basic disciplines God has given us for our spiritual growth. We simply will not grow without consistency in these disciplines any more than a child will grow healthily apart from nutritious food. It is not an issue of God's approval or disapproval (and should not be a matter of our approval or disapproval). It is simply an issue of growth.

Grace Does Not Equal Indulgence. But suppose the person doesn't want to grow or, perhaps more accurately, doesn't want to pay the price of the spiritual disciplines necessary to grow. What do we do then? We do what Paul did. We admonish and teach (Colossians 1:28). We warn them of the dangers of spiritual slothfulness. We teach them the true meaning and intent of the grace of God as portrayed, for example, in Titus 2:11-12. We point out that Jesus died, not just to rescue us from eternal damnation but "to redeem us from all wickedness and to purify for himself a people that are his very own, eager to do what is good" (Titus 2:14).

All the while we are admonishing and teaching, we should do so with an attitude of total acceptance. We should never imply to those we are discipling that God's favor is dependent on their faithfulness; rather, it is based on the merit of Jesus Christ on their behalf. And we should certainly never indicate by our attitude or actions that our acceptance of them is based on their performance.

The grace of God is in my mind shaped like a key,
that comes from time to time and unlocks the heavy
doors.

~DONALD SWAN

But doesn't this teaching of God's unconditional love to us in Christ lead to a careless attitude on the part of some? Yes it does—sometimes even to the point of willful and flagrant disobedience. To these people we must emphasize that God's grace does not negate the scriptural principles that "a man reaps what he sows" (Galatians 6:7), and "The Lord disciplines those He loves" (Hebrews 12:6). God's unconditional love should never be equated with permissiveness and indulgence.

Likewise, our love should be unconditional yet not permissive. It should be like Paul's love as expressed to the Corinthians, "For I wrote you out of great distress and anguish of heart and with many tears, not to grieve you but to let you know the depth of my love for you" (2 Corinthians 2:4).

In all of our discipling relationships, we must remember that we are only ministers of God. If God accepts a person by His grace, we must accept a person on the same basis, loving him unconditionally but not permissively. The foundation of our discipling should be the gospel, not the spiritual disciplines. Only a person who is firmly established in the gospel can handle the important disciplines of the Christian life without falling into legalism.[41] ◄

Called and Empowered

In the church at Antioch there were prophets and teachers: Barnabas, Simeon called Niger, Lucius of Cyrene, Manaen (who had been brought up with Herod the tetrarch) and Saul. While they were worshiping the Lord and fasting, the Holy Spirit said, "Set apart for me Barnabas and Saul for the work to which I have called them." So after they had fasted and prayed, they placed their hands on them and sent them off (Acts 13:1-5).

**Gifts of the
Spirit**
For this reason,
ever since I heard
about your faith
in the Lord Jesus
and your love for
all the saints, I
have not stopped
giving thanks for
you, remember-
ing you in my
prayers. I keep
asking that the
God of our Lord
Jesus Christ, the
glorious Father,
may give you the
Spirit of wisdom
and revelation, so
that you may
know him better. I
pray also that the
eyes of your heart
may be enlight-
ened in order that
you may know
the hope to which
he has called you,
the riches of his
glorious inheri-
tance in the
saints, and his
incomparably
great power for us
who believe (Eph-
esians 1: 15-19a).

Our Work, God's Work

Paul was a "successful" evangelist and pastor. Although his sermons didn't yield 100 percent conversion rates, and his discipleship efforts weren't foolproof, he was an amazingly effective servant
of Christ. Still, Paul clearly knew that everything he did was done in
cooperation with the Spirit of God:

"For we know, brothers loved by God, that he has chosen you,
because our gospel came to you not simply with words, but also
with power, with the Holy Spirit and with deep conviction"
(1 Thessalonians 1:4-5a).

Do we sometimes forget that we also work in cooperation with
God? It's a question Alice Fryling thought worthy of considering.

▶ God gives all of us a choice to follow Him: "See, I set before
you today life and prosperity, death and destruction. For I command
you today to love the Lord your God, to walk in his ways, and to
keep his commands, decrees and laws. . . . I have set before you life
and death, blessings and curses. Now choose life" (Deuteronomy
30:15-16; 30:19). Along the way, people have helped me to choose
life by gently "nudging" me to want to be like them.

On the other hand, I can think of too many friends who have
turned away from God because of someone's ill-suited attempts to
"disciple" them. In our well-intentioned determination to "clean up"
a new believer's life, we may impose standards and expectations that
God never intended.

This, I believe, is because we often forget how God works in our
own lives. He usually works slowly and quietly. He uses circumstances to pattern His own intervention. And He never speaks to me
in exactly the same way He speaks to you.

Who is the third who walks alway beside you?
When I count, there are only you and I together
But when I look ahead up the white road
There is always another one walking beside you. . . .
—T.S. ELIOT

Most important, we must remember that *He* does the work. It isn't our work, our influence, or our ideas that cause real growth in another's life. If we forget that, we can be tempted to manipulate others, and we risk becoming caricatures of people of faith.

As I've experienced God's work in my own life and seen Him work in the lives of others, I've noticed that He does three things: He nudges, He speaks, and He corrects. We grow—we choose life—when we respond to His activity in our lives. We help others choose life, too, when we understand and participate in God's work as He nudges them, speaks to them, and corrects them.

The Holy Spirit knocks us unconscious—so that God can do His work of love within us, which we resist when we are awake.

—FR. JOHN HARPER

God's Loving Discipline. God nudges. God speaks. And God also corrects. I'm thankful for that. Sometimes I miss His nudges. Sometimes I misunderstand His words. And so He needs to correct. But God's correction is not a frightening thing. Rather, it is freeing and invigorating.

Christians who want to reach out to their friends and help them grow sometimes make the mistake of thinking that it's their job to convict their friends of sin. But this is the Holy Spirit's job (John 16:7-10). Our job, if we have the gift of exhortation, is to "stimulate the faith of others" (Romans 12:8, PH), to stand on the sidelines and cheer: "Yes, my friend! Be free! Listen to the conviction of the Spirit! Follow the Word of the Lord!"

Dust as we are, the immortal spirit grows
Like harmony in music.

—WILLIAM WORDSWORTH

Most of the time God's nudging, speaking, and correcting take place in the ordinary moments of our days. Sometimes God seems especially present in a conversation. Occasionally, I sense God leading me to suggest meeting with a friend five or six times to discuss a

**Life Follows
Birth**
While the new
birth is necessary
as the beginning,
it is only the
beginning. We
must not think
that because we
have accepted
Christ as Savior
and therefore are
Christians, this is
all there is in the
Christian life.

In one way physi-
cal birth is the
most important
part in our physi-
cal lives, because
we are not alive
in the external
world until we
have been born.
In another way,
however, it is the
least important of
all the aspects of
our life, because
it is only the
beginning and
then it is past.

After we are
born, the impor-
tant thing is the
living of our lives
in all their rela-
tionships, possi-
bilities, and
capabilities. It is
exactly the same
with the new
birth. 43

—Francis A. Schaeffer

particular issue, book, or passage of Scripture. When that happens, I usually tell my friend that I'd like to give her the gift of focusing on her agenda when we get together. This is not chitchat time. It's not even sharing time. It's a time to look at her life to see if we can discover what God is saying to her. I love it when people show that kind of interest in me. And you can be sure that others will respond enthusiastically to your interest in them.

Thinking back to my childhood, I'm thankful for those whom God has used to nudge me towards the kingdom. I'm delighted that in the years since then, God has used me to help many others "choose life."

God uses ordinary people like you and me, to urge others to follow Him. What a privilege to be part of His work in the world today! 42 ◄

Only God Brings True Spiritual Maturity

Eugene Peterson once wrote a book on discipleship entitled *A Long Obedience in the Same Direction*. That may be one of the best definitions we've heard.

A.W. Tozer explored this theme of perseverance himself:

► "And they continued steadfastly in the apostles' doctrine and fellowship, and in breaking of bread, and in prayers" (Acts 2:42).

So says Luke of the thousands who received the Word and were baptized following the preaching of Peter on the day of Pentecost.

Conversion for those first Christians was not a destination; it was the beginning of a journey. And right there is where the biblical emphasis differs from ours.

---

*Our prayer will be most like that prayer of Christ if we
do not ask God to show us what is going to be, or to
make any particular thing happen, but only pray that
we may be faithful in whatever happens.*

≈FR. ANDREW

Today all is made to depend upon the initial act of believing. At a given moment a "decision" is made for Christ, and after that every-

226

thing is automatic. This is not taught in so many words, but such is the impression inadvertently created by our failure to lay a scriptural emphasis in our evangelistic preaching. We of the evangelical churches are almost all guilty of this lopsided view of the Christian life, and because the foundations are out of plumb the temple of God leans dangerously and threatens to topple unless some immediate corrections are made.

In our eagerness to make converts we allow our hearers to absorb the idea that they can deal with their entire responsibility once and for all by an act of believing. This is in some vague way supposed to honor grace and glorify God, whereas actually it is to make Christ the author of a grotesque, unworkable system that has no counterpart in the Scriptures of truth.

In the Book of Acts faith was for each believer a beginning, not an end; it was a journey, not a bed in which to lie while waiting for the day of our Lord's triumph. Believing was not a once-done act; it was more than an act, it was an attitude of heart and mind which inspired and enabled the believer to take up his cross and follow the Lamb whithersoever He went.

It is, however, only by fidelity in little things that a true and constant love of God can be distinguished from a passing fervor of spirit.

~FRANÇOIS FÉNELON

"They continued," says Luke, and is it not plain that it was only by continuing that they could confirm their faith? On a given day they believed, were baptized and joined themselves to the believing company. Very good, but tomorrow what? and the next day? and the next week? How could anyone know that their conversion had been genuine? How could they live down the critic's charge that they had been pressured into a decision? that they had cracked under the psychological squeeze set up by crowds and religious excitement? Obviously there was only one way: They continued. 44 ◄

Growth Means Maturity

If we are to be mature we must get hold of a mature faith—or better, it must get hold of us. For the immaturities of our faith will soon show themselves in immaturities in our actions and our attitudes. "The creed of today becomes the deed of tomorrow." Nothing can be more immature than the oft-repeated statement: "It doesn't matter what you believe just so you live right." For belief is literally by-lief, by-life—the thing you live by. And if your belief is wrong your life will be wrong.

Don't misunderstand me. I don't mean to say that if you have a correct belief you'll necessarily have a correct life. That doesn't follow. The creed, to be a creed, must be a vital rather than a verbal one. For the only thing we really believe in is the thing we believe in enough to act upon. Your deed is your creed. But it does matter what you hold as the basic assumptions of your life. If you have no starting point, you'll have no ending point. 45

—E. Stanley Jones

Section Five

ISSUES:
Applying God's Wisdom in Changing Times

God never changes, but human culture certainly does. Thus, there's no guarantee that the things that may have worked for the Apostle Paul in the first century or even Billy Graham in the 20th will work for us in the 21st century.

In this section, we will take a look at six major issues through essays that are both timeless and timely. Although not all of these essays deal explicitly with the subject of discipleship, they all wrestle with complex issues that pose important challenges to both individual believers and the worldwide body of Christ as we seek to live out God's call on our lives in the midst of changing and seemingly chaotic times.

Postmodernism: A New Mars Hill

Although there have been many continuities in the ways discipleship has happened during the first 20 centuries of the Christian era, many thinkers believe discipleship will change during the 21st century.

Ravi Zacharias, an acclaimed author and international speaker, addressed some of these changes during a talk he gave at the International Consultation on Discipleship entitled "Discipleship in a Millennium Culture: The Challenge of Postmodernity and Religious Pluralism."

▶ As a Christian I am involved in defending the Christian faith. And I can say that the task of evangelism and the task of discipleship are daunting in this postmodern, pluralist culture.

Malcolm Muggeridge was right when he said that all new news is old news happening to new people. We may think that we are up against an enormous task unprecedented in the history of cultures, but that is just not so.

Look at the cradle within which the gospel came, and look at the worldviews that were in collision then. Look at how it was that a man by the name of the Apostle Paul was born a Hebrew and raised a citizen of Rome. We can begin to see how important it was for him to try to communicate in that age and at that time. If there is any difference between that time and our own, I believe it is this. While the

The Never Changing Good News

The gospel of Jesus Christ has gone forth in every era with power to convert human hearts. Today that gospel is the answer to the longing of the postmodern generation. Our task as Christ's disciples is to embody and articulate the never-changing good news of available salvation in a manner that the emerging generation can understand. Only then we become the vehicles of the Holy Spirit in bringing them to experience the same life-changing encounter with the triune God from whom our entire lives derive their meaning. [1]

—Stanley J. Grenz

231

heart of humanity has not changed, and challenges to the gospel have always been there, the fact is, with the communication capacities we now have, the power to influence and mold and shape a whole generation has much greater possibilities now than ever before in history.

Bishop John Reed told a humorous story that well captures, at least for me, something of the postmodern mindset. There were two foreign sailors who had arrived by boat in England. Their first night ashore, they went into a bar and drank themselves silly. At the end of that long evening of drinking they walked out of the bar and were rather unsteady on their feet. Looking into a dense London fog, they were unable to find their way, and they were staggering around in a miserable condition.

Then they saw a gentleman coming into the bar. Unknown to them, he was a highly decorated British naval officer. One of the sailors approached him and said, "Say, you bloke, can you tell us where we are?" And the officer, rather offended by this insulting way of being addressed, looked at them and said, "Do you men know who I am?" At which point, one sailor looked at the other and said, "We are really in a mess now. We don't know where we are, and he doesn't know who he is."

If ever there was a simple way to indicate what postmodernism is like, that little anecdote tells it. Along the path of measuring ourselves and progress, we really don't know where we are. There is no grade by which to measure progress anymore. And what is worse, we do not even know WHO we are in our essence and in the very core of our being. But the tragedy is not just so much that we, in the church of Jesus Christ, stand back and are unaware of this problem, but, that in many ways, this postmodern culture has subsumed us as well.

Living in a New Cultural Context. Dramatic changes have taken place in our world with which the church must contend. The first is that we are facing the popularization of the death of God, and its ramifications. Somehow, atheism has not only been a way of looking at things, it has also become a driving ideology that is undergirding even the empirical sciences. Here is how one scientist boldly asserted his fear of religion:

"I don't mean to refer to the entirely reasonable hostility toward certain established religions and religious institutions in virtue of their objectionable moral doctrines, social fallacies, and political influence. Nor am I referring to the association of many religious beliefs, with their superstition and the acceptance of evident empirical falsehoods.

"I am talking about something much deeper. Namely, the fear of religion itself. I speak from experience, being strongly subjected to this fear myself. I want atheism to be true and am made uneasy by the fact that some of the most intelligent and well-informed people I know are religious believers. It isn't just that I don't believe in God, and naturally hope that I'm right in my belief; it's that I hope there is no God. I don't want there to be a God, and I don't want the universe to be like that."

Now a whole generation of young people is openly exposed to this kind of hostile, ideological, antagonistic thinking. As a result of this, there is a desensitization that takes place.

Secondly, there's a gathering storm of religious pluralism that has disoriented Western culture. What I mean by that is very simply this. You can go to virtually any campus today in many parts of the globe and give a talk openly on Hinduism, or Buddhism or Zoroastrianism, or Confucianism, or Islam. But as soon as you present a talk on the claims of Jesus Christ you are bound to run into some kind of open castigation or censorship. The Christian faith bears the brunt of that attack.

There are many universities where somebody raises the question, "How can the Christian faith claim exclusivity in a pluralistic world?" But every major religion I know has exclusivity at its core. *Every* major religion. In fact Buddhism was born rejecting two or three of the cardinal doctrines of Hinduism, including the authority of the Vedas. And it is so intriguing that a cultural mood has emerged where mysticism, spirituality of certain strands and stripes, is readily accepted and even propagated. But somehow the Christian faith is marginalized as one of those that doesn't fit in a rather accommodating and tolerant culture.

People often raise the question, "How can the Christian faith claim exclusivity in a pluralistic world?" But every major religion I know has exclusivity at its core.

—RAVI ZACHARIAS

233

A third factor is the power to inform through the visual. How do we disciple a generation that listens with its eyes, and thinks with its feelings? That is a challenge we all must face.

These changes in our cultural context must cause us to reexamine the ways we present the content of our faith.

In the 21st century, we will need a gospel that is not merely heard but is also seen. Not long ago I did an open forum for three nights at the University of Iowa. One night I was on my feet for three hours. There were over a thousand people, faculty and students, listening to a defense of the Christian faith. It was wonderful.

As we got into our car the next morning with the gentleman who had organized the whole thing, he said, "Ravi, do you want to know what my neighbor said about last night?" Then he told me this story:

"She's a medical doctor, a skeptic who would never go into a church and resists all of our beliefs. She agreed to come because of the setting and what you were going to talk about. As my wife was driving her back, this highly intelligent women was asked 'What did you think of the evening?' And there was silence before at last she said, 'Very, very compelling. I wonder what he is like in his private life.'"

And every time I repeat that I cannot resist the surge of a tear in the eye, because she's right. She has a right to raise that question. And it's a scary concept for those of us who are in ministry. People wonder what we are like in our private lives. But unless that life is also seen in this generation, it'll become nothing more than just one of the other ideas present in a hypocritical culture.

Our Faith Must Be Felt. Christianity is a message that must not only be argued, but also be felt. You see, there's a place and there are events happening in our culture that make us incredibly lonely people. And so many things are happening around us that we are not able to cope with the alienation that is so endemic.

I'm years away from my teenage years, but I understand something because I came to know Christ on a bed of suicide when I was seventeen, in the city of New Delhi. I understand what alienation and fragmentation may mean to a certain degree. But what I'm trying to put in my mind is this. We are living in a time when people desperately want to belong and do not know how. And so they cling to even symbols that will intimate their desperate longing to be touched, and to be felt, and to be embraced. This is a generation that will tell you in symbols how much it longs to belong.

―――――――

We are living in a time when people desperately want to belong and do not know how. And so they cling to even symbols that will intimate their desperate longing to be touched, and to be felt, and to be embraced.

―⮞RAVI ZACHARIAS

―――――――

One day my son didn't come home immediately after school. He phoned us and said he would be late, but he didn't want to tell us where he was going. Finally my wife got it out of him. He said, "I'm going to the shopping center. I want to get a necklace, put it around my neck, with the number 13 on it." And it suddenly struck us why. This was a week after the shootings at Columbine High School in Colorado, where 13 people had been killed. And our son Nathan wanted to remind himself that 13 people lost their lives in this carnage. He was willing to hold on to a symbol to tell us how the young community really thinks.

In addition, ours is a message that must not only rescue the ends, but must also rescue the means. Of all the casualties of this time, I am saddened about the casualty of language—what Jacques Ellul would have called the humiliation of the word. I've heard people say that a picture is better than a thousand words. I would like to challenge that. Sometimes a word is better than a thousand pictures.

Think of how Jesus turned the water into wine. I've seen many, many pictorial representations of it. None of them comes even close to Alexander Pope's description of it in one line. He said "The conscious water saw its master and blushed." You see, in the beginning was not video. In the beginning was the Word, and the Word became flesh and dwelt among us full of grace and truth. Yes, He's a God of beauty. A God who gives us the glory of sight and the model of imagination. But truth is distinctly a property of propositions. And He gave to us His Word that conforms to reality and He sent us His Son to show us what reality looks like embodied, when it represents the character of God.

Somehow the Word is going to have to be rescued in our proclamation and in our instruction so that young minds and imaginations will be stirred. And while the pictures may supplement the Word, while the music may take us to heights of splendor and gloriously lift us there, it is the truth of the Word that will dig deeply into our hearts. As Jesus said, "If you hold on to My teaching, you are My disciples, then you shall know the truth and the truth shall set you free."

By understanding our changing cultural context and the ways we must rethink how we present the content of the gospel, we will come to a fresh understanding of the goal of disciple-making.

The Book of Daniel shows us how Daniel was living in a culture that sought to brainwash him, that sought to give him all the literature and the culture of the Babylonians, all the comforts of palatial surroundings. He could have enjoyed a tremendous future at the behest of Nebuchadnezzar. He could have had all that Babylon in its splendor afforded. All of this was within reach because he was one of those choice young men that the Babylonian leadership prized.

But Daniel knew early that if he was going to make a difference for God, after whom he'd been named, he would have to draw his lines and be a good disciple. The goal we have is to train disciples like this who will draw the lines in these places. Where are those lines drawn? When you understand the culture you will understand better where the lines need to be drawn.

I spoke to a doctor friend once who told me he was terribly afraid. In a valiant effort to save the life of a woman in his operating room, he nicked his finger and exposed himself to her blood. Later he found out she was HIV-positive. I asked him, "Are you telling me one paper-thin cut is going to put you at risk to contract something as deadly as that?" He said, "You better believe it."

If a paper-thin cut can take away our resistance physically, think of the cuts in the souls of our young people early in life. What immunity within them is being broken down? Our goal in training disciples is to produce a disciple who will draw the lines in the right places. 2 ◄

Living Out Timeless Truths in a Changing World

F ew aspects of the Christian culture are more idealized but less understood than discipleship. But what is true discipleship? Here, Jerry Harvill seeks to provide a fresh and accurate biblical definition that exposes the full weight of its mandate:

▶ The road to discipleship is lined with hazards. The better we understand these pitfalls the more likely we will be to navigate safely past them.

The first roadblock to true discipleship is the virtually unanimous respect with which men speak of Jesus. Even when it was fashionable to proclaim the death of God, it was also in vogue to acclaim the life of Christ.

This aesthetic admiration is not an asset precisely because in an environment of universal celebration there is no longer anything distinctive or perilous in praising Him. Vague admiration dulls His sword, blunting the original outrage of His mission and inoculating us against the sting of His demands. We substitute homage for obedience. We give Him praise instead of surrender.

Vague admiration of Christ dulls His sword, blunting the original outrage of His mission and inoculating us against the sting of His demands. We substitute homage for obedience. We give Him praise instead of surrender.

~JERRY HARVILL

The second major barrier to contemporary discipleship is the anti-authority posture of our times. The very idea of obeying commands raises hackles today. Modern man assumes that freedom is a supreme value and that assertions of authority destroy freedom.

Rather than submitting to others, people today look to self as the highest authority. The watchwords of the modern cult of self are self-knowledge, self-esteem, and self-actualization. The philosophy is

Becoming Like Jesus

One of the revolutionary truths about the Christian life is that we can be like Jesus in a way that no other disciples can be like their master. In fact, becoming like Jesus is the overarching goal of the entire Christian life. The Apostle Paul declares, "And we, who with unveiled faces all reflect the Lord's glory, are being transformed into his likeness with ever-increasing glory" (2 Corinthians 3:18). This transformation is a process that begins now and is concluded in eternal life.

Do we really believe this transformation is possible? It sounds too good to be true. Or too impossible. Isn't becoming like Jesus reserved for pastors or missionaries and the like? Many of us labor under misconceptions that keep us from entering the life that leads to spiritual abundance, freedom, and change. [3]

—Michael J. Wilkins

self-assertion, and the goal is self-determination. The god Me is intolerant of old-fashioned virtues such as discipline and self-denial.

The third barrier to discipleship is the wide gulf of cultural change separating 1st-century Galilee from 20th-century America. The daily problems facing citizens of New York or Nashville or San Francisco appear wholly different from those of ancient Capernaum. What concerns do a 747 pilot and a Tiberias fisherman share? What pressures are common to modern life in the "fast lane" and the lifestyle of Hebrew shepherds?

These changes affect more than externals. The meaning of words, of ideas, and of actions has shifted decisively so that critical adjustments must be made in our thinking before biblical terms and concepts can be seen to relate to our modern experience. Many are so burdened by the rigors of those adjustments that they abandon the whole project. Alan Richardson, writing in the *Cambridge History of the Bible,* reports a "gradual decay of the ordinary Christian's sense that he can read the Bible for himself without an interpreter and discover its unambiguous meaning." He argues that the Bible has come to be regarded as a book for experts only, requiring elaborate training in linguistic and historical disciplines before it can even be understood.

The net result of the cultural alienation which many now feel from the language and the priorities of the biblical world is the widespread abortion of discipleship. It is seen as an antique, a fossil of a bygone age, no longer functional in an era of microprocessors and artificial intelligence.

The fourth barrier to authentic contemporary discipleship is the distorted role models visible today. For many moderns the institutional church is a liability instead of an asset to discipleship. Francis Schaeffer warned, "I am convinced that in the 20th century people all over the world will not listen if we have the right doctrine, the right policy, but are not exhibiting community." Albert Camus, the French existentialist, saw the role of the Church in the modern world more clearly than some theologians. He wrote, "What the world expects of Christians is that Christians should speak out, loud and clear . . . in such a way that never a doubt, never the slightest doubt, could arise in the heart of the simplest man."

I am convinced that in the twentieth century people all over the world will not listen if we have the right doctrine, the right policy, but are not exhibiting community.

≈FRANCIS A. SCHAEFFER

Instead the Church has skeletons in her closet—the skeleton of disunity, the skeleton of hypocrisy, the skeleton of suburban isolation, the skeleton of guilty silence on world issues while headlining minor concerns.

Together these four deterrents pose formidable obstacles to authentic discipleship. We must remember that we, too, are products of our times; we, too, must negotiate these barriers. None is exempt. In fact, self-deception may well be the greatest hazard of all.

The Divine Pattern for Discipleship. What we need today perhaps more than ever before is an authentic, definitive pattern to follow. We need a flesh-and-blood demonstration of exactly what discipleship is all about.

That is precisely what we have in the Incarnation of the Son of God. His coming is the pattern for our going; his mission the definition of our own. "Peace be with you! As the Father has sent me, I am sending you" (John 20:21). "As you sent me into the world, I have sent them into the world. For them I sanctify myself, that they too may be truly sanctified" (John 17:18-19).

Understanding discipleship is in fact understanding the mind of Christ, and practicing discipleship is following the footprints of Jesus. We are on the right track, therefore, when we define the demands of discipleship not in terms of what we think or feel but in terms of what the Cross meant to Jesus. In Him is God's pattern for discipleship. In Him is the start and the finish of our faith (Hebrews 12:2).

Philippians 2:5-11 sets forth the crux interpretum for the biblical doctrine of Christ's Incarnation. Here, in what may echo an early Church hymn, Paul highlights Christ's pre-existence in heaven (Philippians 2:6), His humiliation on earth (vv. 7-8), and His subsequent enthronement in heaven (vv. 9-11). But what is especially remarkable about this passage is the insight it provides concerning the values and motives of Christ Himself.

Understanding discipleship is in fact understanding the mind of Christ, and practicing discipleship is following the footprints of Jesus. We are on the right track, therefore, when we define the demands of discipleship not in terms of what we think or feel but in terms of what the Cross meant to Jesus. In Him is God's pattern for discipleship.

—JERRY HARVILL

The second chapter of Philippians reveals four dimensions to Jesus' life as Suffering Servant, four rungs in the ladder of His descent into "the lower parts of the earth." It traces the pattern of Jesus' servanthood in the form of God (v. 6), in the form of servant-man (v. 7), under sentence of death (v. 8), death by crucifixion (v. 8). As Motyer sums it up, "He who from all eternity possessed and displayed the divine attributes ended his incredible career of self-abasement under the curse of God."

These four dimensions reflect four essential principles that are not only the rationale of the life of Christ, they are also the indispensable ingredients of discipleship. Here is the divine model for self-renunciation, self-adaptation, self-surrender, and self-sacrifice. Here is divine demonstration of the demands of discipleship.

Self-renunciation. It can never be said that Christ requires of His followers what He did not give; that His demands exceed His own personal investments. In Paul's fourfold summary of what the Incarnation meant for Jesus we see God taking His own medicine; we see the unique Son refusing preferential treatment in order that through His experience of suffering He could be equipped to represent us in heaven (Hebrews 5:8-10). God Himself has shown us the way.

The text says literally, "Himself he emptied" (Philippians 2:7). We should not see the idea of emptying in terms of discarding something. Rather, I suggest we see this passage in the light of Isaiah 53:12, "he poured out his life unto death," and that we understand the "emptying" in the sense of total personal commitment and total self-denial.

Furthermore, it is vital to note the emphatic word order in this verse. The word order of the original Greek points to His humiliation as voluntary, self-imposed. No one took anything away from Christ; what He renounced He renounced of His own will.

With this verse we begin to see the mind of Christ on discipleship. Everything touching self-advantage or self-display must go. There is no limit to self-humbling as long as anything remains that may be poured out. In His self-emptying, Jesus shows us that the most divine act is to give.

How shockingly Christ's act contrasts with contemporary demands for personal rights. The only person in the world who had the right to demand His rights, waived them! His attitude reveals the self-seeking hidden within our exclamations, "I don't have to put up with this!" How many conflicts and church splits would be prevented if our discipleship contained this voluntary renunciation of personal rights? Could we hold grudges and at the same time "put up with anything" for the sake of the gospel? (1 Corinthians 9:12) Jesus poured it all out, emptying Himself. Let us remember His words: "No servant is greater than his master . . ." (John 15:20).

Self-adaptation. Jesus thoroughly identified Himself with the human situation. He was not an angel pretending to be man; He was truly one of us in both essence and detail.

It was not upper echelon humanity that the Son of God incarnated, but slave-man. A play on the word *morphe*, "nature," accents this point as we see Him who was "in very nature God" (Philippians 2:6) now "taking the very nature of a servant" (v. 7). Jesus paid the full price in adaptation in order to be our Elder Brother (cf. Hebrews 2:14-18).

Here is the strongest possible mandate for disciples who are servants. Here is the strongest possible imperative for a Servant-Church. When our churches are content to pamper themselves and to merely "hold services," we have forgotten our calling and we are lying against the divine model we claim to love and follow. The "mind of Christ," which we are to imitate (Philippians 2:5), demands that we roll up the sleeves of our faith and get dirty in the work of redeeming men. No smug suburban isolation; no concern by proxy.

Here is a shattering call for the middle-class, status-conscious American Church to "empty" herself in world service and to "be

241

willing to associate with people of low position" (Romans 12:16).

Self-surrender. The Philippians passage goes further by affirming explicitly Jesus' humiliation: "he humbled himself" (Philippians 2:8). The term *tapeinophrosune,* "lowliness," was transformed by the Cross and redefined by the Gospel. From ignoble, scurrilous, secular connotations it became one of the great words of the Christian vocabulary under the influence of Christ's radical new policy of greatness. Jesus taught that to be great in His kingdom is to be servant of all. In His service the way up is down.

Tapeinophrosune describes a condition of unself-consciousness in which one has a humble opinion of oneself. It is the opposite of egotism, self-seeking, and assertiveness. One of the definitive features of Jesus' personality was humility (Matthew 11:29). It is not surprising that His supreme act of love and service is described as lowly surrender.

More specifically, the term means in this context a willingness to seek others' advantage instead of our own. Paul exhorted, "Do nothing out of selfish ambition or vain conceit, but in humility *(tapeinophrosune)* consider others better than yourselves" (Philippians 2:3). The whole Christological section that follows is but a practical application of the Incarnation to enforce this lesson of humility in Christian discipleship. The intended message is plain: your attitude toward serving others should be the same as that of Christ Jesus; model your thoughts on His.

How many of us are more likely to defend our own interests than to humbly defer to others? Yet one of the marks of the Spirit-filled man (or church, or organization) is not self-assertion, but submission. H.A.A. Kennedy once observed, "It is a strange phenomenon in religious history that intense earnestness so frequently breeds a spirit mingled of censoriousness and conceit." May the Lord hasten the day when our earnestness is matched by our humility.

Self-sacrifice. Philippians 2:8 goes beyond saying that the Son of God surrendered to the extent of dying. At its climax, it asserts the most awful of deaths as His sacrifice: "Even death on a cross!" The type of construction Paul uses here stresses the kind or character of Jesus' death: death-by-crucifixion. A.T. Robertson says, "Here is the bottom rung in the ladder from the throne of God. Jesus came all the way down to the most despised death of all, a condemned criminal on the accursed cross."

In our consumer culture indulgence, not sacrifice, is the norm. Sadly, instead of challenging this spirit of our age in the name of Christ I see the Church smuggling consumerism into discipleship under religious labels! Christianity and Madison Avenue's "good life" become hopelessly confused. In our churches bigger is equated with better, motion with growth, and success with celebrity. We pamper and indulge ourselves while we preach about sacrifice and praise self-denial.

Surely, for the Christian to see his Elder Brother pour-
ing Himself out in total sacrifice is to learn not only
what each disciple ought to do, but
also to learn why he must do it.

JERRY HARVILL

The Incarnation of the Son of God is the divine model for true discipleship. To have the "mind of Christ" is to know the rigors of demanding servanthood. To follow Him is to practice self-renunciation, self-adaptation, self-surrender, and self-sacrifice. Surely, for the Christian to see his Elder Brother pouring Himself out in total sacrifice is to learn not only what each disciple ought to do, but also to learn why he must do it.

Putting On the Mind of Christ. Here, then, is both the problem and the solution. The flesh that frustrates our desires to serve the Lord according to "the attitude of our minds" can be effectively overcome only by putting on "the new self, created to be like God in true righteousness and holiness" (Ephesians 4:23). Both the model and the means for the demands of discipleship are found in the mind of Christ.

By modeling our thoughts on His we can overcome the threats of aesthetic admiration, aversion to authority, cultural changes, and defective models. By adopting as our goal the mind of Christ we will know that His loving, coming, and serving is the mandate for our loving, going, and serving. In Him we will find the pattern and the power for a life of self-renunciation, self-adaptation, self-surrender, and self-sacrifice. [5] ◀

The Challenge of Community

Portions of the Book of Acts read like a manual to Christian community building. "When the day of Pentecost came, they were all together in one place," reads the opening verse of chapter 2. Later, we read: "All the believers were one in heart and mind. No one claimed that any of his possessions was his own, but they shared everything they had" (4:32).

Today, however, such committed Christian community is rare. Here, Dave and Neta Jackson, who have lived in Christian community for many years, explore the reasons why:

▶ Most men in our church eagerly anticipate the annual men's retreat. Memories of getting lost on dark country roads late Friday night or coming home with muscles stiff from too much football are all forgotten (or glorified) when the leaves turn and plans for another weekend circulate. But Rick was new to our church, and he wasn't "ready for anything quite that intimate."

How could anyone be afraid of a fun-filled men's retreat—for just one weekend? You might guess that Rick was a new Christian or possibly not even a believer. Not so.

Rick had been a prominent leader in his former church, but he and his family had been burned by some unpleasant experiences as his church attempted to practice Christian community. Rick was still recovering—holding other Christians at a distance while he tried to rebuild trust in the Body of Christ as he knew it should exist.

Rick's response represents just one of several barriers to developing genuine, biblical community in the church today. Most people long for Christian community, but for one reason or another it remains an ideal that teases them from just beyond their reach. Sometimes the barrier is internal—unhealed attitudes and experiences from the past. Sometimes the church creates unnecessary barriers by its own life or structure.

What are those barriers, and how can they be overcome?

Fear of Intimacy. An eight-week discipleship class was coming to an end, and the participants were considering whether to continue as a small group designed for sharing and community building within the church.

"I'd like to be in the group," Larry confessed. "But I don't know if you would like me if you really knew me."

Ethel had another concern: "I want to be assured that what I say to the group will never leave this room."

And Phyllis said, "I've lived through the era of sensitivity training and guilt trips, and I'm not sure I want to be manipulated by people who think they know my motives well enough to judge everything I do or say."

Three fears of intimacy: the fear of rejection, the fear of broken confidences, and the fear of manipulation. They are all valid in the sense that bad things can happen when we make ourselves vulnerable to others. But they shouldn't happen. So how can we guard against them and help people like Larry, Ethel, and Phyllis overcome their fears?

1. *Come alongside . . . slowly.* Larry may not be able to allow the group to know him yet, but what about one person? He might take a risk with one person who has special affinity for him. If that person accepted him and acted as his support and advocate, Larry might be able to open himself to others. But the process must not be rushed.

2. *Avoid gossip.* If group members talk about other people without their permission—even under the guise of praying for them—then the fearful newcomer can be sure of getting stabbed by gossip, too.

There is only one limit to confidentiality—when group leaders need to seek spiritual or professional help with overwhelming situations. When someone wants to swear us to secrecy before confiding in us, our policy is to say: "Then you'd better not tell us. If you don't trust us enough to allow us to get help if we need it, then you don't trust us." But that is different from maintaining basic confidentiality, which everyone deserves.

3. *Suspend judgment.* There is an appropriate role for church authority, as we'll see in the next section. But people feel manipulated if they are not heard and if their positions are "typed" without serious consideration. If a person is labeled defensive, racist, selfish, chauvinist, ignorant, not open, or anything else before his ideas are really heard and before anyone considers whether he has reason to respond as he does, he probably will withdraw.

Scars from Excessive Authority. Many evangelistic ministries that began in the 1970s to reach countercultural youth developed genuine aspects of Christian community—the sharing and caring, the discipleship and interdependence modeled after the New Testament church. These ministries ranged in size from independent house-church fellowships to sprawling, nationwide outreach ministries. Unfortunately, to confront the thoroughly pagan background of their new converts effectively, many of these groups evolved a highly structured, somewhat austere lifestyle under strong, authoritarian leadership.

Thousands of today's baby boomers had their first authentic encounter with Jesus through those ministries, an encounter for which they and we should praise God. But now the church must overcome their fear that excessive authority will dominate them again if they become involved in the close life of a small group or any other expression of Christian community.

Joe Peterson, the caretaker of the property of Shiloh Youth Revival, a Jesus-people ministry based in Oregon, estimates that, before its breakup in 1978, more than 30,000 young people passed through this ministry alone. Peterson's recent research among Shiloh "alumni" shows that most considered their experience "the best of times and the worst of times." They remain cautious about groups that use the language of "community."

Bob and Sally are one couple from Shiloh who ended up in our church. They love the Lord deeply, but in spite of their rich background, they were not eager for community in our setting. They feared commitment and were even more apprehensive about small-group intimacy.

The so-called shepherding movement of the 1970s and early 1980s also left many people afraid of community. Bill is an example. As a new believer, he was told by his small group that he needed to "get under the authority" of a mature Christian man. So he began to meet weekly with Ted, five years his senior.

When Ted learned that Bill was divorced, had remarried, and had a new baby, he immediately pronounced the second marriage an adulterous relationship and told Bill to end it. Bewildered and angry, Bill stopped meeting with Ted, dropped out of the small group, and even stopped attending church.

Besides the thousands who have been personally burned by excessive authority, there are many more whose opinions of community have been influenced adversely by what they've heard it's like and who therefore are afraid of it. How can we overcome this fear? And how can we keep from repeating the mistakes of others?

We need to distinguish legitimate from excessive church authority and take care never to cross the line separating the two. Then we will be less likely to hurt others by imposing our standards under the guise of God's. If we make this distinction and our commitment to uphold it clear, those who have been burned in the past, or who have heard of others getting burned, will be reassured by the boundaries within which we intend to operate.

We need to distinguish legitimate from excessive church authority and take care never to cross the line separating the two. Then we will be less likely to hurt others by imposing our standards under the guise of God's.

☙DAVE AND NETA JACKSON

This difference can be pictured as a spectrum on which God's will and the role of church authority are aligned. True, the church must speak out in many matters concerning the life and practice of its members. But it must also preserve God-given liberty and personal differences. When these understandings are taught and practiced, we are less likely to abuse others, and the fearful are reassured that they will not be violated.

Unhealthy Individualism. In their book, *Habits of the Heart,* Robert Bellah and his colleagues wrote, "Individualism lies at the very core of American culture. . . . We believe in the dignity, indeed the sacredness, of the individual. Anything that would violate our right to think for ourselves, judge for ourselves, make our own decisions, live our lives as we see fit, is not only morally wrong, it is sacrilegious."

This "deepest identity," as Bellah calls it—without suggesting that it should be abandoned—influences how we experience community in our churches. As much as we want community, we shy away whenever it infringes on our autonomy.

It's hard, of course, to face the potential of disapproval without becoming defensive or going on the offensive (which frequently is also a defense). Christian community shouldn't stifle independent thinking, initiatives, language, styles, etc., but too often it appears to do so. Too often everyone in the church begins thinking, acting, sounding, and looking alike.

This conformity happens because only the exceptionally mature can be really close to others while espousing divergent—though biblically legitimate—differences. Consider questions of Christian activism, family finances, family size, child rearing styles, home or private or public school, the priority of various ministries, simple living, war and peace. Strongly held differences in such areas cause most of us to feel acutely uncomfortable when we're close.

The community of faith performs an important function for its members by building them up through corporate encouragement of right behavior. It should challenge sin (but never morally neutral personal preferences) through—let's face it—group disapproval.

How can we encourage acceptance of people with different (though not unbiblical) ideas and lifestyles? How can we reassure each other that differences are valued?

1. *Emphasize the diversity in the Body of Christ.* Teachings from 1 Corinthians 12:12-31 remind us that "The eye cannot say to the hand, 'I don't need you!'" A spiritual gifts discernment process might be of help in this. C. Peter Wagner's book *Your Spiritual Gifts Can Help Your Church Grow* is one of several sources for understanding and deliberately identifying each person's spiritual gifts. Studying it helped our church members appreciate one another.

2. *Allow plenty of latitude for disagreement over issues not clearly decided by Scripture (Romans 12).* In many instances, political preferences, educational choices, decisions about standard of living, and so on, must be left to the conscience of the believer once the community has given counsel based on careful evaluation of biblical principles and surrounding circumstances.

Exhausting Busyness. Busyness is a barrier both inside and outside the community. Jean tells how the consuming pace within her Christian community made her inaccessible to a neighbor:

"Alice had come over to chat. I felt pressed with all the things I had to do that day, but I took time out to sit in the backyard.

"Then the phone rang, and I went in. It was a call from Gail about a committee meeting. I set out lunch for the kids as I cradled the receiver and listened to her 'one quick question.' The kids arrived home squabbling, so I promised to call Gail back. As I got the kids settled, I realized that I had not yet finished my shopping list for the Friday night community supper, and I had to get the stuff that afternoon because all the next day I was to substitute at the community's daycare center.

"I finished the list about twenty minutes later just as Alice walked in and said, 'Guess I'll be going now.'

"I couldn't believe it; I had totally forgotten her!"

An excessive pace of life within the community is not the only barrier to community. The pace of life outside it can be equally distracting.

In our city most families have to work 60 or more hours per week to survive financially. This means some combination of two jobs or an extensive amount of overtime by one parent. Baby boomers are reaching the age of greatest responsibility to provide for teenagers, college education, aging parents, and a mortgage. School activities, civic involvement, and career advancement consume hours.

But building community demands time, too. From where will it come?

Usually there must be flexibility on both ends. Too many churches pay no attention to this problem, scheduling ministries and activities on every night of the week. Dennis Guernsey, in *A New Design for Family Ministry,* suggests coordinating events to fall on no more than one or two nights of the week. This means people can't be involved in more than one or two ministries, but that ought to be enough.

Other churches have tried to ensure that more of their events foster community. No longer are there just Bible study classes, there are fellowship groups that study the Bible together. Ministry teams become small sharing-and-caring groups for their members. While this doesn't always work, it is a step in the right direction.

On the other end, some families need help managing their finances so that more overtime isn't the only means to a balanced budget.

Inward Focus. When community begins to function, this last barrier sometimes arises and turns others away.

Most efforts to build Christian community go through a cycle of intense internal focus. It is the ultimate common goal, and it does develop a certain kind of community, even a strong community. But it can be a very selfish goal. And in the long run, God cannot bless selfishness. Unfortunately, some groups never emerge from their internal focus and either dissolve or calcify into sociological relics.

Three steps can help a group emerge from or avoid too much internal focus:

1. *Become willing for the group to die.* Thinking the group must go on forever is probably the hardest attitudinal barrier to surmount. A group enchanted by its experiences together rightly values them and appreciates their biblical base. But what Jesus said of the individual is equally true of the community: "Whoever wants to save his life will lose it, but whoever loses his life for me will find it" (Matthew 16:25). In the end, Christian community is a gift that cannot be produced or preserved by our own efforts.

2. *Conduct evangelism only on behalf of Jesus Christ and His Church, not for the purpose of recruiting members into your specific community.* No matter how much you may want the experience of community for others, their relationship with Jesus is far more important. He may then guide them to the gift of community, but if you campaign on its behalf, you will risk becoming sectarian. And sectarianism is one of the greatest temptations whenever a church develops Christian community. Why? Because community is so spiritually rewarding that the members begin to think that nothing else could be worthy or right.

No matter how much you may want the experience of community for others, their relationship with Jesus is far more important. He may then guide them to the gift of community, but if you campaign on its behalf, you will risk becoming sectarian.

—DAVE AND NETA JACKSON

---

3. Deliberately develop outreach and service ministries. The community can expend its corporate strength and help itself focus outward by supporting a wide variety of "works of the kingdom": crisis pregnancy centers, family and personal counseling, shelters for the homeless, low-cost housing for the poor, care of refugees, drug rehabilitation, daycare centers for children or the elderly, and employment for people coming out of prison. Ministries that are service-oriented and have a low potential for recruiting new members will do the most to combat too much inward focus.

The community that doesn't graduate from its inward focus will lose its image of Christ and its members will become brittle and bitter.

Christian community, like all significant relationships, requires major investments and care. In most cases, mistakes will be made, and forgiveness needs to be liberally extended. In the end we must trust in the Lord. Then we "will be like a tree planted by the water that sends out its roots by the stream. It does not fear when heat comes; its leaves are always green. It has no worries in a year of drought and never fails to bear fruit" (Jeremiah 17:8).7 ◄

Confusing Discipleship with Citizenship

Throughout the world today, one can see a disturbing pattern which reasserts itself in many countries and cultures.

The pattern is this: through complex processes such as modernization, urbanization, and secularization, centuries-old cultural norms are challenged.

Then, as a response to these disruptive changes, fundamentalist movements based on Christian, Jewish, or Muslim faith systems have risen up in an effort hold back what many believe to be a destructive tidal wave of change.

Sociologist and Christian writer Tony Campolo has watched such a pattern emerge in his country—the United States. But his comments can be applied to similar culture battles all around the globe:

continued on the
next page

Winsome Ambassadors for Christ

We are ambassadors of Christ, and like any ambassador, we may at any moment be summoned home to give an account of what is going on at our post. Though looming judgment ought not terrify us, since we are saved by grace rather than works, it should change us. It should make us ask with each new morning, "Lord, knowing that today may be the last day of my life—perhaps even of the world—how shall I make things more suitable for your coming?" It should inspire us to continue in well-doing, even in the face of opposition, because, for all we know, the Lord of goodness may be on hand in five minutes. Zeal for the coming Christ and love for people go together. Our practice of public goodness aims not to put people down but to win people to him before it is too late. What our culture needs these days is a vibrant, plausible, winsome Christianity. Intellectual and philosophical arguments are important and good, but they

▶ Christianity is clearly at risk in America today. But the ACLU and the PC police are not our greatest enemies. Today, as always, the greatest danger to those who would follow Jesus is not overt persecution by society, but subtle seduction by its values. Compromise with the culture has always had more potential for annihilating true faith than has intellectual skepticism or the threat of being thrown to the lions.

Before we attempt to "clean up" America, before we try to remove the log from the eyes of humanists, feminists, atheists, and abortionists, we would do well to engage in a personal eye exam. Are our own lifestyles biblically pure? Let me suggest three areas that beg for evaluation.

Materialism. American Christians today have been lulled into an attractive, comfortable, and emotionally gratifying form of slavery. The socially prescribed affluent, middle-class lifestyle has become so normative in our churches that we discern little conflict between it and the Christian lifestyle prescribed in the New Testament.

Think about it. American society will survive only if its people adopt a lifestyle that makes buying things we do not need our ultimate reason for existence. If we do not buy what we do not need, we will not buy enough to support the industrial production that forms the economic backbone of our society. If industries close down, unemployment will soar, and America, as we know it, will come to an end.

But as we get sucked into the buying mania that is required of us if we are to be "good citizens," we ought to become aware of the biblical warnings against allowing our lives to revolve around buying things (Matthew 6:19-34). And we ought to remember that a certain rich young ruler was told that he had to choose between gaining eternal life or having the possessions that money can buy (Mark 10).

Ironically, even our churches give us the message—spoken or unspoken—that radical sacrifice for the poor and disengagement from the culturally prescribed lifestyle are not really necessary for Christian discipleship. We have reduced being Christian to agreement with some doctrinal propositions and have ignored the call to radically sacrifice in the name of Christ for the poor and the oppressed.

The primary culprit in this seduction is the ingenious ads that come from the gang on Madison Avenue. They have been so effective in creating a hunger in us for things we do not need that their artificially created wants take on dimensions of ultimate good. We are so convinced that we have to have them that we are willing to sacrifice to get them, even if we have to neglect our families, sacrifice intimacy, and renege on our religious commitments. To satisfy real need takes time, but we have to give all our time to earning enough money to satisfy our artificially created wants. Consequently, the typical American father talks to his children about four and a half minutes a day. He talks to his wife about eleven and a half minutes a day. This is the result of being enslaved to our culture's values.

Political Power. Over the last few decades, we Christians also have become acquainted with the allurements of power. In the old days we looked on political involvement as something that was, at best, a necessary evil. We stayed away from the political process, and were convinced that those who used political power to effect social justice were in danger of being led away from their real calling, which was to win people to Christ.

Today's evangelicals have moved beyond that naïveté and have come to see the wisdom of Edward Burke's famous dictum, "All that is necessary for evil to triumph is for good people to do nothing." We have learned how to organize and to flex our voting muscle. And in the process we have been infected by a triumphalism that parades under the slogan "Take America Back for God!" We are increasingly convinced that we are God's chosen instruments for imposing biblical principles as the guidelines for the general population.

What got us started was the abortion issue. We decided that we had had enough from the "liberal political establishment," and we weren't going to take it any more.

Once we got rolling, we showed the old politicos that we weren't as dumb as they thought we were. In short order we learned all the techniques of the pros. We even learned how to manipulate with propaganda. We discovered we could sway elections and put into office candidates who espoused our political agenda. When we found that the media, which we believed held a liberal bias, was against us, we created an alternative information highway with radio and TV stations of our own. Soon we had our own "spin doctors" who were giving our own biased slant to the news.

cannot stand alone. They must come from lives of people who have evidently been changed for the better by the God they profess. Do we love people enough, we must ask, to showcase—by how we talk, how we do business, how we do politics, and how we treat people—something of the goodness, justice, loyalty, beauty, and love of our true home? Why does Christ get such bad press in our day—or why does he often get no press at all? Could it be, at least in part, because we are not the winsome ambassadors we should be? [8]

—*Charles D. Drew*

253

Our successes were amazing. There are many who would argue that we gained the power to significantly influence elections all the way up to the White House. And when we found the Oval Office occupied by someone who was not of our political stripe, we outdid ourselves in the art of vilification. We resorted to the worst "dirty tricks" of the profession. We readily broadcast innuendoes and rumors. And the President of the United States came to be seen by many as fair game for any unsubstantiated accusations we could muster up. We relished every bit of evil gossip about the President or the First Lady. Somewhere along the line we forgot the words of Scripture that read, "Finally, brethren, whatsoever things are true, whatsoever things are honest, whatsoever things are just, whatsoever things are pure, whatsoever things are lovely, whatsoever things are of good report; if there be any virtue, and if there be any praise, think on these things" (Philippians 4:8, KJV).

Having tasted the intoxicating effects of political power, we soon became addicted. In fighting the dragon, as one philosopher suggests, we have become the dragon. In our conflict with those we believed were twisting the truth and embracing "the low road" in politics, we have gradually become more and more like them. In order to fight the evils of the world, we have resorted to the ways of the world. And this may have been Satan's most subtle and successful way of seducing us.

People-pleasing Ministries. But strangely enough, we have most compromised with the world in the ways we promote our own ministries. It takes money to carry out new forms of evangelism. Religion, of necessity, we say, has become big business. Multi-million dollar budgets for Christian organizations have become normative.

What is even more significant and dangerous is that almost every Christian ministry I know about is operating right up to the edge of its financial resources. The loss of five or ten percent of its constituent support for a month or two would prove nothing short of disastrous.

All of this means that it is very difficult for ministries to be prophetic. Anything that offends even a small number of the financial supporters of a ministry can send shock waves from the top office of the organization down to the lowliest echelons. For ministry leaders, taking stands on controversial social issues has to be evaluated in terms of financial costs. "The Work of God" ends up being controlled by the opinions of those who give money, rather than being under the control of the Holy Spirit and Scripture. Thus we once again find ourselves following the ways of the world, almost unaware of what has happened.

---

*We must find ways of transcending what class con-
sciousness does to our thinking. We must somehow get
hold of "the pure and sincere milk of the Word," as
opposed to the diluted baby formula that has become
the diet prescribed by society. We must escape the
tendency to conform to society—even within
our most crucial spiritual disciplines.*

—TONY CAMPOLO

Standing Firm on Scripture. Paul once wrote, "We know in part, and we prophesy in part." But between now and the time in which "that which is perfect is come," we must try to break out of our culture's mindset and seek to discover "that good and perfect will of God." In short, we must find ways of transcending what class consciousness does to our thinking. We must somehow get hold of "the pure and sincere milk of the Word," as opposed to the diluted baby formula that has become the diet prescribed by society. We must escape the tendency to conform to society—even within our most crucial spiritual disciplines.

It seems to me that only a strong doctrine of the Holy Spirit offers us any hope of reading Scripture without being influenced by our culture. There has to be something of a miracle involved in true revelatory Bible reading. And the good news is that such miracles happen. As I read the Scriptures, more times than not, I am conscious of His Spirit's presence. There is revelation, and in it the Spirit applies what I read to my life. I sense I am "breaking out" of culturally controlled modes of interpretation, even as I sense the "breaking in" of God.

The direct reading of the Word of God, without the help of commentaries or interpreters' notes, becomes a special event for me.

Something that transcends the intellect occurs. The truth I receive not only is untainted by the culture, it gives me a detached perspective on the culture. There is a mystical quality to all of this. It is from this new perspective that I often discern how the culture has gained control over my spiritual life and what I must do to escape its iron grip. As I read the Bible, the Spirit often "bears witness with my spirit" in ways that the culture cannot control.

Finding Strength in the Body. The major problem with all of this is that, as in all mystical experiences, there is a tendency toward subjectivism. Private interpretations of Scripture, in which individuals claim to have received a word directly from God, are always dangerous. From such come heresies and cults.

That is why I take the traditions of the Church so seriously. The Church has been around for almost 2,000 years, and over the centuries its people have struggled to understand Scripture. The same Spirit has been at work in their lives that has been at work in mine. I read Scripture "in the Spirit"; consequently, I learn to be sensitive to this "great crowd of witnesses." When I get something out of Scripture that runs contrary to what the saints through the ages have gotten out of God's Word, I have to call my own reading into question. The tradition of the Church stands as a counter-cultural standard not only to what the world is about, but also against cultural influences that permeate my personal reading of the Bible.

But even when a counter-cultural reading of the Scripture under the power of the Holy Spirit takes place, and obedience by the reader follows, there is still a threatening difficulty. And that is how to keep from being sucked back into culturally prescribed ways of thinking and acting. It is extremely difficult to maintain the counter-cultural perspective that is essential for Christian living. This is especially true when we try to go it alone.

That is why a "support group" is so crucial. Each week I meet with three friends for the expressed purpose of revitalizing our commitment to Christ. We get together to remind each other that it's the world that is crazy and not the values we find in the Word of God.[9] ◄

Compassion for the Poor

J esus once said, "The poor you will always have with you." But His statement was not, as some suppose, intended to encourage believers to ignore their plight or the church to turn its back on its responsibility to help them.

The Parable of the Good Samaritan, after all, was more than a nice story. At its conclusion, Jesus commanded: "Go and do likewise" (see Luke 10:25-37).

Gordon Aeschliman, who has spent much of his adult life encouraging Christians to live lives of compassion, writes here about "God's Heart for the Poor":

▶ I was born in South Africa, and lived there as a missionary kid until my college years. That country has always been my emotional home.

In the mid 1980s, I attended a meeting in Washington, D.C., to listen to the U.S. government's position on South Africa. The policies emerging from our state department at that time were particularly harsh toward the blacks of South Africa. In fact, the policies clearly supported the bigoted laws of the apartheid government. The President's staff was committed to influencing clergy toward their view, and the day-long gala I attended at the state department headquarters was quite a show.

The particularly embarrassing part was their defense of racism in South Africa as the only reasonable policy that would keep violence at a minimum. I confronted the head of this government program because I knew he was a Christian. I asked how he could advance a policy that was so clearly against the well-being of millions of blacks in South Africa. His response, simple and direct, was, "Gordon, I am an ambassador of the government. I represent the government and speak on its behalf only, not mine."

Hmmm. A very sharp and clear response.

That meeting taught me something critical about my faith. It's this: I do not have the right to represent God apart from His character. No matter what my life's vocation may be, I am always under God's government. We might not usually use government language to indicate

257

The Spiritu-ally Poor

In our culture, we think being poor means you drive an old car, you can't afford life insurance, and you don't go out to eat very often. But what if being poor means that you have noth-ing? That you're reduced to beg-ging? That your only hope of keeping body and soul together is the generosity of someone else—someone who'll provide for you what you can't provide for yourself?

What if being spiritually poor means the same thing?

Could Jesus be saying that disci-pleship begins only when we understand just how spiritually desititute, just how God-dependent we really are? [10]

—Tim Woodroof

our submission to Christ, but we who have accepted the grace of Cal-vary into our lives now serve in the kingdom of God. We are, in fact, ambassadors of the heavenly kingdom. All of our speech and actions should reflect our submission to heaven's ways, just as those actions and words are to point others to the way of the kingdom.

A Kingdom for the Poor. When we explore the Bible's teach-ings about God's concern for the poor, we discover that we belong to a compassionate kingdom, one wide enough to take in all the lost, oppressed, haggard, hungry, homeless, and dispossessed.

The Bible gives us a picture of a God who is taken by the plight of the poor. The psalmist teaches us about this God. In Psalm 14:6 we hear: "You evildoers frustrate the plans of the poor, but the Lord is their refuge." And in Psalm 72:12-13: "He will deliver the needy who cry out, the afflicted who have no one to help. He will take pity on the weak and the needy and save the needy from death." Again, "He raises the poor from the dust and lifts the needy from the ash heap" (Psalm 113:7). It is the poor who usually live in the most des-olate of places—barren land, garbage dumps, and such. The psalmist was speaking to a very real situation in his day, and those words are absolutely relevant to the plight of today's poor.

The Prophet Isaiah contrasts Israel's religious life with what God considers a righteous life. In Isaiah 58 he describes their tithing, sac-rifices, keeping of the Sabbath, and such as the wrong kind of "fast." What God wants, says the prophet, is true fasting, demonstrated in these behaviors: "to loose the chains of injustice and untie the cords of the yoke, to set the oppressed free and break every yoke. Is it not to share your food with the hungry and to provide the poor wan-derer with shelter—when you see the naked, to clothe him, and not to turn away from your own flesh and blood?" (Isaiah 58:6-7) Isaiah continues, "If you spend yourselves in behalf of the hungry and sat-isfy the needs of the oppressed, then your light will rise in the dark-ness, and your night will become like the noonday."

This theme of caring for the poor as a good calling, appearing throughout Isaiah, is echoed by other prophets who were sent by God to call Israel's attention to a God who loves the poor. Amos teaches us about God's heart for the poor through his cautions to the people of Israel who had forsaken the needy. Israel became a wealthy nation after conquering the Promised Land, and it quickly forgot its history of poverty and captivity in Egypt. Amos warned Israel of its errant ways: "You trample on the poor and force him to give you grain. Therefore, though you have built stone mansions, you will not live in them; though you have planted lush vineyards, you will not drink their wine. For I know how many are your offenses and how great your sins. You oppress the righteous and take bribes and you deprive the poor of justice in the courts" (Amos 5:11-12). Jeremiah wrote, "Sing to the Lord! Give praise to the Lord! He rescues the life of the needy from the hands of the wicked" (Jeremiah 20:13).

We learn from the Bible that God provides for the poor (Psalm 68:10), delivers the poor (Psalm 72:12), secures justice for the poor (Psalm 140:12), hears the poor (Job 34:28), shows no partiality against the poor (Job 34:19), protects the poor (Psalm 12:5), will not forsake the poor (Isaiah 41:17), and gives food to the poor (Psalm 146:7).

So, this is the kingdom to which we belong. We are called to be ambassadors of this kind of God, and as such, we are called to stand up on behalf of the poor. To do less is to rebel against God. Worse, to do less is to falsely represent the character of God to the world, to slander His name among the nations.

Jesus Cared about the Poor. The Scriptures display Jesus as one who could not bypass the needy. The crowds that followed Jesus knew this, and they would always appeal to His mercy.

When Jesus was in Tyre, a Canaanite woman whose daughter was tormented by a demon asked Jesus to heal her: "Son of David, have mercy on me," she pled (Matthew 15:22). After the Transfiguration, a man begged Jesus to heal his epileptic son: "Lord, have mercy on my son. . . . He has seizures and is suffering greatly. He often falls into the fire or into the water" (Matthew 17:15). How could Jesus not respond?

Jesus not only showed compassion to the needy of the day by healing them, He lived a good amount of His life with them and took criticism from the religious leaders of the day because of it. He identified personally with the poor and outcast and defended His calling to them. He lived among the poor, not being concerned about His reputation with those who did not appear to have needs. And if we claim to follow Jesus, our lives will reflect the same compassion.

Remember the story of the lawyer who came to Jesus to make

sure he was "saved"? (Luke 10:25-37) He essentially approached Jesus to see if there was any fine print in the Law. There was. Upon being asked how to inherit eternal life, Jesus put the question back to the young man and asked him what the requirements were. The lawyer gave Jesus the two love commands—to love God with all our heart and to love our neighbor as ourselves. The lawyer wanted to understand the limits of the command and asked Jesus, "Who is my neighbor?" Jesus told the Parable of the Good Samaritan. The neigh-bor, it turns out, is the one who lived with compassion. This is the person who fulfills the requirement of the Law.

Those who are hard of heart will look for loopholes, scapegoats, rationalizations, or complex explanations on why love for the poor can't always be a good idea. The Bible is not friendly to that orientation.

⁓Gordon Aeschliman

The idea of compassion for the poor is quite central to our faith. It is not complicated or hard to understand. Those who are hard of heart will look for loopholes, scapegoats, rationalizations, or complex explanations on why love for the poor can't always be a good idea. The Bible is not friendly to that orientation. It quite simply requires a true faith that is marked by the character of God and the lifestyle of Jesus.

A Friend of the Poor Is a Friend of God. When we choose to follow the way of God's heart for the poor, we become friends with God. The Bible speaks very highly of those who serve on behalf of the poor and promises them good outcomes.

Proverbs 19:17 tells us that those "who [are] kind to the poor lend to the Lord." And in Proverbs 14:31: "He who oppresses the poor shows contempt for their Maker, but whoever is kind to the needy honors God." The Prophet Jeremiah wrote of good King Josiah, "'He defended the cause of the poor and needy, and so all went well. Is that not what it means to know me?' declares the Lord" (Jeremiah 22:16). In the New Testament Church we are given a picture of believers who shared so completely among themselves that there were no poor among them (Acts 4:34). And in the same book we learn that Cornelius, searching for God, is found precisely because of his sensitivity to the poor: "Cornelius, God has heard your prayer and remembered your gifts to the poor" (Acts 10:31).

All of us marvel at history's friends of the poor. We look at the life of Francis of Assisi, who left the fortunes of his father's textile industry to live with the poor. There was something right about his life, something we want to emulate. Our modern-day Francis is Mother Teresa. She quietly left her home country and emigrated to India where she took on citizenship to serve the lepers. Mother Teresa would have quietly slipped into the grave had she not been discovered by the famous author Malcolm Muggeridge, who told her story to the world. We must wonder how many other friends of the poor quietly go about their work on behalf of the kingdom, living out the mystery of God's love for the poor.

I had the privilege of befriending Bishop Festo Kivengere before his death. When I first met him he was serving as an Anglican priest under the cruel and pathetic dictator of Uganda, Idi Amin. Amin's demonic campaign of terror in the 1970s left hundreds of thousands of orphans and widows in its wake. Kivengere, defying Amin's threats against his life for helping the orphans and widows, stayed in Uganda to minister God's mercy to the poor even though he had several invitations from abroad to serve as bishop in safer regions.

Once Amin was deposed, I asked Bishop Kivengere how he managed to live in the middle of such pain and destruction, how he was able to persist on behalf of the poor. "Doesn't such poverty overwhelm you?" I asked. Kivengere's sweet spirit, forged through his friendship with Christ, shot right back at me: "No, Gordon, Christ's compassion does not overwhelm us. It sharpens our vision, sensitizes our hearts, and compels us into action." I found myself desiring his deeper life because it was clear he was a friend of God.

Faith Without Love for the Poor Is Dead. Those of us who have placed our faith in Jesus have to live with a certain amount of doctrinal tension. There are passages in Scripture that link our works to our faith. The Apostle James gives us that famous call to consider—that faith without works is dead. He compared the notion to a body without a spirit. True religion, said James, is "to look after orphans and widows in their distress and to keep oneself from being polluted by the world" (James 1:27). Works describe our faith, true—but more, works are linked to our faith.

Jesus offers a disturbing picture in Matthew 25 of this same idea. He tells His followers that at the end of time all humanity will be separated into two groups. The one group—the "goats"—He will condemn into outer darkness. This group will be stunned, because, as they put it, they have performed great miracles in His name, and have referred to Him as "Lord." Not impressive to God, apparently, who tells them that He doesn't know them because they did not feed the hungry, visit the prisoner, clothe the naked, and take care of the orphan. And He will tell the "sheep" they are welcome into heaven because they did just that.

Is Jesus suggesting that the work of Calvary was not going to be sufficient to save us? Of course not! But He does leave us with the conclusion that if the work of Calvary were present in our lives there would be evidence of a compassionate lifestyle. Jesus is so convinced of this that He will apparently divide people along those lines.

Faith without compassion is dead. The message of this warning takes the question "Do Christians need to be compassionate?" and turns it on its head. The question now is, "Can we be Christians without being compassionate toward the poor?" [12] ◄

Avoiding the Excesses of Abuse

L ook up the subject "discipleship" in any number of esteemed Christian reference works and it won't take long for you to come across an examination of the dangers of spiritual abuse. How can one distinguish between healthy discipleship and relationships that are unhealthy and controlling? Gordon MacDonald, former president of Inter-Varsity Christian Fellowship, explains the differences:

► Child abuse, police brutality, sexual harassment: shocking terms that have entered our modern vocabulary in recent years. They refer to painful and often destructive patterns in human relationships when one person misuses a privileged position in order to exploit or dominate another.

Add another term to the list: disciple abuse. It happens with alarming frequency.

A man in his early thirties visits with me to talk of disillusionment with his spiritual life, his marriage, and his personal disciplines. As we talk, he refers back to his college days when he and his fiancée (later his wife) had come under the influence of a Christian leader known for a heavy emphasis upon discipling.

"What I realize now," he says, "is that we were pressed to become extensions of him rather than more mature versions of what we ourselves really were. Both of us became too tightly tied in the relationship with him.

"We always lived with the fear of disappointing him, of letting him down. He had this way of indicating strong displeasure if you disagreed with him. And when my wife and I decided that we were in love and wanted to get married, he simply turned his back upon us. He didn't come to our wedding; he never made contact with us again. It was a terribly disillusioning experience, and to this day (years later) we find it very hard to trust anyone in spiritual leadership."

My visitor is describing some of the results of what I call disciple abuse.

The act of discipling—what I like to refer to as "person growing"—is among the most intimate of human relationships. And when there is potential for great intimacy between people, there is the possibility for either growth and development or oppression and destruction.

There are five critical dimensions of discipleship. And as we will see, each of these critical dimensions has potential for abuse.

We need to talk often of the marvelous possibilities which come from discipling relationships, but we ought not to ignore the dark side—when such intimacy turns sour and disciples are abused.

Here is a look at the five areas.

1. Calling and Commitment. Discipling usually has a starting point. Jesus encountered Matthew, the toll-taker, for example, and said, "Follow me." And Matthew did! A relationship began, and he was slowly shaped into Christlikeness and prepared for a mission.

Why did Jesus pick him? Why, for that matter, did he pick any of the Twelve? There are none of them to whom I would have been drawn. Certainly there is no indication that they were compliant, that

---

Five Mistakes to Avoid in Mentoring

1. Don't be too dominant in establishing the purpose of the mentoring relationship. Draw the mentoree into it for his or her motivation, ownership, and appropriate focus.

2. Do not give out too many tasks too early. Let the mentoree set the pace.

3. Watch out for midway relational "sag." The mentoring relationship tends to lose its original zest at about the midpoint. Ensure that the mentoree makes bite-size progress, and keep frequent contact.

4. Assess and select mentorees carefully. Check motivation, responsiveness, and right timing.

5. Be careful of "weak closure" and sloppy accountability. Be faithful to the mentoree during the mentoring experience, and end well. [13]

—*Paul D. Stanley and Robert J. Clinton*

they were hero-worshipers, or that they were unemployed or needed something to do. Credit Christ with taking on a strange, diverse, hard-to-control team.

Abusive disciplemaking begins when someone seeks people with the conscious or unconscious aim not of growing or leading them, but of controlling them.
≈ GORDON MACDONALD

But not every disciple-grower does it that way. Abusive disciple-making begins when someone seeks people with the conscious or unconscious aim not of growing or leading them, but of controlling them. Sadly, this can be—and often is—effectively done in the name of discipling. The extremity of this tendency is cultism.

Such controlling does not produce disciples who are Christlike; it rather provides psychic gratification for the one doing the controlling. The product is an abused disciple.

Some would-be disciple-growers like to control others because they are themselves insecure, uneasy in normal peer relationships, or simply driven to manipulate others for personal emotional gain. Perhaps Diotrephes (cf. 3 John 9) was one of these.

When these sorts of people emerge in a Christian context (and we must not fail to face this reality), they cloak their intentions in theological vocabulary and defend their motives and methods in a most impressive Christian framework. Their preferred relationship with a "younger Christian" promises spiritual maturity but in fact leads to relational domination.

The corollary to this potentially abusive situation centers on the one being discipled. For there are many potential "disciples" who are not that at all. Their motive for accepting a mentoring relationship is not a genuine quest for maturity but an emotional need for a surrogate father or mother.

In our modern times of absentee parents, it is not unusual for young adults to possess a subconscious need for parenting which they did not experience in childhood or adolescence. They seek to fill the voids where there was no authority, affirmation, or rebuke.

For the abusive discipler who wants to control, these are ripe for the picking. For the genuine disciple-grower, they are a drain to his energies, and it is important to discern such inadequate motives before it is too late. Certainly these people need help, but what they need is not discipling but counseling.

2. The Mentoring Process. There is a delicate balance to be maintained in the discipling relationship. The objective of authentic discipling is to point a person toward maturity measured by what we call Christlikeness.

Abuse comes when Christlikeness is abandoned for cloning. In the former, the eyes of both parties in the relationship are set upon what it takes to follow Christ; in the latter, the subtle shift comes when the mentor pressures the disciple to become a copy of himself.

The Christian community was never meant to be a collection of "cookie-cut" human beings. The gospel delights in a Christlike individuality for each disciple.
―GORDON MACDONALD

We can see examples of this not only in personal discipling relationships but sometimes in religious movements where scores of followers become "duplicates" of the leader who becomes a father or hero figure. Pressure can be exerted on the "disciples" through the selective use of guilt, fear, anger, threat of ostracism from the larger group, and through a constant barrage of adulation directed toward the leader. In this form of disciple abuse, the disciple-grower sets out to create a clone or a replica of himself or (what may be more the truth) what the discipler wishes he himself could be.

The Christian community was never meant to be a collection of "cookie-cut" human beings. The gospel delights in a Christlike individuality for each disciple. One never sees Jesus, for example, squelching the dynamism of Peter. Rather, He simply seeks to envelope Peter's temperament in wisdom and spiritual character. The Apostle Peter, who so wisely gives leadership to the Jerusalem church in its early days, is the same Simon Peter of earlier days who was marked with impulsiveness and a competitive spirit. The only difference between the apostle and the fisherman is maturity, not suppressed individuality.

The disciple-grower abuses his son/daughter in the faith when there is disregard for the disciple's gifts, temperament, and personality style. When these things are forcefully modified, they do not disappear; they are simply suppressed and usually await another time to spring out. And when they do, they emerge in their original immaturity. The process is defeated; the disciple is left abused.

3. The Broadening Effort. There has been considerable abuse in the ministry of discipling when the one in spiritual directorship has attempted to single-handedly and exclusively control the "world" of the disciple.

It can happen, first of all, when a mentor attempts to assert domination over virtually all personal decision making. The disciple may not be permitted to engage in interpersonal relationships without the leader's approval; he is not to discern the will or purposes of God without consultation; there is no freedom to make decisions without fear of being berated or rebuked; the use of one's time is carefully controlled and critiqued.

Sadly, there are many people who are only too glad to submit to such an arrangement. They are afraid to think, to make decisions, to take the risks involved in healthy Christian living. They thus open themselves to those who in the name of disciple-making would handle these matters for them by imposing rules, arbitrary expectations, and demands for consultation on all personal matters. The process eventuates in a dangerous dependency which denies maturity to the disciple and provides unwholesome psychic gratification to the mentor.

This sort of suppression is not always easy to observe at first. The disciple is not aware that he is being manipulated or controlled. In fact, it may only become clear that this is what is happening when the disciple dares to appeal to other authorities or to his own inner awareness.

In such cases the disciple is liable to be ridiculed or threatened with relational isolation, told he is departing from the will of God, or accused of diminishing spiritually. If the disciple has come to love the discipler (or fear him) this can be a powerful deterrent to independent growth. And the result is a serious kind of abuse.

We need to remind ourselves how easy it is for this sort of abuse to occur in Christian circles. If we were talking about the context of business, the dominating person would be threatening the novice with a loss of job. But in the Christian context, one can abuse young believers by appealing to a superior relationship to God which appears to bring with it deeper insight. One can effectively claim mysterious authority and impose the threat of some sort of spiritual judgment. All of this can be seriously intimidating to an impressionable young Christian. And it, too, results in abuse.

4. Releasing and Sending. The dimensions of discipling involve not only a beginning moment which I have labeled "calling/commitment," but also all healthy discipling relationships terminate with what could be called a "release/send" component.

This is a time when the definitions of discipling and friendship ought to be contrasted. Theoretically, friendships are based upon a peer experience; discipling relationships are not. In mentoring there is clearly a predominant leader in the equation, and that does not exist in the simple friendship.

Furthermore, friendships are not thought of in terms of a termination point; but healthy discipling relationships must always have an end. While friendships emphasize a level of companionship for its own sake, discipling implies the preparation of someone for a function or a level of character quality.

Disciples are abused when disciple-growers disregard these contrasts and either permit the discipling relationship to become solely a friendship, without goals of growth and development, before the discipling is completed, or—worse yet—choose never to release and send the disciple to the goal of the original call and commitment.

I find it fascinating that Jesus seems always to have sent His disciples out to tasks just before most of us would have felt they were ready.

~GORDON MACDONALD

Disciple-growers, as a rule, have a difficult time letting go of their proteges. And this is a natural, human tendency. Parents, as many of us have discovered, do not easily face the fact that their children are growing up and no longer need strict parental supervision. In the same way a discipler is frequently tempted to think that his/her charge is in need of continuing protection, training, or consultation. Thus, no release; limited, if any, sending out to responsibility.

I find it fascinating that Jesus seems always to have sent His disciples out to tasks just before most of us would have felt they were ready. At one point He says to them in a rather ironic turn of words, "I am sending you out like sheep among wolves" (Matthew 10:16). It was His way of saying that His men were going to get kicked around, bitterly opposed, and probably humiliated. But that was okay with Him. The learning experiences would be invaluable. And when they returned, they'd have a serious mind to listen to further teaching. They would be bursting with questions instead of drowning in cockiness.

Disciple-growers do find it difficult to release disciples. There is a loss of relational power and influence. There is the risk that the disciple may actually move out and begin to beat the disciple-grower at his own "game."

Thus, abuse occurs when the disciple-grower—consciously or subconsciously—refuses to let go. The mentor may constantly criticize the disciple, making sure that short strings are maintained. He may give the disciple little satisfaction that growth is taking place. The abusive discipler may want to make the disciple think that the relationship is still needed and that the release cannot happen yet (if ever).

When this sort of holding-on happens in families between parents and children, there is often a rebellious atmosphere. There can be serious tension as the younger tries to prove himself to the older and the older attempts to demonstrate through superior knowledge and expertise that the younger is not yet ready for the real world. Everyone loses, and it is not unusual for there to be a long lasting break in the relationship between parent and child.

The very same negative dynamic occurs in mentoring experiences in which there is a reluctance to release and send. The evidence that this is happening will be seen where a strong leader keeps a never-changing group of people about him, each discharging the tasks assigned to him but never released to pursue God's call for himself.

The abused disciple who is not released and sent never has the satisfaction that he has proved his worth to either the mentor or God. The result is stunted growth often ending in frustration, anger, and rebellion.

5. Continuing Affirmation and Appreciation. There is a final aspect of the discipling process that often goes ignored. And that is the importance of a continuing flow of affirmation and appreciation between the disciple-grower and the disciple.

Once there has been a release (healthy or unhealthy) of the disciple, it is not unusual for some mentors to cut themselves off from the disciple. The result: a strange silence!

Though releasing and sending disciples may be painted as beautiful and satisfying, it is painful nevertheless to release a disciple whom one has loved and cared for no matter how right and ready the time is.

—GORDON MACDONALD

I have been on the receiving end of that silence from some who helped disciple me. And I have also become silent toward some whom I had helped disciple. I now understand why that sometimes happens.

Though releasing and sending disciples may be painted as beautiful and satisfying, it is painful nevertheless to release a disciple whom one has loved and cared for no matter how right and ready the time is. The humanness in us sometimes is tempted to believe that the disciple—newly released—cannot make it without us. He is sure to stumble, we hear ourselves reasoning, sure to come staggering back for help and advice, to admit that he didn't realize how much he needed us. And when it does not happen—when the disciple lives a confident, fruitful life without constant oversight—the discipler is tempted to feel unneeded and unwanted. Thus—silence. While the disciple-grower waits . . . and waits . . . and waits for a return that may never happen.

Usually the disciple does not come back, and he may even go on to prove that he not only is everything his discipler originally wanted him to be, but even more.

It is a credit to Christ that He not only trained His disciples to go far beyond the quantitative limits of His own ministry, but also outwardly told them that this was exactly what would happen. "I tell you the truth, anyone who has faith in me will do what I have been doing. He will do even greater things than these, because I am going to the Father" (John 14:12).

This pain of parting sometimes causes the insensitive disciple-grower to assume that his protege does not need continuing affirmation or to be told that what the disciple is achieving and becoming is pleasing to the mentor. Nothing could be further from the truth. Usually, the released and sent disciple is aching for a word of "well done" from his teacher, and hurts badly when it does not come.

Perhaps *abuse* is a strong word at this point, but it is a fact that the unaffirmed disciple always wonders if the one who taught him really still cares or is interested. With regularity the disciple looks over his shoulder wondering if the old mentor is proud or pleased with what the novice has become, and when no word comes, he is left puzzled and hurt.

Avoiding Disciple Abuse. It is possible to abuse disciples. In fact, it is easy to do it. How can we avoid it? Several thoughts.

The disciple-grower must first of all realize that his approval and disapproval through words, the giving of love or the withholding of it, the modeling of his life is often perceived by the disciple at a far louder and stronger level than the disciple-grower ever meant it to be. My wife often reminds me that what I say at a "4" (on a 1-10 scale) is usually heard at an "8." When I forget that, I often abuse people I really meant to assist.

A disciple-grower must also never forget that the goal of discipling is to present every man mature in Christ (Colossians 1:28). Disciple-growers are not out to change people; they are out to grow them. The gardener does not try by the force of his will to make peas into roses. He merely cultivates the ground in which peas are planted, freeing them to become what God meant them to be.

Finally, the disciple-grower must discipline himself to affirm his disciple and delight in what the disciple is doing. He must be the temporary conveyer of the words, "Well done!" (Matthew 25:21) until they are heard from the Father Himself.

Disciple abuse is a serious matter. Examples abound. The man I described at the beginning is one of them. As we talk together about his past experience, I try to point out to him that his discipler was quite human after all. He had his needs, his blind spots, his sins. We pray asking for forgiveness for abusive things done years ago that have their effect even today upon a person, a marriage, a concept of

God. And when we finish our conversation, I feel as if there has been a release and a healing of some sort.

But I'm also very much aware that it is just a beginning. A lot more forgiving and forgetting will have to happen. A very powerful ministry called discipling has been misused; a man and a woman have been spiritually abused. Those of us trusted with spiritual leadership must be careful not to let this happen through us. [14] ◄

APPENDIX:
Recommended Resources

The editors of this volume consulted hundreds of books, magazine articles, Web sites, and other resources during the process of compiling this book. Two CD-ROM collections proved particularly helpful.

Time after time, the *Discipleship Journal Anthology* CD-ROM, which features the contents of issues 1–111 (1981–1999) proved to be the best single source we could find. Searchable by topic or author, the PC-only anthology features articles and pointers on a multitude of topics. For availability information, contact iExalt Electronic Publishing (1-800/888-9898).

We also valued some of the older, out-of-print resources collected on *The Master Christian Library* and *Reformation History Library* CD-ROMs published by AGES Software (1-800-297-4307).

Also helpful was the *Disciple's Study Bible* (Holman, 1988).

Experts Nominate Best Books

In 1997, *Discipleship Journal* published its 100th issue. To commemorate the event, the magazine's editors asked top discipleship experts to recommend the ten best books. Here are their selections:

• *Words to Winners of Souls* by Horatius Bonar (Presbyterian & Reformed). Recommended by Jerry White, president of The Navigators: "This book pierces to the heart and soul of a person who is committed to reaching out in the world. It emphasizes the living of a holy life for the one engaged in God's work. I return to it again and again."

• *The Pursuit of God* by A.W. Tozer (Christian Publications). White calls this "a classic in challenging a person to live a life of committed discipleship. It addresses the hard issues of our motivations and walk with God."

• *The Cost of Discipleship* by Dietrich Bonhoeffer (Simon & Schuster). Chuck Colson, the founder of Prison Fellowship Ministries, recommends this classic. A German theologian who was put to death for his stand against Hitler, Bonhoeffer is perhaps best known for his words,

"When Christ calls a man, He bids him come and die." Colson describes his book as "a heroic call to obedience."

• *The Pursuit of Holiness* by Jerry Bridges (NavPress). Colson says this book helps us understand God's role in making us holy and our role in pursuing holiness. It comes with an excellent study guide that helps the reader apply the principles from the book to daily living.

• *A Long Obedience in the Same Direction: Discipleship in an Instant Society* by Eugene Peterson (InterVarsity). Recommended by Ravi Zacharias of Ravi Zacharias International Ministries. Using the psalms known as the Songs of Ascent, Peterson focuses on the need to persevere as disciples and pilgrims rather than look for quick success.

• *Following Christ* by Joseph Stowell (Zondervan). Recommended by both Ravi Zacharias and Tony Evans, senior pastor of Oak Cliff Bible Fellowship in Dallas. Stowell examines the voices that distract us from Christ's "follow Me." He then proclaims the compelling simplicity of a life devoted to following a single voice.

• *The Spirit of the Disciplines* by Dallas Willard (HarperSanFrancisco). Recommended by Bill Hybels of Willow Creek Community Church and Michael J. Wilkins, dean of the faculty of Talbot School of Theology. Wilkins says, "This is must reading for understanding who we are as God's creatures and what it means to grow in Christ. . . . Offers a mature theological reflection on human nature and Christian growth."

• *As Iron Sharpens Iron* by Howard and William Hendricks (Moody). Recommended by Chuck Swindoll, president of Dallas Theological Seminary. Chuck describes this book on mentoring as "a thoroughly biblical yet up-to-date, extremely practical volume that helps us get involved and stay accountable. This stuff works!"

• *The Master Plan of Evangelism* by Robert Coleman (Revell). Recommended by Chuck Swindoll as "an outstanding study of how our Lord trained His twelve disciples and how we can emulate some of the same principles. A terse, insightful volume acquainting us with many of the behind-the-scenes moments we easily overlook in our hurried approach to the gospel accounts. Whoever digests Coleman's observations will find timeless guidelines worth following."

• *The Lost Art of Disciplemaking* by LeRoy Eims (Zondervan). Recommended by Lorne Sanny, former general director of The Navigators.

Disciples have as their marching orders the command to "make disciples of all nations." This book points out the biblical mandate to disciple young believers into mature, fruitful Christians and gives how-to's for doing so.

Contemporary Writers Praise the "Classics"

Every year, thousands of new books are published around the world. Though many of these new titles are valuable and helpful, some contemporary authors believe that many of the newer books will never surpass some older books that still speak to us across the ages.

Here, six respected writers discuss the classic books that moved them and provide a brief excerpt from these favorite classics:

Elisabeth Elliot, author, speaker and missionary
When I was 14, I went to a boarding school where the headmistress often quoted Amy Carmichael, an Irish missionary who traveled to India in the late 1890s to reach the village women of Muslim and Hindu faiths. Later, Carmichael founded an amazing mission for children in moral danger. I was hooked by her books, and in particular the gripping book *If.*

The meaning of the cross is the red thread that connects her writings, and from them I've learned much about Calvary love. She would often tell interested missionaries, "We cannot offer you anything especially interesting and certainly not exciting. What we can offer you is a little pile of red sand in the southern tip of India where you can have a chance to die." She used those words "a chance to die" to mean opportunities every day to give up your right to yourself. That is the first condition of discipleship. Jesus tells us to take up the cross and follow Him. To me, Amy Carmichael's words are the closest thing to Jesus' own—only provided in modern English and with application.

From *"Toward Jerusalem"*:
Lord Crucified,
O mark Thy holy cross
On motives, preference, all fond desires,
On that which self in any form inspires
Set Thou that sign of loss.

And when the touch of death is here and there
Laid on a thing most precious in our eyes,
Let us not wonder—let us recognize
The answer to this prayer.

Luis Palau, evangelist

There is a book with a life-changing message for which I've thanked God for more than 35 years. It is the now out-of-print classic *The Saving Life of Christ* by Major W. Ian Thomas. When I was a first-semester student at Multnomah Bible Seminary in Portland, Oregon, Major Thomas, the founder and general director of the Torchbearers (the group that runs the Capernwray Hall Bible School in England), spoke at one of our chapel services. His message—thankfully preserved in his book—was, "Any old bush will do, as long as God is in the bush." Thomas said the burning bush that Moses came upon in the desert was likely a dry bunch of ugly sticks. Yet, Moses had to remove his shoes. Why? Because this was holy ground.

God was in the bush! I realized I was that kind of bush: a useless bunch of dried-up old sticks. I could do nothing for God. All my reading and studying and asking questions and trying to model myself after others was worthless. Everything in my ministry was worthless unless God was in the bush. Only He could make it work. That day marked the intellectual turning point in my spiritual life. The practical working out of that discovery would be lengthy and painful, but at least the realization had come. It was exciting beyond words.

From *The Saving Life of Christ:*

Moses lost his sense of God, and maybe you have lost your sense of God for the same reason. You are not called upon to commit yourself to a need, or to a task, or to a field. You are called upon to commit yourself to God! It is He then who takes care of the consequences and commits you where He wants you. He is the Lord of the harvest! He is the Head of the body—and He is gloriously competent to assume His own responsibilities! Man is not indispensable to God. God is indispensable to man!

Philip Yancey, author

A journalist asked G.K. Chesterton what one book he would want to have along if stranded on a desert island. He paused only an instant before replying, "Why, *A Practical Guide to Shipbuilding,* of course." Apart from the Bible, the book I'd choose if stranded is Chesterton's own spiritual autobiography, *Orthodoxy,* first published in 1908. Past its formidable title are words from which my faith has never recovered.

I was experiencing spiritual dryness when I first read *Orthodoxy.* It brought me freshness and a spirit of new adventure. More than any facts or intelligent arguments, I gained from Chesterton a new, Romantic way of looking at my faith. I also appreciate Chesterton because he seemed to sense instinctively that a stern prophet will rarely break through to a society full of religion's "cultured despisers." Instead, he preferred the role of the jester.

Today, in a time when culture and faith have drifted even further apart, we could use Chesterton's brilliance, his entertaining style, and above all his generous and joyful spirit. When society becomes polarized, as ours has, it is as if the two sides stand across a great divide and shout at each other. Chesterton had another approach: He walked to the center of the swinging bridge, roared a challenge to any single-combat warriors, and then made both sides laugh aloud.

From *Orthodoxy:*

Because children have abounding vitality, because they are in spirit fierce and free, therefore they want things repeated and unchanged. They always say, "Do it again"; and the grown-up person does it again until he is nearly dead. For grown-up people are not strong enough to exult in monotony. But perhaps God is strong enough to exult in monotony. It is possible that God says every morning, "Do it again" to the sun; and every evening, "Do it again" to the moon. It may not be automatic necessity that makes all daisies alike; it many be that God makes every daisy separately, but has never got tired of making them. It may be that He has the eternal appetite of infancy; for we have sinned and grown old, and our Father is younger than we.

Os Guinness, senior fellow at the Trinity Forum

There are certain things about Blaise Pascal's life I cannot identify with. He was a mathematical genius; I have zero gifts in math. He also practiced the strict aesthetic practices of Jansenism, which I find opposed to the gospel and the freedom we have in Christ. But there are also certain things I absolutely love about him.

In such a short, intense, flame-burst of a life—only 39 years—he lived his belief that our days are numbered and we should live them to the fullest, especially doing that which we do before the Lord to the greatest extent. I also admire his passion for Christ. In 1654, at age 31, he had an extraordinary mystical experience—a second conversion of sorts. It was so precious to him that he wrote it down on parchment and sewed it into the lining of his shirt. He wore it next to his heart for the rest of his life; it was only discovered after his death.

In an age when so many thinkers were solely cerebral, Pascal was passionately in love with Christ. Finally, I love Pascal for his book *Pensees,* which was published in 1670 after his death. *Pensees* was his collection of notes for what would have been a book of apologetics. Although we only have the architectural blueprint, that blueprint has become one of the great classics. It is filled with profound, suggestive, searching aphorisms that engage us as human beings and beg to be read again and again.

From *Pensees:*

People despise Christian faith. They hate it and are afraid that it may be true. The solution for this is to show them, first of all, that it is not unreasonable, that it is worthy of reverence and respect. Then show that it is winsome, making good men desire that it were true. Then show them that it really is true. It is worthy of reverence because it really understands the human condition. It is also attractive because it promises true goodness.

What does all this restlessness and helplessness [of mankind] indicate, except that man was once in true happiness which has now left him? So he vainly searches, but finds nothing to help him, other than to see an infinite abyss that can only be filled by One who is Infinite and Immutable. In other words, it can only be filled by God Himself.

The Christian faith teaches men these two truths: There is a God whom men are capable of knowing, and they have a corrupt nature which makes them unworthy of Him. . . . It is as equally dangerous for man to know God without knowing his own sinfulness as it is for him to know about his sinfulness without knowing the Redeemer who can cure him. Knowing only one of these aspects leads either to the arrogance of the philosophers, who have known God but not their own sinfulness, or to the despair of the atheists, who know their own wretched state without knowing their Redeemer.

Luci Shaw, author, poet and writer in residence at Regent College in Vancouver, Canada

Dorothy Sayers' book *The Mind of the Maker* made an enormous impression on me as a writer and poet, in terms of understanding that what I do is not just what I do. It is a reflection of the creative mind of God, in whose image I am made. Sayers was a British writer who lived from 1893–1957. Although she wrote several books, *The Mind of the Maker* (1941) is top of the ladder for me as a statement about her philosophy of life. In it, she discusses the Trinity, the various roles of the Godhead, and how our own creative lives parallel the activities of the Father, Son, and Holy Spirit. It's a stretching book —dense in the sense that it's tightly packed with fascinating information, philosophy, and psychology.

Because it is so provocative and profound, you have to pick it up, read a couple of pages, and then let them digest. That is a step beyond the superficial reading many of us are used to. But if you wish to develop your own philosophy of what the Christian faith is and not just be spoon fed, this is for you. I believe God is pleased when we take Him seriously, and this was the pattern of Dorothy Sayers' life.

From *The Mind of the Maker:*

The Jews, keenly alive to the perils of pictorial metaphor, forbade the representation of the person of God in graven images. Nevertheless, human nature and the nature of human language defeated them. No legislation could prevent the making of verbal pictures—God walks in the garden; He stretches out His arm; His voice shakes the cedars; His eyelids try the children of men. To forbid the making of pictures about God would be to forbid thinking about God at all. For we are so made that we have no way to think except in mental pictures.

Calvin Miller, author

The tenderness of her style makes Julian of Norwich one of my favorite writers. This Anchorite nun of the 14th century was England's first woman writer. And through her writings, she has given me three gifts. First, she's taught me the art of laughing Satan out of my life. Derision is a strong way to handle an enemy who is not to be converted. Satan has already been conquered by Christ, so he is no serious threat to us. We have to laugh and rejoice in God because of this.

She also teaches us to see ourselves as the prize of Christ's passion. Jesus is deeply in love with us. If you'd been the only one that needed Him, He would still have come and welcomed you into His bliss. We evangelicals think we invented the personal relationship with Jesus!

Her last gift is the concept of eternity as the ultimate "oneing." All our lives we seek union with Christ. Then we die and have it immediately. Death for the ardent believer is the instant realization of the intent that we've had all our lives—to merge into oneness with Christ. There may be those writers who are more pregnant with literary style, but nobody writes more sweetly of Christ than Julian of Norwich.

From *Showings:*

He kindles our understanding, He prepares our ways, He eases our conscience, He comforts our soul, He illumines our heart and gives us partial knowledge and love of His blessed divinity, with gracious memory of His sweet humanity and His blessed Passion, with courteous wonder over His great surpassing goodness, and makes us to love everything which He loves for love of Him, and to be well satisfied with Him and with all His works. And when we fall, quickly He raises us up with His loving embrace and His gracious touch. And when we are strengthened by His sweet working, then we willingly choose Him by His grace, that we shall be His servants and His lovers, constantly and forever.

ENDNOTES

Introduction

1. *Christianity Today,* 25 October 1999, 28.

SECTION ONE:
Come, Follow Me:
Being a Disciple of Jesus

1. Elisabeth Elliot, *Discipline . . . The Glad Surrender* (Old Tappan, N.J.: Fleming H. Revell, 1982), p. 14.
2. Joyce Rupp, *May I Have This Dance?* (Notre Dame, Ind.: Ave Maria Press, 1992), pp. 11-12.
3. St. Clement, *Epistle to the Corinthians,* in *Reformation History Library CD-ROM,* version 2 (Rio, Wis.: Ages Software, 1998).
4. St. Bernard of Clairvaux, *On Loving God,* in *The Master Christian Library CD-ROM,* version 6 (Rio, Wis.: Ages Software, 1998).
5. Brother Lawrence, *Discipleship Journal,* No. 54.
6. Thomas à Kempis, *The Imitation of Christ,* in *The Master Christian Library CD-ROM.*
7. Amy Carmichael, *Discipleship Journal,* No. 33.
8. Ken Gire, "He Looks at Me with Delight," *Discipleship Journal,* No. 102.
9. à Kempis, *The Master Christian Library CD-ROM.*
10. David Brainerd, *Discipleship Journal,* No. 54.
11. Cynthia Heald, "Becoming a Friend of God," *Discipleship Journal,* No. 54.
12. St. Ignatius, *Epistle to the Ephesians,* in *Reformation History Library CD-ROM.*
13. Vernon Grounds, *Radical Commitment* (Sisters, Ore.: Multnomah Press, 1984), pp. 15-16.
14. Richard Baxter, *The Reformed Pastor,* in *The Master Christian Library CD-ROM.*

15. John Henry Newman, *Parochial and Plain Sermons,* ed. Ian Ker (Mahwah, N.J.: Paulist Press, 1994), in *Discipleship Journal,* No. 105.

16. Dallas Willard, *The Divine Conspiracy* (San Francisco: HarperSanFrancisco, 1998), pp. 283-84.

17. David Watson, *Called and Committed* (Wheaton, Ill.: Harold Shaw, 1982), pp. 5-6.

18. Brennan Manning, *The Signature of Jesus* (Grand Rapids, Mich.: Chosen Books, 1988), pp. 66-68.

19. William MacDonald, *True Discipleship* (Kansas City, Kans.: Walterick Publishers, 1975), pp. 6-9.

20. John Bradford, "A Sweet Contemplation of Heaven and Heavenly Things," in *Reformation History Library CD-ROM.*

21. *Epistle of Mathetes to Diognetus,* in *Reformation History Library CD-ROM.*

22. John Flavel, *The Method of Grace: How the Spirit Works,* in *The Master Christian Library CD-ROM.*

23. Rene Padilla, *Discipleship Journal.*

24. Jeremiah Burroughs, *The Rare Jewel of Christian Contentment,* in *The Master Christian Library CD-ROM.*

25. à Kempis, *The Master Christian Library CD-ROM.*

26. Grounds, *Radical Commitment,* p. 42.

27. St. Clement, *Epistle to the Corinthians,* in *Reformation History Library CD-ROM.*

28. Ibid.

29. à Kempis, *The Master Christian Library CD-ROM.*

30. Teresa of Avila, *Majestic Is Your Name,* arranged and paraphrased by David Hazard (Minneapolis: Bethany House Publishers, 1993), in *Discipleship Journal,* No. 79.

31. à Kempis, *The Master Christian Library CD-ROM.*

32. Andrew Murray, *The Believer's Secret of Living Like Christ* (Minneapolis: Bethany House Publishers, 1985), p. 111.

33. Roy Hession, *The Calvary Road* (Fort Washington, Pa.: Christian Literature Crusade, 1950), in *Discipleship Journal,* No. 10.

34. John Bunyan, *Pilgrim's Progress,* in *The Master Christian Library CD-ROM.*

35. Dietrich Bonhoeffer, "Costly Grace," in *The Martyred Christian,*

ed. Joan Winmill Brown (New York: Collier Books, 1983), pp. 64-65.

36. George MacDonald, *Unspoken Sermons,* in *Discipleship Journal,* No. 74.

37. à Kempis, *The Master Christian Library CD-ROM.*

38. Hadewijch of Brabant, "The Way of the Cross," *Discipleship Journal,* No. 98.

39. Brother Lawrence, *The Practice of the Presence of God,* in *The Master Christian Library CD-ROM.*

40. J. Hudson Taylor, *A Ribband of Blue and Other Bible Studies,* in *The Master Christian Library CD-ROM.*

41. Jerry Bridges, *The Pursuit of Holiness* (Colorado Springs: Nav-Press, 1978), pp. 18-28.

42. Polycarp, *Epistle to the Philippians,* in *Reformation History Library CD-ROM.*

43. Bridges, *The Pursuit of Holiness,* p. 14.

44. William Law, *A Serious Call to a Devout and Holy Life,* in *The Master Christian Library CD-ROM.*

45. St. Clement, *Reformation History Library CD-ROM.*

46. Law, *The Master Christian Library CD-ROM.*

47. Francis A. Schaeffer, *True Spirituality* (Wheaton, Ill.: Tyndale House Publishers, 1971), p. 94.

48. à Kempis, *The Master Christian Library CD-ROM.*

49. Agnes Sanford, "The Healing Light," in *Spiritual Classics . . . Selected Readings for Individuals and Groups on the Twelve Spiritual Disciplines,* ed. Richard J. Foster and Emilie Griffin (San Francisco: HarperSanFrancisco, 2000).

50. Jeanne Guyon, *Experiencing the Depths of Jesus* Christ (Newnan, Ga.: Seed Sowers Christian Books Publishing House), p. 85.

51. Richard J. Foster, *Celebration of Discipline* (New York: Harper & Row Publishers, 1978).

52. Murray, *The Believer's Secret of Waiting on God* (Minneapolis: Bethany House Publishers, 1986), pp. 15-17.

53. Eugene H. Peterson, *A Long Obedience in the Same Direction* (Downers Grove, Ill.: InterVarsity Press, 1980), p. 127.

54. Bunyan, *The Master Christian Library CD-ROM.*

55. Jerry Bridges, "Staying Faithful Through the Years: How Can You Keep Walking with God Throughout Your Life?" *Discipleship Journal,* No. 58.

SECTION TWO:
Go and Make Disciples:
Helping Others Follow Jesus

1. Thomas Coke, *The Duties of the Minister of the Gospel,* in *The Master Christian Library CD-ROM.*

2. John Bradford, "A Prayer for the Obtaining of Faith," in *Reformation History Library CD-ROM.*

3. Waldron Scott, "What Can I Do?" *Discipleship Journal,* No. 7.

4. Gottfried Osei-Mensah, "Driven by Compassion," *Discipleship Journal,* No. 7.

5. Elton Trueblood, *The Company of the Committed* (New York: Harper & Row Publishers, 1961).

6. St. Augustine, in *Spiritual Classics,* ed. Richard J. Foster and Emilie Griffin, p. 69.

7. Hadewijch of Brabant, in *Spiritual Classics,* pp. 200-201.

8. Thomas à Kempis, *The Imitation of Christ,* in *The Master Christian Library CD-ROM.*

9. Hannah Whitall Smith, *The Christian's Secret to a Happy Life,* in *The Master Christian Library CD-ROM.*

10. A.B. Bruce, *The Training of the Twelve* (Grand Rapids, Mich.: Kregel Publications, reprint 1971), pp. 37-38.

11. Ibid., pp. 146-53.

12. Ibid., p. 41.

13. à Kempis, *The Master Christian Library CD-ROM.*

14. Brennan Manning, *The Signature of Jesus,* pp. 73-74.

15. Michael Yaconelli, "Reckless Grace," *Discipleship Journal,* No. 109.

16. A.B. Bruce, *The Training of the Twelve,* pp. 138-39.

17. François Fénelon, "Serving God in the Ordinary Business of Life," *Discipleship Journal,* No. 87.

18. Walter Wangerin, Jr., *Little Lamb, Who Made Thee?* (Grand Rapids, Mich.: Zondervan Publishing House, 1993), in

Discipleship Journal, No. 79.

19. Georg Strumpf and J. Stephen Lang, "Racing Down Main Street," *Discipleship Journal,* No. 97.

20. Jim Petersen, *Evangelism as a Lifestyle* (Colorado Springs: Nav-Press, n.d.), in *Discipleship Journal,* No. 3.

21. Rebecca Manley Pippert, "The Best Time to Share Your Faith May Be When You Don't Have It All Together," *Discipleship Journal,* No. 57.

22. Pippert, *Out of the Saltshaker and Into the World* (Downers Grove, Ill.: InterVarsity Press, 1979), pp. 88-90.

23. Dorothy Day, *Dorothy Day: Selected Writings,* ed. Robert Ellsberg (Maryknoll, 1983), in *Discipleship Journal,* No. 77.

24. Ted W. Engstrom with Ron Wilson, "Unconditional Love—The Key to Caring," *Discipleship Journal,* No. 27.

25. William Law, *The Master Christian Library CD-ROM.*

26. Charles Colson, "Doing Justice, Loving Mercy, Walking Humbly," *Discipleship Journal,* No. 63.

SECTION THREE:
I Am With You:
We All Do the Work of Discipleship

1. Manuel Scott, "Accomplished in Our Generation: He Uses Whom He Chooses," *Discipleship Journal,* No. 7.

2. Dawson Trotman, "The Need of the Hour," *Discipleship Journal,* No. 7.

3. William J. Petersen, *The Discipling of Timothy* (Wheaton, Ill.: Victor Books, 1980), in *Discipleship Journal,* No. 6.

4. Jill Briscoe, "The Life of a Disciple-maker," First International Consultation on Discipleship.

5. Richard A. Cleveland, "Follow-Up: Person to Person," *Discipleship Journal,* No. 6.

6. Clyde S. Kilby, "Holiness in the Life of C.S. Lewis," *Discipleship Journal,* No. 22.

7. St. Gregory the Great, *Pastoral Care,* ed. and trans. Henry Davis (Newman Press/Paulist Press, 1950), in *Discipleship Journal,* No. 108.

8. Bruce Demarest, *Satisfy Your Soul* (Colorado Springs: NavPress, 1999) pp. 244-45.

9. Joseph M. Stowell, *Following Christ* (Grand Rapids, Mich.: Zondervan Publishing House, 1996), pp. 71-72.

10. Rachel Crabb, *The Personal Touch: Encouraging Others through Hospitality* (Colorado Springs: NavPress, 1990), in *Discipleship Journal,* No. 69.

11. Judith Couchman, "Hospitality in a Hectic World," *Discipleship Journal,* No. 98.

12. Pamela A. Toussaint, "Homemade Disciples," *Discipleship Journal,* No. 102.

13. Stephen Sorenson and Yvonne Baker, "Evangelistic Home Bible Study," *Discipleship Journal,* No. 59.

14. Toussaint, *Discipleship Journal,* No. 102.

15. Karl Rahner, "Encounters With Silence," ed. Richard J. Foster and Emilie Griffin, in *Spiritual Classics*, pp. 217-218.

16. Doug Sherman and William Hendricks, "Does Your Job Matter?" *Discipleship Journal,* No. 45.

17. Richard Baxter, *The Reformed Pastor,* in *The Master Christian Library CD-ROM.*

18. Dawson Trotman, "Follow Up," *Discipleship Journal,* No. 1.

19. J. Oswald Sanders, *Spiritual Leadership,* rev. ed. (Chicago: Moody Press, 1980), in *Discipleship Journal,* No. 95.

20. Baxter, *The Master Christian Library CD-ROM.*

21. Paul Borthwick, *Discipleship Journal,* No. 106.

22. Richard Halverson, *Discipleship Journal,* No. 41

23. Elisabeth Elliot, "A Shortage of Leaders" *Discipleship Journal,* No. 41.

24. J. Oswald Sanders, *Spiritual Leadership,* pp. 29-30.

25. Amy Carmichael, *Discipleship Journal,* No. 69.

26. John of the Cross, *The Collected Works of St. John of the Cross,* trans. Kieran Kavanaugh and Otilio Rodriquez (Washington, D.C.: ICS Publications, 1979, 1991), in *Discipleship Journal,* No. 109.

SECTION FOUR:
Teaching Them to Obey:
Disciple-making Methods and Models

1. *The Master Christian Library CD-ROM.*

2. Dallas Willard, *The Divine Conspiracy,* p. 301.

3. Jim Petersen, *Lifestyle Discipleship* (Colorado Springs: NavPress, 1993), pp. 15-16.

4. Willard, *The Divine Conspiracy,* p. 350.

5. Ibid., pp. 321-22.

6. Ibid., pp. 351-52.

7. Stowell, *Following Christ,* n.p.

8. Bob Briner, *Roaring Lambs* (Grand Rapids, Mich.: Zondervan Publishing House, 1993), pp. 27-31.

9. Waylon B. Moore, *Multiplying Disciples: The New Testament Method for Church Growth* (Colorado Springs: NavPress, 1981), in *Discipleship Journal,* No. 6.

10. George Barna, "How's Your Vision?" *Discipleship Journal,* No. 58.

11. Walter A. Henrichsen, *Disciples Are Made, Not Born* (Colorado Springs: Chariot Victor, 1988), p. 90.

12. Howard Baker, *Soul Keeping* (Colorado Springs: NavPress, 1998).

13. J. Oswald Sanders, *Spiritual Leadership,* p. 65.

14. Henri Nouwen, *Seeds of Hope,* ed. Robert Durback (New York: Doubleday, 1989), pp. 98-99.

15. Jack Griffin, *Man to Man: How to Do Individual Disciplemaking,* in *Discipleship Journal,* No. 10.

16. Roger Fleming, "Disciplemaking—A Life on Life Approach," *Discipleship Journal,* No. 30.

17. James Houston, "Discipleship: The Mentoring Process," First International Consultation on Discipleship.

18. Houston, "Discipleship Training Through Mentoring," First International Consultation on Discipleship.

19. Joyce W. Sackett, *Discipleship Journal,* No. 104.

20. Stephen Sorenson, "14 Ways to Love Your Neighbors," *Discipleship Journal,* No. 78.

21. Dietrich Bonhoeffer, *Life Together* (San Francisco: HarperSanFrancisco, 1954), pp. 26-27.

22. Stuart Briscoe, "The Church Where Disciples Are Made," First International Consultation on Discipleship.

23. Deryck Stone, "Discipleship and the Cell Church," First International Consultation on Discipleship.

24. LeRoy Eims, *The Basic Ingredients of Spiritual Growth* (Wheaton, Ill.: Victor Books, 1992), p. 80.

25. Carl Wilson, *With Christ in the School of Disciple Building* (Grand Rapids, Mich.: Zondervan Publishing House, 1976), pp. 63-65.

26. Dawson Trotman, *Discipleship Journal,* No. 1.

27. Eims, *The Basic Ingredients of Spiritual Growth.*

28. Paul E. Little, *How to Give Away Your Faith* (Downers Grove, Ill.: InterVarsity Press, 1962), pp. 11-12.

29. Billy Graham, *The Faithful Christian: An Anthology of Billy Graham*, compiled by William Griffin and Ruth Graham Dienert (New York: McCracken Press, 1994), p. 316.

30. Thomas à Kempis, *The Imitation of Christ,* in *The Master Christian Library CD-ROM.*

31. William Law, *An Humble, Earnest, and Affectionate Address to the Clergy,* in *The Master Christian Library CD-ROM.*

32. Robert E. Coleman, *The Master Plan of Evangelism* (Fleming H. Revell Company, 1963), in *Discipleship Journal,* No. 2.

33. Eugene H. Peterson, "In Other Words," *Discipleship Journal,* No. 76.

34. Monte Unger, "Lessons from the Master," *Discipleship Journal,* No. 82.

35. Jeanne Guyon, *Experiencing the Depths of Jesus Christ,* p. 117.

36. Jeff Jernigan, "Not According to Plan," *Discipleship Journal,* No. 67.

37. Randy Raysbrook, "Cookie-Cutter Discipleship?" *Discipleship Journal,* No. 55.

38. C.S. Lewis, *The Joyful Christian* (New York: Macmillan, 1977), pp. 135-36.

39. Jan David Hettinga, *Follow Me* (Colorado Springs: NavPress, 1996), pp. 177-78.

40. Michael J. Wilkins, *In His Image* (Colorado Springs: NavPress, 1997), pp. 111-13.

41. Jerry Bridges, "How to Develop Learners, Not Legalists," *Discipleship Journal*, No. 74.

42. Alice Fryling, "In His Steps," *Discipleship Journal*, No. 67.

43. Francis A. Schaeffer, *True Spirituality* (Wheaton, Ill.: Tyndale House Publishers, 1971), p. 4.

44. A.W. Tozer, *A Treasury of A.W. Tozer* (Grand Rapids, Mich.: Baker Book House, 1980), pp. 85-86.

45. E. Stanley Jones, *Christian Maturity* (Nashville: Abingdon Press, 1957), p. 3.

SECTION FIVE:
Issues: Applying God's Wisdom in Changing Times

1. Stanley J. Grenz, *A Primer on Postmodernism* (Grand Rapids, Mich.: Eerdmans, 1996), p. 174.

2. Ravi Zacharias, "Discipleship in a Millennium Culture: The Challenge of Postmodernity and Religious Pluralism," First International Consultation on Discipleship.

3. Michael J. Wilkins, *In His Image,* pp. 25, 36-37.

4. Ibid.

5. Jerry Harvill, "The Road to Discipleship," *Discipleship Journal,* No. 33.

6. M. Scott Peck, *The Different Drum* (New York: Simon & Schuster, 1987), pp. 67-68.

7. Dave and Neta Jackson, "The Commitment Quandary," *Discipleship Journal,* No. 51.

8. Charles D. Drew, *A Public Faith* (Colorado Springs: NavPress, 2000), n.p.

9. Tony Campolo, "Getting Out of the World Alive," *Discipleship Journal,* No. 86.

10. Tim Woodroof, *Walk This Way: An Interactive Guide to Following Jesus* (Colorado Springs: NavPress, 1999), pp. 38-39.

11. Ibid.

12. Gordon Aeschilman, "God's Heart for the Poor," *Discipleship Journal,* No. 93.

13. Paul D. Stanley and Robert J. Clinton, *Connection: The Mentoring Relationships You Need to Succeed in Life* (Colorado Springs: NavPress, 1992), p. 211.

14. Gordon MacDonald, "Disciple Abuse," *Discipleship Journal,* No. 30.

NAMES INDEX

The Bible Knowledge Commentary (OT & NT) edited by John F. Walvoord & Roy B. Zuck. An Exposition of the Scriptures by Dallas Seminary Faculty

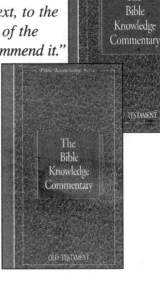

"The Bible Knowledge Commentary *is true to the text, to the point and yet meaty enough to give serious students of the Bible something to chew on. I need it. I use it. I recommend it.*"

Charles R. Swindoll, Chancellor,
Dallas Theological Seminary

The Bible Exposition Commentary (OT Pentateuch) By Dr. Warren W. Wiersbe.

Study the Scriptures in digestible sections that emphasize personal application as well as biblical content.

The Victor Journey through the Bible by V. Gilbert Beers
A unique resource that brings the Bible to life in full color, story by story.
- ◆ Over 400 colorful pages of photographs, drawings, maps and charts
- ◆ More than 100 drawings from objects or monuments of Bible times
- ◆ Over 200 photographs of Bible lands today
- ◆ Photographs of more than 50 archaeological discoveries
- ◆ Scores of reconstructions and diagrams and dozens of colorful maps

Find these books at your local Christian bookstore or visit us at:
iVictor.com or call 1-800-323-7543

Victor DISCIPLESHIP—APOLOGETICS

Know What You Believe
by Paul E. Little (personal and group study questions now included.) A practical discussion of the fundamentals for the Christian faith.
"There are just a few timeless treasures in Christian literature. Know What You Believe *is one of them."*
Joseph M. Stowell, President, Moody Bible Institute

Know Why You Believe
by Paul E. Little (personal and group study questions now included.) A clear affirmation for the reasonableness of the Christian faith.
"Know Why You Believe *is a valuable piece of work."*
Ravi Zacharias

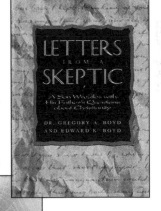

Letters from a Skeptic
by Dr. Gregory A. Boyd & Edward k. Boyd
A son wrestles with his father's questions about Christianity.
Why is the world so full of suffering? How can you believe that a man rose from the dead? Why do you think the Bible is inspired? Do all non-Christians go to hell? *Letters from a Skeptic* will help you wrestle with the rational foundation of your own faith. It will also help you know how to share that faith with the skeptics you love.

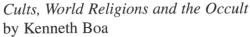

Cults, World Religions and the Occult
by Kenneth Boa
What they teach. How to respond to them.
Ken Boa explains: The history of each religious movement; the distinctive teachings of each; how their followers live; how you can respond to these spiritual counterfeits with biblical truth and compassion.

Reflective Living Series by Ken Gire

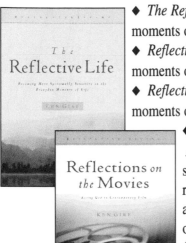

♦ *The Reflective Life:* Becoming more spiritually sensitive to the everyday moments of live

♦ *Reflections on Your Life:* Discerning God's voice in the everyday moments of life.

♦ *Reflections on the Word:* Meditating on God's Word in the everyday moments of life

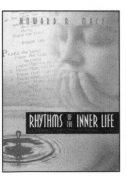

♦ *Reflections on the Movies:* Seeing God in contemporary film
Are you hungry for a more intimate relationship with God? If this speaks to the passion of your heart, there is hope. Ken Gire reveals the "habits of the heart" practiced by Jesus, the apostles and Mother Teresa that will enable you to see God at work in all of life's moments.

"I eagerly await any book from the pen of Ken Gire. His writing speaks to the heart, soul and mind."
Norm Wright

♦ *Rhythms of the Inner Life:* Yearning for closeness with God by Dr. Howard Macy
Explores seven movements of the heart in the psalms: longing, waiting, trembling, despairing, resting, conversing and celebrating.

"Howard Macy skillfully guides us through the waiting and despairing that we all know so well, and ultimately into the joyful celebration that we all long for. I recommend it highly!"
Richard Foster

♦ *After the Leap:* Growing in Christ, the basics of discipleship by Carol Vance
"After the Leap is a wonderful, clear, teachable book of the tenets of the Christian life by my good friend Carol Vance."
Chuck Colson

♦ *Disciples Are Made, Not Born:* Equipping Christians to multiply themselves through ministry to others by Walter Henrichsen. **Over 500,000 copies in print!** This book is not a collection of dry, doctrinal dust, but is eminently practical and provocative. The writer constantly hits the nail on the head."
Howard G. Hendricks

Heritage Builders—A Ministry of Focus on the Family
"Helping you build a family of faith"

♦ *Your Heritage; Family Fragrance; Family Traditions; Family Compass*

♦ *Family Nights Workbooks Vols. 1-12:* Clear, practical, and family-fun tested ideas designed to make a lasting impression on children of all ages.

Heritage Builders strives to equip, train and motivate parents to become intentional about building a strong, spiritual heritage.

Website: www.heritagebuilders.com

♦ *Daddy's Blessing:* Bestowing a biblical blessing by Randy & Lisa Wilson. *Daddy's Blessing* includes:

  ♦ Keepsake gift tin
  ♦ Scented blessing candle with decorative gold cord
  ♦ Beautifully illustrated *Daddy's Blessing* book—both a powerful story and an inspring model for practicing this biblical concept in your family

♦ Simple instructions and practical suggesions for creating your own blessing

♦ *The Joshua Basket:* Remembering the Faithfulness of God by Randy & Lisa Wilson

Throughout the Old Testament, God continually reminds the Israelites, "Remember, remember, remember" because their future hinged on their memory of God's faithfulness in the past. The Joshua Basket, based on Joshua 4:4-7, comes complete with Memory Stones and *The Joshua Journal* for parents and children to record the family's significant spiritual moments of the past week, month, or year.

♦ *Celebrate! I Made a Big Decision:* creating a spiritual scrapbook with your son or daughter by Pam Farrel

Based on Deuteronomy 6:4:9, this unique scrapbook enables parents to intentionally celebrate the significant spiritual moments in their child's life. Everything from his first expressions of faith, early prayers and baptism, to her church programs and traditions of special significance. The entire spiritual development of his or her early years are yours to capture with this one-of-a-kind tool.